The Divin

Tad Mann received an architecture degree from Cornell University and practised in New York City and Rome before becoming a professional astrologer. He gives lectures and workshops world-wide as well as writing on astrological subjects.

By the same author

The Round Art
Life★Time Astrology
The Mandala Astrological Tarot
Astrology and the Art of Healing

The Divine Plot

Astrology and Reincarnation

A. T. MANN

Shaftesbury, Dorset • Rockport, Massachusetts

© Tad Mann 1986

First published by Allen & Unwin

Published in Great Britain in 1991 by
Element Books Limited
Longmead, Shaftesbury, Dorset

Published in the USA in 1991 by
Element, Inc
42 Broadway, Rockport, MA 01966

All rights reserved.
No part of this book may be
reproduced or utilized in any form or by any means,
electronic or mechanical, without permission in
writing from the Publisher.

Cover design by Max Fairbrother
Printed and bound in Great Britain

British Library Cataloguing in Publication Data

A catalogue record for this book is
available from the British Library

Library of Congress Catalog Card Number available

ISBN 1–85230–232–1

★ *Table of Contents* ★

astrological structure of history. The Time Scale. The Octave of Mythology: Aries, Taurus, Gemini and Cancer. The Octave of Civilization: Leo, Virgo, Libra and Scorpio. The Octave of Realization: Sagittarius, Capricorn, Aquarius and Pisces. The End of the World Age. Panoramic Memory. Historical Shock Points. The Tibetan Bardo States between lives. Media, Fashion and unconsciousness. The Last Judgement of History. Higher octave Aries, Taurus and Gemini. Disidentification is liberation.

★*Papyrus Anana*★

"Behold it is written in this roll. Read ye who shall find in the days unborn, if your gods have given you the skill.

Read, O children, of the future and learn the secrets of the past which to you is so far away, and yet truth is so near.

Men do not live once only to depart hence forever, they live many times in many places, though not only in this world.

That between each life is a Veil of Darkness. The doors will open at last and show us all the chambers through which our feet wandered from the beginning.

Our religion teaches us that we live on eternally. . . now eternity, having no end, can have no beginning: it is a circle. Therefore, if one be true, namely that we live on forever, it would seem that the other must be true also. . . namely, that we have always lived.

To men's eyes God has many faces and each swears that the one he sees is the only true God, yet they are all wrong, for all are true.

Our Kas, which are our spiritual selves, show themselves to us in various ways. Drawing from the infinite veil of wisdom, hidden in the being of every man, they give us who are instructed glimpses of truth and the power to work miracles.

Among the Egyptians, the scarabeus beetle is no god, but a symbol of the Creator, because it rolls a ball of mud between its feet, and gets therein its eggs to hatch; just as the Creator rolls the world around, which seems to be causing it to produce Life.

All gods send their gift of love upon this earth, without which it would cease to be. My faith teaches me more clearly, perhaps, than yours, that life does not end with death, and therefore that love being life's soul, must endure for all eternity.

The strength of the invisible time will bind souls together long after the world is dead. In the end, however, all the various pasts will reveal themselves."

Anana, Chief Scribe and companion to Pharaoh Jentle Leti II; about 1320 B.C.

★ *Acknowledgements* ★

To past and future generations of seekers after the truth.

The author would like to thank Margo Russell for her penetrating and necessary reading of the manuscript. To Painton Cowen for early support and the mathematical understanding required for the tables and historical times. To my particular inspirations in history: Plato, Pythagoras, Giordano Bruno, Nietzsche, Gurdjieff and Rodney Collin.

★ *Prologue* ★

The apocalyptic fury of the "Last World War" coincided with an ecological breakdown to accompany the end of the world age. Collective physical and psychological shocks devastated humanity. The final fifty years of chaos and anxiety negated thousands of years of civilization.

Foolish humanity had challenged nature and reaped a self-imposed ejection from Eden. The population had exploded into emaciated billions fanatically ravaging the land in search of anything to eat, eliminating all life in the process. The bio-sphere barely admitted a vague sun, creating a hostile Ice Age. The depletion of fossil fuels and poisoning by nuclear reactor leakages accompanied the collapse of technology and completed the irreversible. The momentous event everyone feared had come.

The civilized world had consumed itself. Total panic fanned across every continent. The most civilized people were the first to die – shrieking with terror, barricaded within concrete deserts, surrounded by powerless instruments of leisure and destruction. Domesticated pets and servants devoured obese bodies. Scores which had been grossly uneven since the dawn of time were finally settled. Humanity had finally achieved its wildest fantasy: return to the unconscious, to the source, and found a nightmarish brutality, both natural and organic.

Survivors wandered through lost Eden, having forgotten the fantasy of humanity's evolutionary position as apex of some quaint cosmic pyramid of ordained, scientific development. The backslide to prehistoric survival happened with absurd ease and great speed. Cultural, religious and racial schisms accelerated the descent into an abyss that alienated father from mother, brother from brother, and parents from children until the confusion was absolute. The primary aim of the dying age was to quench perpetual hunger.

Fighting for survival was quite natural for the least civilized as it was not far from their lot throughout history, but there were few people exempt from centuries of civilization. Most isolated primitives had been rooted out, featured in documentaries, had their homelands become the sites of exotic package holidays, and then "civilized". World population plummeted rapidly from its peak of more than five billion to a few million. The survival rate was less than one in a thousand. It was like a science-fiction fantasy of multiple plagues of locusts, army ants and man-eating jungle beasts translated into quasi-human form. The atrocities of previous wars, famines and repressive governments seemed like child's play by comparison.

The survivors tried to get further and further away from the others. Classic psychotic behaviour was dominant – there was no relief from the nightmare. It was truly hell on earth. Kill or be killed was the name of the game.

The political and economic structure of the world before the fall mirrored its anthropology afterwards. The protagonists in the final battles were the industrialized one-tenth of humanity, including the USA, Russia, Japan and western Europe, against the agrarian nine-tenths of humanity including South America, Africa, the Middle East and Asia. Four billion starving have-nots surged into and devastated civilization. When the dust cleared, the Caucasian races were virtually non-existent. The situation was reminiscent of anthropological descriptions of the millennia before the modern age when only the strongest and most brutal survived.

The industrialized races were finally destroyed by the poison of their own pollution, acid rains sterilizing lakes and rivers and baring trees, faulty diet, cruelly propagated animals, chemically corrupt foods, unnatural medical practices, sexual plagues and genetic experiments – in the latter days the only manner of conception was artificial. Humanity degenerated to proto-primate reality, as survivors wandered aimlessly over the earth like Neanderthalers seeking whatever growing things gradually began to appear after the radiation dispersed. Mutations caused by the cumulative effect of pollution and radiation upon genetic code produced wild deviations in most species. Frightening extremes in climate assisted in generating a virtual "Planet of the Apes".

Eventually the earth was battered by volcanoes and earthquakes, and purified by shifting tectonic plates which devastated and cleansed its surface. Advancing and retreating walls of ice played with metamorphosing continental land masses. Supposedly permanent monuments and great sprawling cities were devastated, pulverized and blasted back into their component parts. They were submerged under newly created seas and sandwiched between layers of thousand-foot high mountain chains. It happened at an unimaginable scale and speed. By the time equilibrium was restored, all traces of the previous world age had been eradicated from the face of the earth, except in the minds of the survivors.

The conditions described above echoed the disappearance of great ancient civilizations during the earliest historic eras, but infinitely more rapidly and completely. The technological world before the Apocalypse, believing itself to be eternal and non-biodegradable, vanished without trace.

Geographical localities which escaped annihilation were rare, but there were islands of amnesty for the survival of the spirit of humanity, places distinguished by natural fortification or stability of position which allowed vestiges of existing life to carry on amidst the chaos outside. These refuges were buffered from the madness of the outside world by being protected, if not totally sealed, as the fabled "lost continents" which existed in fantasy beyond man and time. Isolated valleys, thousands of feet up in great mountain chains, protected by sheer walls of stone; fertile valleys shifted upwards by congenial fluke upheavals of nature; islands arisen from voracious seas. Benign ecology cleared the air, purified the prime materia and began the re-establishment of life, but also prevented access, creating safe havens during the cosmic storm. References to these places permeate mythology as the *Garden of Eden, Valhalla, Noah's Ark, Mount Meru* and *Paradise*.

The natural strongholds were what the previous age had recognised as spiritual centres. The indefinable qualities which made them revered lay in their unimagined purpose, and they possessed an attraction which could only be called "cosmic". They radiated the finest levels of energy and thus adduced individuals of the most benign understanding to them. During the collapse of the world age they sent out their subtle call to all those refined enough to hear it. It was as though the guiding hand of destiny operated to preserve the world order through the end of an age.

Small enclaves of enlightened survivors of the obliterated world age lived with single-minded joy, yet with the proposterous limitations of Adam and Eve in Paradise. The restricted environment provided eternal peace and happiness, yet the threat of instant destruction through any contact with the world beyond. The survival of utopia rested upon total containment. The taboo upon the outside world depended upon regulating sexuality and perpetuating insularity over many generations. The tree of good and evil – knowledge of world ages – grew just beyond their domain.

Although the surviving founders knew the fate of the rest of the world and of their mission, the survival of civilized humanity, succeeding generations could only speculate upon what seemed exaggerated myths of great wars and the wild primitive half-humans populating the world beyond Eden. The survivors had experienced the death and rebirth of a world age, but did not escape unchanged. The extreme shock to their psycho-physical organisms had eradicated conscious awareness. Although enlightened, they were as infants. They had no link back to their heritage in the last world age, nor an inkling of their future. The sheer enormity of the demise of civilization had erased their memories, removed all elements of logic, and so affected their mental perpective that they reverted to pure spirit. It evoked the worshipping of epileptics as sacred channels in ancient times.

It was as though the survivors had been given cosmic pre-frontal labotomies and emerged as illiterate adult-children in the Garden of Eden – incorruptible, naive and innocent to the point of simple-mindedness. They had achieved the state which had been the aim of ecstatic mystics throughout history: total union with nature.

The description of the end of a world age, as one approaches, is also a description of the end of the last world age, fifty thousand years ago, which is called "The Destruction of Atlantis". It has all happened before.

★Chapter One★
★The Divine Plot★

The grand plan of the universe. Special Creation. The relativity of life in time. Celestial magic. Cyclic vs linear time. Linking back. The return at the end of time. Genetic Code and reincarnation. Electronic recurrence. Revolutions in science. The unity of history. Biology, perception and astrology. The Book of Life.

> The world indeed is sacred; but paradoxically, one cannot see the sacredness of the world until one discovers that it is a divine play.
> Mircea Eliade

The Divine Plot is the grand plan of the universe, carried through the mechanism of time. The Divine Plot requires a divine plotter – the plotter is god. God manifests through the universe, which comes into being in time, and yet god is beyond time. Without time there is no space, and without space-time there is no universe. In all creation myths, space and time come into being simultaneously at the beginning. The Divine Plot is the "great secret". Definitions of *"plot"* are as follows[1]:

plot, sb.
> *– The site, situation, of a building, town, city, etc.*
> *– A ground plan of a building, field, farm, etc.; a map, a chart.*
> *– A sketch or outline of a literary work.*
> *– The plan or scheme of a play, poem, work of fiction, etc.*
> *– A plan or project, secretly contrived; a conspiracy, a sly plan, an innocent scheme.*

plot, v. 1588
> *– To make a plan, map or diagram; to lay down on a map; to represent by a plan or diagram (the course of any action or process.)*

> − *To make a plan of (something to be laid out, eonstructed, or made.)*
> − *To plan, contrive or devise (something to be carried out or accomplished.)*
> − *intr. To scheme, lay plans, contrive, conspire.*

As The Divine Plot makes clear, god is the creator and time is the vehicle by which creation is organized, from the smallest sub-atomic particles to the largest galaxies. Every part is organized in the same way as every other part; everything is alive, from apparently inert lead to the infinite electron; everything intercommunicates at all times and in all ways; and every component of the universe is represented in the human being. The microcosm is the macrocosm. As above, so below.

Cosmologists project the history of the universe backwards to ever denser compactions of radiation energy, to shrinking volumes and into shorter durations. But, from what does the universe come in the first place? It is apparently created with its entire history already implicit. The universe cannot be anything other than what it is. There is either another universe which, having been destroyed, is the nucleus of the creation of the known universe, or there is a "special creation", a creation as a divine action of god. In modern times the dispute is being enacted by scientists and fundamentalist Christians.

We recapitulate the entire life of the universe in life from conception to death. The burst of pure energy at conception elongates time sense. The white light of life is infinite and eternal, arising from the Big Bang of creation. It can only come into being at creation − not earlier nor later. Conception is creation. Our development within the womb recapitulates the process of all life and gradually slows down, but the soul perceives the process of gestation taking fifteen billion years. By the time of birth, we are oriented at the emergence of consciousness 50,000 years ago. At the moment of death, the universe ends. It can only be this way, and no other.

The stars are the key to the great secret. When a world age ends, as thousands have ended and thousands more will end, the only possible orientation is by the stars. Astrology, probably the oldest system of knowledge, was not originally used for fortune-telling, but as a way for organizing the psyche. The stars receive projections of all knowledge, awaiting the time when the knowledge may be retrieved. Celestial magic was practised in the Renaissance as an attempt to gain knowledge of time, which means knowledge of god. God is in everything, moves everything and creates everything. The only liberation is disidentification from the reality of things and concentration, over many lives, on the godlike process of things.

Circular Time

The Prologue relates, from some future time, the end of a World Age and its implications. The description is evocative of the present century, but also prehistory fifty thousand years ago. The end and beginning of world ages form the basis of all religions, mythologies, philosophies, mysticisms, cosmologies and sciences. Craving utopia, world revolution or return to Eden are all reflections of a universal desire to recapture the purity of primal paradise.

Before linear, mechanist Darwinian evolution, many cultures accepted the eternal repetition of time and history and based their cosmologies and mythologies on circular, recurrent time. Egyptians, Buddhists, Stoics, Hindus, Jews, Zoroastrians and Ismailis understood that individual and world cycles repeat eternally. Recurrent great years have been postulated as being from 7000 years to an inconceivable 864,000,000,000 years long.

The Divine Plot is a creation theory of eternal recurrence, where time is circular and repetitive. Within the fabric of time are woven many diverse strands of history, mythology, mysticism, religion, science, psychology, mathematics, philosophy, art and medicine into a "unified theory" of life in the universe, organized according to the celestial science and art, astrology. By reconciling archetypal historical concepts with the biologically-based Life★Time Astrology, truly relative history is discovered.

The spiralling pattern of the solar system as it hurtles through space is similar in form to genetic code which encapsulates the patterns of growth of species and individuals. Just as planetary patterns may be projected into the past, so the reincarnations of every being are available within the genetic code. The mathematics of astrology is the key to deciphering genetic code, and all previous incarnations may be determined with elementary tables. The present moment is the culmination and sum of all past and future experience.

Humanity faces the threat of extinction and it is essential to discover a model which explains reality more profoundly than destructive science or obscure philosophy. Most people assume the world situation to be unique and without prototype, but there is evidence that virtually identical circumstances have occurred in previous world ages.

The schism in the human race even extends to projections of what will or should happen in the future. Some believe that with the dawning of the *"Age of Aquarius"* all men and women will instantaneously recognise true love and life in peace together. Others believe that it is already too late to reverse the destruction of life on earth. What is clear in either view is that a dramatic transformation is immanent.

The Link Back

Every person now on earth is the result of 100% successful experiment in evolution because everyone has had parents who reproduced successfully, as their parents did, and so on, back to the first humans, before that to the first life, back to the origin of the universe. At no point could anyone have entered the system from outside, as there is no outside. Those of us alive today are not necessarily the fittest, the strongest, the most intelligent or the most successful – but we are the survivors. We link back to the origin (*ab-origine*) through genes, the matter from which our body is made, the structure of our brain, the fabric of the time and in our deeper spiritual reality. Many religions transmit the spiritual inheritance through time by successions of prophets or gurus. (Fig. 1) To track our origin we must reconstruct the unfolding of all life in time. The most natural starting point is human embryological development. We embody the universal creative mechanisms that lie behind psychology, philosophy, mysticism and science. The ancient term for the process by which previous influences affect the world is reincarnation. Every person has specific prototypes in the biological, mythological and individual being which can be determined mathematically, dated and deciphered.

At conception the universe begins and at death the universe ends. While usually taken as a metaphor, it is quite literally true. The universality of human life makes everyone a participant in the cosmic drama from the beginning, just as we all participate at the end. The mysteries of life are experienced by everyone who has lived. Mircea Eliade realized that a prominent characteristic of modern society is the obsession with history. Until the last century, history was recorded as a behavioural guide, while now it is worshipped for its own sake. The passion for the past reflects a troubled world situation. Many folklores carry the belief that at the moment of death, our

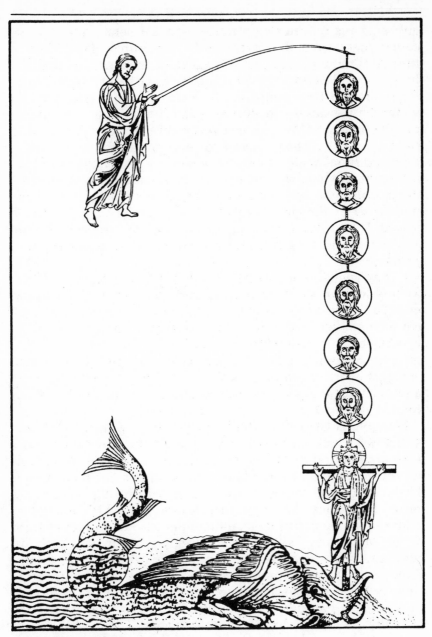

Fig. 1: Sacred Christian Lineage
The lineage of David shown as fishing tackle for catching the Leviathan of time, with the crucifix as bait. As there are seven images, the tackle also represents the planets as a sequence of transformational influences. *(Herrad, Hortus deliciarum, 12th cent.)*

entire past is relived down to the smallest detail, and that we cannot pass from the body until all personal and collective history is remembered. This "panoramic memory" is the Last Judgement described by Buddhism, Christianity, Hinduism, Egyptian and other religions. Considered from this point of view, the passion for history is a sign portending humanity's imminent death.[2] We can see everywhere the anxiety similar to the fears of the savage about to undergo an initiation which involved ritual death, the extinction of the personality and ego, a descent into hell, and finally rebirth as a new being. Woman's initiation dramatizes the process of gestation and birth, while men abstract the processes of life and death. The initiate is shocked into remembering and revaluing the whole life – when world ages end the entire population reconstructs all history.

It is estimated that as many people will live from 1950 to 2000 as have lived in the last fifty thousand years, since Cro-magnon emerged from the mists of time and humanity became conscious. Every individual from the world age is returning to experience the possibility of rebirth into the New Age. The ancient religions, cultures, artifacts and their behavioural surrogates are returning, as though a choice must be made about where (and when) we wish to find our centre of gravity in the next world age.

Electrons exist in all matter in the universe by forming atomic structures which exist for seconds or millennia, until they decay into an unbound form. When they decay, other electrons rush to replace them, reproducing other atoms in their place. Electrons create patterns in time into which their successors recur. Molecules also die (break down into their component atoms) at a rate of five to six million per second and regenerate at the same rate. Cells recur so exactly that the cellular body only gradually reflects its changes in appearance. Many millions of generations of such recurrences are required for there to be noticeable change in atoms or cells. The same is true of stars and galaxies. They recur in time as they reproduce virtually the same developmental stages. There is a formal similarity between the nature of atoms and galaxies. Just as atoms continuously die and are re-created, so galaxies explode and re-form. All existence in the universe, from atoms to galaxies, are only concentrations of energy fields which recur in time. An eternal flux of energy enfolds all processes in universal space-time, at every scale from the sub-molecular to the galactic, so that there is a reflection of the whole in every fragment, at every time. A great paradox is that we accept recurrent processes everywhere in the universe except in ourselves, an acceptance which is the key to transcendence. *We must understand the circular and cyclic nature of ourselves and the universe.*

The world view of physics has undergone a radical change in recent years. The Euclidian-Newtonian universe was rectilinear, time was absolute and clocks would keep the same time wherever they were. In a relativistic universe there are no preferential reference points, and time is variable, making the universe curved. Time is therefore cyclical rather than linear. The emphasis has shifted from particles to patterns of events, including history in physics. With no preferential reference points, there is an interaction between the observer and the observed. Every person is the centre of their own universe, a state foreshadowed in ancient models of reality thousands of years ago.

In biology a similar revolution has been initiated by questioning the logic of disassembling bodies in order to discover how they work. Must all life on earth be extinguished to find out where life came from? The patterns governing life processes do not reside in particular parts of the brain, but are inherent in the morphogenetic fields which affect all living beings and may well be the invisible medium by which heredity, body form and even esp are transmitted from individual to individual and from generation to generation. The keys to the organization of the universe exist within everyone.

There are formal structures inherent in the universe but the actual nature of such structures is still unknown to science. Circular, recurrent patterns are required to restructure our destructive views of the universe and to restore balance and wholeness to life on earth. Such a pattern has existed for thousands of years in the most ancient science and art, Astrology. Astrology describes the pattern in time which fulfils the requirements of science, psychology, history and mythology. It is a map which has been used since the dawn of mankind and provides the Key to unlocking the secrets of the universe. When the history of the universe is restructured along astrological lines, it becomes possible not only to identify the cycles of life at every level from electron to galaxy, but for the first time the matrix of the universe may be glimpsed. That itself may be the purpose of the next stage in the development of intelligent life.

The Unity of History

> But before the curtain falls, there is one more task for the historical Faustian spirit, a task not yet specified, hitherto not even imagined as possible. There has still to be written a morphology of the exact sciences, which shall discover how all laws, concept and theories inwardly hang together as forms and what they have meant as such in the life-course of the Faustian Culture. The re-treatment of theoretical physics, of chemistry, of mathematics as the sum of symbols – this will be the definitive conquest of the mechanical world-aspect by an intuitive, once more religious, world-outlook, a last master-effort of physiognomic to break down even systematic and absorb it, as expression and symbol, into its own domain.
>
> Spengler, *"The Decline of the West"*[3]

In order to unite history, it is essential to join many disparate belief systems with mathematical methodology. The synthesis is accurate both as a model for organizing time, and for linking subjective, personal experience which animates our history transmitted through the generations. This is no less than linking the universe with its invisible mirror anti-universe, the left and right halves of the brain, science and mythology, white and black, male and female, west and east. The unification of opposites integrates the entire range of qualities in the universe. Division and fragmentation is within everyone in the way reality is categorized, qualified and constructed. Dreams are dreamed in a unitary state within which time does not exist, but to express the remembered dream it is necessary to apply sequence and temporal order to its timelessness. The same principle operates in the individual within which history occurs. We are beings in time, but we also exist beyond time.

The individual horoscope is a context for describing the life pattern and the transpersonal realm, as outlined in my books *"The Round Art: The Astrology of Time and Space"* (1979) and *"Life★Time Astrology"* (1984).[4] Life★Time Astrology is a mechanism for unlocking knowledge of time, the mysteries of the psyche and of the world. Instead of grading time additively, the logarithmic time scale reflects the relativity of perception in time. Time sense changes with age. The earliest developments in life, within the womb, happen very rapidly. As we age time seems to pass more and more quickly. Days in childhood take much longer to pass than days in maturity, a mechanism inherent in the way metabolism determines time perception – a biological time sense. When the lifetime is graded logarithmically, it is possible to describe twelve developmental stages from conception to death through which every individual passes during life. The positions of the planets signify events, archetypal mechanisms of behaviour and the cast of characters in life.

Schopenhauer and Freud accepted that individual life recapitulates the life process of the species. The microcosm is the macrocosm. A record of the collective past is carried within everyone and its symbolic language can be understood. The Divine Plot is a symbolic system which allows just such a communication, through a logarithmic Universal Time Scale, a series of repetitive cycles from the big bang to the lifetime of subatomic particles, the longest to the shortest cycles known. The intermediate cycles are graded continuously, and the ends joined like the ouroboros snake eating its tail – an image of eternity. The result is a description of universal time.

Every individual carries the history of creation and remains as an energetic pattern until the end of time. Every being is eternal and immortal. But, it is necessary for every sentient being to understand and accept the whole transcendent reality. At the transition shock points at the beginning and end of world ages individuals have a unique opportunity to pass beyond the mundane world to higher levels of reality. Approaching the year 2000, every person on earth has an opportunity, if only we can experience. Everyone will experience the Last Judgement or Grand Resurrection to have the singular chance to pass through the ultimate vortex, *T I M E*.

> And I saw the dead, small and great, stand before God, and the books were opened: And another book was opened, which is the Book of Life, and the dead were judged out of those things which were written in the book, according to their works.
>
> Book of Revelations

The Book of Life is within you!

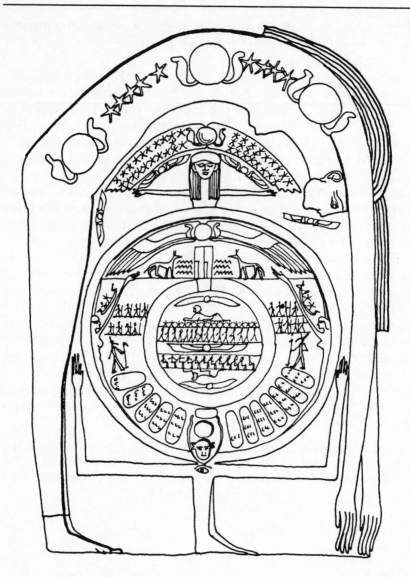

Fig. 2: Egyptian Sky Goddess Nuit
Nuit, the sky goddess, swallows the sun each evening and brings it
forth into the world again at dawn. Hathoor, the moon goddess, is
enthroned in the process, creating vegetation on earth.

★Chapter Two★
★Life History★

Individual life as history. The Collective Unconscious. Stories and myths. The soul and death memory. The conspiracy of linear time. Cyclic world ages of the Buddhists, Hindus, Christians, Jains, Babylonians, Mandeans and Jews. The Great Year. Precession of the Equinoxes. Myths of the World Axis. Flood Legends. Atlantis.

All theories of the nature of time, man and the universe are conditioned by a very important fact: they all happen within history. Every theory is created within and conditioned by the attitudes, belief systems, needs, language and levels of consciousness of those from whom they issue. Even when ideas come from archetypal levels or beyond reality, they must be translated into a medium, a language, symbol system or specific vocabulary in use at a particular time and place. Profound ideas ahead of their time, or presented to cultures unready for them are rejected or ignored, and their originators dismissed or persecuted. As civilizations gestate, are born, mature and die, their symbol systems, ideas, concepts and realities die with them. Only rarely do ideas really transcend their civilization of origin and affect others who follow.

The Buddhist prophet Nichiren described a human truth when he stated:

> The learning of just one word or phrase of the Right Law, if only it accords with the time and propensity of the learner, could lead to the attainment of the Way. The mastery of a thousand scriptures and ten thousand theories, if they should not accord with the time and the propensity of the one who masters them, would lead nowhere.[5]

Whatever the message, the time of its saying is critical. To understand history, all times must be compacted into the eternal present. There is no such thing as "objective" history – history exists only within each person. All time is contained in the present moment. In order to understand time, it is necessary to define its mechanism.

Throughout recorded history humanity has measured time. Initially time was measured only by the cycle of day and night, generated by the rotation of earth around its axis. The moon's cycle begins with the sliver crescent (the beginning of Hebrew and Islamic months), becomes fuller until it dominates the sky, and then shrinks until it disappears for three days, only to be reborn from the "underworld". The solar year is a cycle of four seasons of Spring, Summer, Autumn and the death of nature in Winter. The basic natural cycles are astronomical.

A second, minute, hour, day, year, decade and century are absolute units of time agreed by convention. Worldwide time standards are now based on the vibration of cesium atoms, measured to thousandths of a second. Universal Time is the timekeeping standard for science. In spite of the apparent accuracy of timekeeping, in the context of Eastern mysticism, psychology and more recently physics, time is not absolute, but is subject to great variance and distortion, and may be an illusory perception.

In the pre-relativistic Cartesian theory space was a rectilinear grid and time simply another dimension, but in Relativity Theory the speed of light in a vacuum is the universal constant. Space and time are inseparable in a space-time continuum which is curved. Time expands or contracts according to the velocity of the perceiver, and since everything in the universe moves at a great speed, every being and object has its own unique time sense, and its own relative history. An oak tree exists just as we do, only for a vastly longer duration.

History is taught as though it is fact accepted by everyone, but history is also relative, being written by the victors and passed on as a fait accompli. Goethe said, "History, that error of hodge-podge and brute force. Each of us who feels his worth starts from the beginning!"[6] Each successive civilization assimilates the history of its predecessors and extends its own influence into the future by teaching its successors. It is natural for each culture to see itself as the culmination of all previous ages – and they usually are because previous cultures are necessary roots. The same may be said about religions, scientific attitudes and individuals, all conditioned by inherited structures and beliefs inherited from earlier times. We believe that our reality is the only one, and that our beliefs are special in history.

The history of individual life is modified with age. The earliest events in life are known primarily through stories told by parents, who have told these stories for years and years, altering them from telling to telling to make them more interesting. Bits are forgotten, exaggerated or included until the past becomes a collage of stories. With or without realizing it, parents censor the stories which present them in an unfavourable light and delight in telling the stories which present them favourably. The quality of the stories is largely determined by the reality of the parents. By the time we are old enough to be able to understand the implications of our life story, the stories are assumed to be fact without distortion.

Most of what we know about ourselves is carried by stories. When meeting someone new, we display ourself by selecting, editing and telling stories in particular sequences, with certain points made. Individual histories are transmitted and stored as stories.

A world view is constructed in the same way. Information is presented at school and conditioned by the home and family system as though it is the objective reality of the events told. History is presented as absolute fact. By maturity we are governed by a world and set of values that are deemed fact. Our attitude to the world is dependent upon relationship or adaptation to other individuals and the collective values of the environment. The unwillingness or inability to adapt is considered either rebellious or insane.

Freud introduced time and history into a category of phenomena that had previously been approached from without, rather in the way that a naturalist treats his subject.[7]

> The lives of each of us comprise a history, whether that history be articulated in a full narrative account or array of accounts or remain fragmentary, incomplete or latent. No life is without its personal experiences of myth, epic, romance and tragedy. These exemplary and recurrent themes of experience belong for Freud to the species as much as they do to each of us. Yet what helps in part to animate these processes as history is that each one of us actually sustains in his own person that which the species, our ancestors, or a character we will read about is said to have passed through. And what also helps to animate them as history is that each one of us can testify to goings-on in the past that appear to have the warrant of actuality; but the shape of that testimony is invariably a conjectural reconstruction, a fabrication, something we have made, a history.[8]

The nature of the continuum in which our life is lived must be understood in reference to the collective reality of our entire race, the "collective unconscious" of Jung. "The world of archetypes of Jung is like the Platonic world of ideas, in that the archetypes are impersonal and do not participate in the historical time of the individual life, but in the time of the species – even of organic life itself."[9] The collective unconscious is not a receptacle of repressed contents as for Freud, but rather a deeeper layer of innate structural forms which exist in every individual beyond space and time. What is relevant for the entire species is the basis of individual psychology, and leads naturally to the study of history and individual life as integrated subjects.

History is thus endowed with ego and personality, and as such must be understood as a "series of stages which must be traversed, and traversed moreover in an ordered and obligatory sequence. For everything organic the notions of birth, death, youth, age, lifetime are fundamentals – may not these notions possess a rigorous meaning which no one has as yet extracted?"[10]

Mythic Reality

There are many ways in which the world can be understood. While not obviously histories, all views of individual life imply a particular attitude to history.

Earliest humanity had no history. Primitives lived one day at a time as though each day was all of time, much like children. The most basic fear was that when the sun set in the evening it might not rise the following morning. Many cultures worshipped the sun because they connected the appearance of the sun with the power of the sun to create them and their lives. One of the earliest myths is that of the Egyptian goddess Nut or Nuit (Night), who swallowed the Sun at sunset and gave birth to him at dawn. (Figure 2) A myth is the description of natural processes transmitted as a story.

With the advent of language, the human perspective enlarged. The experiences of previous hunts were told as stories – stories which carried great power because they were not just hollow tales but formulae for survival. The more stories of the hunt were told, the more efficiently information required for survival was retained and passed on. Stories were passed on from generation to generation, a fund of knowledge which became a legacy and inspiration for the whole tribe. Although hunts occurred in time, the myths associated with them were transhistorical; they happened outside of time, in a sacred world. The teller of the story was in a powerful and responsible position because of the implication of access to the divine world.

In Thomas Mann's "*Joseph and His Brothers*", Joseph noticed that his tutor Eliezer's ego was not clearly demarcated; ". . . it opened at the back, as it were, and overflowed into spheres external to his own individuality both in space and time; embodying in his own experience events which, remembered and related in the clear light of day, ought actually to have been put in the third person".[11] Eliezer remembered stories of previous tutors of the same name and telescoped their histories into his own, just as he accumulated the exploits of all his and his predecessors' masters and attributed them to his master. An entire lineage found its summation in those alive in the present, making flesh of the past. History is a statified past embedded within us. Its deeper levels precede the earliest records and live beyond the fleshy confines of our ego as they feed and condition us.

The stories of the earliest tribes or cultures were transmitted in the form of myths, fairy tales, heroic sagas or religions, in which time was circular, repetitive and recurrent, an echo of the timeless days of the ancestors. The vast times back to the dawn of history are repressed or ignored by most people, yet everyone has a direct connection back to those times. A record of the developmental process of all life exists within the electrons, particles, genetic code and physical bodies of which everything living is made. The Chinese reverence for ancestors is the basis of their culture, and reflects such a linking back to the origin.

Central mythic themes are the creation and destruction of the world, both of which exist in a mystical realm of the spirit always connected to each other. Sacred moments of birth and death, initiation, healing and sacrifice are "rites of passage", echoing the two primary events in time and essentially making mundane events participate in the sacred.

The search for origins embodied by myth is evident in the world today, but in different guises: theories of the Big Bang and the origin of life; the genealogy of individuals and humanity; the inner search of psychoanalysis into the mythology of early childhood; and the return to nature. Disciplines investigating origins are everywhere, as though to satisfy a deep instinctive desire to return to the paradise which existed before the Fall. The primary impetus is the terror we face in the degeneration of modern life.

The world is dying in preparation for the attainment of a different mode of existence and it is only through knowing about creation that what the future holds can be known. Psychotherapy encourages individual return and in society there is a collective going back. The initiation ceremony was a symbolic death and rebirth, and in order to find immortality and liberation from time and karma, the womb of nature must be re-entered.[12] The only way to become master of one's destiny is to remember births, former lives and relive the origin of the world. "Being in the womb, I knew all the births of the gods."[13] (Figure 3)

Fig. 3: The Alchemical Womb
In alchemy the base for transformation was the furnace, the womb of Mercurius, which was round in imitation of the spherical cosmos so that the stars might contribute to the success of the operation. *(Barchausen, Elementa chemicae, 1718)*

Early humanity recorded history to transmit models of culture and behaviour patterns, but since the last century the aim of history is to reconstitute the entire past of the species and make us conscious of it.

Let us now look at the passion for history from a standpoint outside our own cultural perspective. In many religions, and even in the folk-lore of European peoples, is the belief that, at the moment of death, one remembers the entire past life down to the minutest details, and that death cannot happen without a remembrance and re-living of the whole personal history. Upon the screen of memory the dying human once more reviews the past. Considered from this point of view, the passion for historiography in modern culture would be a sign portending its imminent death.[14]

The ancients believed that the further back to the origin individuals existed, the closer to gods they were in manifesting the universal order in their lives. It is clear that the creator, triple goddess, divine king, great mother and hero are embodiments of a transcendent reality which the present world craves. Humanity searches within the atom, in outer space, in the depths of the oceans and on the highest mountains for the meaning of the origin of life and neglects the origin: within each one of us.

The nature of time, particularly primordial time, is the most profound mystery. The historical approach works backwards until knowledge dissolves into myths, dreams or fantasies, analogous to the seemingly irrational quantum world of particle physics or the realm of the psyche in psychology – in these realms intuition and pattern are the only stepping stones. The meaning of the psyche is as elusive as that of the atomic nucleus. The complexity of creation mythology evokes a similar feeling to the Big Bang – both exist in seemingly familiar inner and outer worlds, and yet cannot be described.

Due to the repetitive nature of myth it is impossible to know how far back the original event setting a pattern occurred. Not only does each telling not clarify the mystery, but renews its magic. In early times "what concerns us is not calculable time. Rather it is time's abrogation and dissolution in the alternation of tradition and prophecy, which lends to the phrase 'once upon a time' its double sense of past and future and therewith its burden of the potential present".[15] Ancient mythologies generate strong feeling about the future, almost as though the earliest memories are simultaneously prophecies. Past events continually repeat until they are accepted as prototypical. Repetition is a reminder that not only is the past as mysterious as the future, but they are firmly linked to each other, if not identical.

A human paradox is the coexistence of the desire for freedom from the constraint of time with the wish for a continuity of individuality from life to life. To have both is impossible. Understanding time as an infinite straight line is a rejection of the possibility of redemption, while salvation is understanding the circular and repetitive nature of time.

The Greeks believed that after death the soul passed in purification through the River Lethe, the stream of forgetting. Death is the annihilation of consciousness and memory and an exit from time. At the moment of death the soul is severed from the individual world, but also re-enters wholeness, an initiation into the realm of the spirit. Death is not an end, but rather a joining of soul with boundless spirit. The ultimate primordial event has its surrogates in ordinary life; birth, death and healing.

The soul enters the underworld after death, a descent into ever darker and denser realms, devoid of movement, where life is absent and time sense is greatly slowed down. The soul slides down a scale of energy, consciousness and organizational levels, from the pure light of god-consciousness to the mineral realm. In Dante's *"Inferno"* and the *"Tibetan Book of the Dead"*, the souls of the dead are in a state of eternal torture, chained to or trapped within rockhewn caverns, subjected to enormous heat and restriction of movement, cut into pieces and inundated with molten metals – precisely like life in the mineral realm. The vast times of the mineral realm, the pressure, heat and crystallized forces in operation would be experienced in this way. The duration of life in the mineral realm dwarfs that of humanity so totally that it does not have what we define as consciousness.

The descent into hell traces evolution back through human life into the geological life of matter, back by definition to the origin of the universe. The human body contains all known elements, therefore the link is not only theoretical, but tangible. The body and psyche carry both the history of the universe and the solution to its origin.

Cyclic World Ages

All forms of time in their measurable cycles imitate eternity.
Plato[16]

The current view is that time, history and evolution are linear, one-directional and irreversible. Development always occurs from simple to complex, implying that humanity is the apex of the development of life, the highest form. Humanity can only evolve higher and become wiser.

In the study of the universe however, cyclic behaviour is the rule in the macrocosm and the microcosm because molecules, small and large cells, simple organisms, planets, moons, suns, galaxies and even universes all recur in time. Does humanity not partake of circularity?

An early formulation of linear time was St Augustine's AD 427 recantation in *"The City of God"* of his cyclic Manichaean beliefs and his acceptance of the Christian dogma that the world was less than six thousand years old, history was not cyclic and Christ died only once for our sins. As Augustine was highly respected well into the renaissance, he represented the watershed of the earlier cyclic theory of the world.

The cosmologies of Heraclitus, Pythagoras and Plato were cyclic and astral and after Augustine were reinforced by Albertus Magnus, St Thomas Aquinas, Roger Bacon and Dante until the Renaissance philosophers Joachim of Floris, Galileo, Tycho Brahe, Kepler, Cardan, Bruno and Dee kept the tradition alive. These profound and spiritual men all believed that "the cycles and periodicities of the world's history are governed by the influence of the stars, whether this influence obeys the will of God and is his instrument in history or whether – an hypothesis that gains increasing adherence – it is regarded as a force immanent in the cosmos".[17] Even the acceptance of heliocentricity did not lessen the interest of great thinkers.

Leibniz applied the final blow to cyclic theory and shifted opinion toward the linear view by proclaiming faith in infinite progress, later popularized by Darwinian materialist science. At present, even mention of cyclic theory is rare. But, the revival of recurrence by Nietzsche, Spengler, Toynbee, Haldane, Gurdjieff, Collin, Ouspensky and Eliade shows that cyclic theory is awaiting resurrection.

The cycles of early cosmologies were defined by periodic cataclysms – an extension of the eternal daily cycle of pre-historic ancestors. Cyclic life was natural and obvious for agrarian cultures governed by lunar months and solar seasons.

It is more important to understand the circular mechanism transmitted by myths of cataclysms followed by burgeoning world ages than exact chronologies. Literal study of the world is an illusory trap, but to transcend the world of time and history is to enter a godlike realm of the spirit. The sacred myth of the eternal return permeates all important early cultures and religions including Egyptian, Chinese, Hindu, Buddhist, Jain, Ismaeli, Hebrew, Roman, Mexican, Hawaiian, Polynesian, Icelandic, Scandinavian, Greek, Incan, Aztec, American Indian and especially the shamanistic cultures of North America and Russia.

The variable in a cyclic world view is the duration of the cycle and the way in which one cycle transforms into another. The dating was more than a measurement of quantity; it was the mathematical relationship of man to god. Each culture defined its antiquity by the length of its world ages, from the 7000-year Jubilee cycles of the Jews, to Hindu yugas of thousands of years, to Buddhist paras of hundreds of billions of years.

The Hindus and Buddhists graded creation with a variety of cycles, each with its own function. Each world age was the creation and then destruction of parts of the world. Successive world ages decreased in duration and quality, as the lifetime of beings living in the age shortened. World ages regress and deteriorate from an originally perfect state, opposite to modern evolutionary views but consistent with the concept of entropy. Primordial rhythms contract through time until a cataclysm ending an even greater series of cycles starts the process over again. There are endless series of cycles within cycles from the lifetime of the universe to a fragment of a single breath, within which human life-span varies from 80,000 to 10 years, and sizes from the colossal to one foot high.[18]

The duration of the Hindu universe is the life of Brahma. After the void following a cataclysm Brahma, due to his previous karma, is the first being to be reborn. He is lonely and wishes for company, so other beings arise spontaneously because of their karma, but Brahma falsely believes that he has created them as he created himself. Brahma rules the sphere of form as creator and originator of time, labouring from his delusion of grandeur.

The smallest Hindu time cycle is the blink of 1/5th second, followed by the muhurta of 48 minutes. Thirty muhurtas make up one day, and the thirty day piturah is a day of the fathers. A year is a day of the gods, and it takes 360 earth years to make one divine year of the gods. The proportion amplifies the transitoriness of humanity. The major unit of time is the *yuga*. Four yugas make a mahayuga, or Great Yuga of 12,000 divine years, with a length in earth years of 4,320,000 years (12,000 x 360). Within a mahayuga, the four yugas diminish in length as they succeed each other. Krita Yuga is a golden age of 4,000 divine years during which men live very long lives in perfect peace and wisdom, preceded by a dawn of 400 years and followed by a twilight of 400 years. The destruction following Krita Yuga yields Treta Yuga of 3,000 divine years with its dawn and twilight of 300 years; then Dvarupa Yuga of 2,000 divine years and its dawn and twilight of 200 years; and finally the present Kali Yuga of 1,000 divine years (360,000 earth years) and its dawn and twilight of 100 years. We now live in the twilight of the Kali Yuga, called the "Age of Misery" because lifetimes are shortest and reality is the most decadent of all the ages. The end of the Kali Yuga twilight is a dissolution of the universe, the "*praylaya*".

To illustrate the immensity of these concepts, when 1000 mahayugas have elapsed, they constitute a kalpa, one day and night in the life of Brahma. One kalpa is 8,640,000,000 earth years, and since Brahma lives one hundred such days, his lifetime of one para is one hundred kalpas or 864,000,000,000 earth years. According to the sacred Vishnu Purana, at the beginning of the present kalpa half the para had elapsed. Brahma therefore has just had his fiftieth birthday.

The truly astronomical length of these cycles of existence was compared by the Hindus, Buddhists and Jains to the *Wheel of Samsara* with twelve spokes, symbolic of the dominion of time over humanity. Salvation is escape from the karmic wheel – freedom from time. (Figure 4) The immense lengths make it quite clear that the gods live in exalted realms separated by immeasurable time.

The elaborate cosmologies of the East come from civilizations and religions which recognized the necessity for transmitting a world view through many dissolutions of humanity. The action of diminishing cycles through time is very important and the changing nature of the ages foreshadows the concept of entropy – the binding of energy in information through time. In the East these ideas are not understood as metaphors, but as images of great spiritual forces within a system which is replicated, albeit in inferior form, from world age to world age. The manifestation of the universe is guided by the universe itself, in the form of Brahma, who is reflected in the spirit of every being.

When the universe ends, Brahma retreats into the void for immeasurable time, until:

> When the world-night comes to an end, Brahma wakes up and has the world come out of him. There arises from him first the great being which still counts as the undifferentiated. From the great being springs thought (manas), which already belongs to the realm of the differentiated. Thought is then the origin of the elements. From it comes ether, from ether wind, from wind fire, from fire water and from water earth. This concludes the creation of the

underlying essences of which all things are constituted, and the creation of living creatures and worlds begins. First there arises the creator god Brahma, alias Prajapati. He creates the gods, father, and mankind; also the worlds with all that fills them. . . finally he creates the Vedas and sacrifices, the orders of society and the stages of life.[19]

Universal cycles are never-ending and the scheme of the organization of the world bears a striking resemblance to modern cosmological theory of the Big Bang.

Darkness was in the beginning hidden by darkness; indistinguishable, all this was water. That which, coming into being, was covered with the void, that One arose through the power of heat.[20]

Fig. 4: The Wheel of Karma
The Tibetan lamas represented the course of human existence in various forms, centring around the cock of amorality, the serpent of hatred and the pig of ignorance. Liberation is freedom from the wheel.

Mind stirs in the water, a symbol of time, and the act of creation is a golden germ of fire which springs up within the water.

The world-egg is a metaphor for the universe. The proportions of the layers of the egg vary from sect to sect, but the overall concept is consistent. The outermost layer is undifferentiated matter; within it is a layer of intelligence; within that is a layer of egocentricity; and within that layers of ether, wind, fire and at the centre, water (time). Each layer is ten times as thick as the next one in, and there are seven layers in all. It is significant that the structure is similar to that of atomic electron shells. In Hebrew mysticism the layers of reality are actually called *"qlipthoth"*, literally translated as *"shells"*.

In the cosmos described by the Hindu sacred Puranas, two sets of seven layers define the universe from the realm of unreincarnated immortals at the top to the lowest hells of the nagas (snakes) below, with the realm of earth in the middle. The layers are defined by their distance above and below the surface of earth and by their temporal periods.[21] The snake is a common symbol of time, often shown encircling the world egg. (Figure 5)

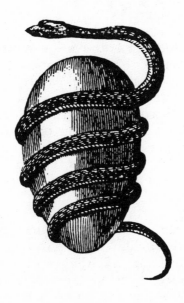

Fig. 5: The Snake of Time encircling the World Egg
An alchemical image of the dominance of time over life on earth.

The Jain cosmos is composed of concentric circles around the eternal wheel of time. The lifetime of the world is divided into 12 ages divided into two equal sets of ascending and descending series of developmental stages. The scheme is similar to those described in *"Up From Eden"* by Ken Wilber and *"The Reflexive Universe"* by Arthur M. Young. (See Chapter Eight)

All early cosmological schemes describe periodic contractions and evolutions of the universe, endless series of great aeons punctuated by destructions of various sorts (by water, fire and wind), Brahmas who command each world, and structures which represent circular layered levels of reality, like the symbol of creation, the lotus. The lotus appears on the surface of the primordial waters, unfolds to become the universe, and when it has finished its cycle, enfolds all being back into itself. The unfolding of the universe happens within the domain of time.

The Babylonian and Sumerian *"Epic of Creation"* states that in the beginning Alala (Earth) and Belili (Time) alone existed, and Anu (Heaven) descended from them, an image evocative of the space-time continuum of modern physics. The world was seen as a repetitive cosmic drama enacted periodically throughout the durations of worlds.

Mandaean world ages telescope in a similar fashion to the Hindu-Buddhist and are additive. A great cycle is 480,000 years, with sub-cycles of 60,000, 240 and five years. Fifty days each year are allotted to the worship and ceremonial repetition of the grand life of time.[22]

Early eastern cyclic cosmologies contain obvious correlations to modern views of the unfolding of the universe, but are ridiculed by science as meaningless and insignificant on the grounds that the mathematics is absurd, with the notable exception of *"The Tao of Physics"* by Fritjof Capra and *"The Dancing Wu Li Masters"* by Gary Zukov. Within the context of such early cultures, the poetic description of universal processes is remarkably accurate and relevant, besides possessing a spiritual quality missing from the modern view of the world. The Shemitah, a Jewish theory of cosmic cycles, is based on a sequence of seven cycles, each composed of 6000 years with a 1000 year sabbath, similar to the organization of the week, and also related to planets. Each 7000 year cycle is the enactment of a variation of the torah (the law). Seven complete cycles culminate in 49,000 years with a Great Jubilee of 1000 years. Every 50,000 years the whole cycle begins again and recurs almost identically.[23]

The Great Year

The ancients attempted to justify cyclic theory by determining when world ages began and ended. There was a belief that the beginning moment was when the seven known planets conjoined in a specific alignment, for example, in the equinoctial sign Aries, then the planets continued on their predictable but complex cycles. It required truly astronomical calculations to discover when such a constellation would occur, so even the most sophisticated cultures were only able to estimate the duration of the Great Year. The positions of the planets were believed to determine appearance, behaviour, parents, fate and events in the world, and it was thought that repetitive astronomical cycles would produce identical repetitive world ages.

The Greek Stoic philosophers Zeno, Chrysippus and Eudemus believed that world ages repeated themselves identically, down to the smallest detail. Plato reasoned that identical world cycles were probable, originating as they do in the Idea, and that the cycles of men were shorter than the cycles of all nature. Plato's *"Timaeus"* describes a story told by the Egyptian priests at Sais to Solon: "There have been and will be many different calamities to destroy humanity, the greatest of them by fire and water, lesser ones by countless means." Plato then told the story of Atlantis, a tale which was "real" but also a metaphor for a previous world age. "We will transfer the imaginary citizens and city which you (Socrates) described yesterday to the real world, and say that your city is the city of my story and your citizens those historical ancestors of ours whom the priests described. They will fit exactly, and there will be no disharmony if we speak as if they were the men who lived at that time." Plato taught the idea of identically recurrent world ages, repetitive down to the character of individuals, even those present in the dialogue. He personified time as a living being, the nature of which is eternal: "it was not possible to bestow this attribute of eternity fully on the created universe; but he (God) determined to make a moving image of eternity which remains for ever at one." The eternal moving image is the soul of the universe contained within the bowl of the heavens, "and when he had compounded the whole, he divided it up into as many souls as there are stars, and allotted each soul a star. And mounting them on their stars, as if on chariots, he showed them the nature of the universe and told them the laws of their destiny".

Origen and Hipparchus believed in Great Years of 36,000 years of identical recurrence, as did Bartholomeus Anglicus (ca.1230), Siger of Brabant (ca.1277) and Pietro d'Albano (d.1316) – they all thought that even minute details of each age were duplicated exactly.[24] I Hsing of eighth century China proposed a cycle of 96,961,740 years and the philosopher Wu Lin-Chuaun (1249-1333) a cycle of 129,600 years.[25] The Greek Lindos astronomer of Rhodes believed in a 290,000 year cycle. The Mandaeans followed cycles of 480,000 years, as well as minor cycles of 5,240 and 60,000 years.[26] Heraclitus assumed a cycle of 10,800 years and Aristarchus of Samos 2484 years.

The Bible describes the creation and destruction of the world. The Old Testament begins with seven days of Creation and ends with Elijah's admonition that "the day cometh that shall burn as an oven".[27] The New Testament reiterates the theme by applying the life, death and resurrection of worlds to the life, death and resurrection of the cosmic man, Jesus Christ. The mystery of resurrection reflects the lifetime of the Universe, of humanity, the seven sacraments of life, the sacred round of yearly festivals and the daily cycle of prayers. The process of the universe is reenacted by every being every day, reflected in the Christian sacraments.

In the Christian church the length of world ages was derived from the Bible, and renowned churchmen such as Clement of Alexandria (c.150-220), Minucius Felix (c. AD 175) and Arnobius (c.285-340) believed in an Annus Magnus (Great Year), the Biblical Creation dated in history. Scholars and churchmen worked out Biblical lineages and tried to date Creation itself, with considerable variation. Septuagint dated Creation at 5960 BC, Josephus at 3952 BC, the Venerable Bede at 3949, Abraham Judeus at 3761 BC, and one creation time was even given as six o'clock in the evening on 22 October, 4004 BC.

The Precession of the Equinoxes

The most common length of cycle was based on the phenomenon called the *Precession of the Equinoxes*, first identified by the Egyptians. The Earth rotates on its inclined axis imperfectly, acting like a pointer moving backwards through the zodiac, a phenomenon called "precession of the equinoctial (spring) point". The polar axis appears to move around the true north pole of the ecliptic in about 25,000 years, called the Platonic Year by the Greeks, subdivided into twelve Platonic Months of about 2,000 years each. Initially the Platonic Year was believed to be 36,000 years, but the true figure was eventually computed. Over the ages estimates of the duration of the Platonic Year have been as follows:

36,000	Original Platonic Year
28,800	Ptolemy (1st Century AD)
26,000	Medieval[28]
25,920	Man and Time
25,725.6	Modern Astronomical[29]
25,411	Ancient[30]
24,120	Tycho Brahe

The equinoctial pointer is the Sun's position at the Vernal (Spring) Equinox, when day is equal to night and the days are getting longer. If at sunrise on the day of the equinox a pointer were projected into space, it would intersect the ecliptic in its sign of precession. In ancient times major deities correlated with the then current precessional sign. (Figure 6) During the precessional Age of Taurus the Bull from approximately 4000 to 2000 BC, the primary gods were bull-gods, the prototypes of the later Egyptian Apis and Hathoor, the Hebrew Golden Calf or the bull-headed Minotaur of Crete. During the Age of Aries, from 2000 BC to the time of Christ, the Ram cults of Ammon in Egypt and the sacrifice of the ram by the "two-horn crowned" Moses replaced the Bull. The Piscean Age from the birth of Christ to AD 2000 saw the Christian motif of the Fishes: "*Ictheos*" which means fishes in Greek is also the word for Christos.

The twelve zodiac constellations in the night sky are not exact thirty degree segments of the ecliptic so the dates for the entrance and exit of the ages are unspecific. The coming precessional Age of Aquarius could begin anytime from the middle of the 19th century to the end of the 21st century.

Myths of the World Axis

"*Hamlet's Mill*" by Giorgio Santillana and Hertha von Dechand presents a theory that myth is the original form of science; that the basis of myth is not terrestrial but celestial. Before writing was invented, counting and measure provided the armature on which the texture of myth was woven. The most potent myths of creation — of whirlpools, shamans and smiths, cosmic axes, world trees, the Garden of Eden, Mount Meru and others — are all representations of the precessional movement

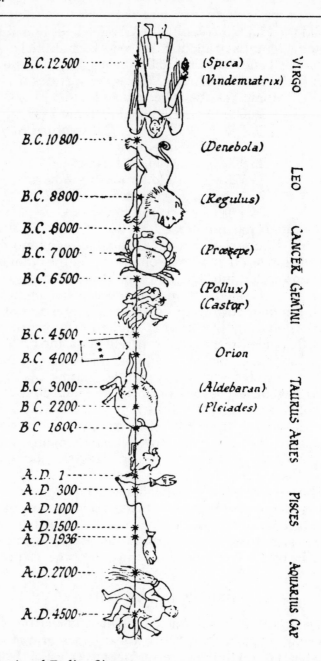

Fig. 6: Precessional Zodiac Signs
Symbols of the zodiac signs superimposed on the ecliptic showing at which time the equinox point passes into and out of each sign. It can be clearly seen that although the signs are considered equal 30° divisions of the ecliptic, that the constellations are uneven and their equivalent precessional periods vary considerably.

Fig. 7: Omphalos at Delphi
The stone omphalos at Delphi, set on the site of the landing of the ark
of Deucalion (the Greek Noah), showing clearly the mesh
symbolizing the latitude and longitude grid of earth. The sun god
Apollo was also reputed to have slain Python, a serpent representing
time, and bound time to earth at Delphi. *(Photo by Margo Russell)*

of the equinoxes. The Pole Star pointer is the axis of the world
and is analogous to the tent-pole because the world axis can be
located anywhere. The Greek *omphalos* (navel) symbolizes the
same idea, and decorations spiralling around the omphalos at
the Temple of Apollo at Delphi clearly show that it is a "centre
of the world". (Figure 7)

Representations of drilling or churning in Hindu, Chinese,
Egyptian, Babylonian and Mayan mythologies as well as the
central Norse myth of Hamlet's Mill reiterate the theme that
the millstone represents the precessional mechanism. In
these myths power over time resides in the centre of the mill,
navel or wheel. Mount Meru in Hindu religion is an image of
the centre of the world and presents another common concept
– enlightened souls ascend to heaven via the world axis.

In Persian Ismaeli theosophy there never was a time when the world did not exist. The present world is only one of 18,000 successive cycles of humanity. Adam is not unique, but always the last survivor of the Cycle of Epiphany preceding our cycle of occultation. As grave symptoms of the end of a world age appear, Koranic dignitaries are obliged to restore the discipline of the arcanum of the *"Gnosis of Resurrection"*. The doctrine does not refer to the outward forms of Islam but to the secret inner transformation of the last Imam (Adam) of each world – every human is potentially last and first. The Eve of Adam is the spiritual, secret meaning of the esoteric law, which he craves in his nostalgia for paradise.[31]

Myths of the end of the world abound. Those cultures which possess a cataclysmic mythology are legion. Bertrand Russell said that only a few of the names of twenty-one past civilizations are known, and then only the names, but that another fourteen have disappeared without a trace.[32]

The following is a partial list of cultures which accepted cyclical world ages, with an indication of the number of the present recurrent world age:

1. Hindu – Fifth Pralaya of an era of decline
2. Buddhist – Kali Yuga of the First Descending interval period of an uncountable in an evolved state (Kali Yuga began in 3102 BC)
3. Mexican – IVth Ixtilxochiti
4. Roman – Fifth World Age (according to Lucius Ampelius)
5. Hebrew – Eighth Jubilee Cycle (Era of Creation 3761 BC)
6. Hawaiian – end of the Ninth
7. Icelandic – end of the Ninth leading to the Tenth
8. Ismaeli Iranian – more than the 18,000th cycle
9. Mayan – Third World Cycle (began 3375 BC)
10. North Borneo – Eighth
11. Chinese – the neo-Confucians accept the idea
12. Norse

Myths of the end of the world also describe the rebirth of a renewed world. An example is the primary Norse myth, the Volpuspa, which tells about the end of the world embodied by the fate of the gods. Both are called *Ragnarok*, the "twilight of the gods", simultaneously the end and the entire process of events, fate and destiny. The collapse affects and is affected by giants, gods and men and is fought on a battlefield one hundred leagues each way. Morality is rejected, brothers slay each other and kinship is profaned. All actions are criminal and bloody, and decay reigns. The primary cause is that the gods begin to disregard their promises to men and to each other. The tempo of downfall increases, the sun darkens and storms rage over the earth. Myriad demons enchained within the earth break loose and arrive to persecute humanity. A yellow eagle shrieks at the prospect of carrion and the ship of death shatters its moorings. The world groans, mountains crash, the sky is rent and the demons demolish the gods with their fiery swords. The stars vanish, smoke and fire abound and the earth falls back into the sea. It is the end of the world, and its termination sounds like a primitive description of now! Even though men and gods die, the world does not disappear forever. The great fire of Ragnarok is followed by the terrible winter, and when it has passed the remaining gods raise the earth from the sea. Two men survive, hiding in the forest Hoddmimisholt, eating only the morning dew, and from them a new race of men descends.

The history of the survivors of a World Age describes the fate of the deceased world age and a pattern for its renewal. All images which carry the exegesis are included. As world ages are endless and repetitive, so the stories and eventually myths of the end and every fragment of history become magnified, distorted and grafted onto personal stories and histories. Every battle is the battle with the gods.

After thousands of generations and tens of thousands of years creation myths assume the character of a cosmic drama, The Divine Plot. In retelling the stories, the reality of the end of a previous highly developed world becomes foggy, misunderstood and seen as fantasy, much as few individuals on earth now could claim to "understand" the state of the world in the present time, including the leaders of the major nations of the earth. Successive generations of elders appropriated the tales told them during childhood and assume their burden and authority. The responsibility for the transmission became so great that the stories themselves assumed godlike proportions. The transmission gradually became sacred.

The Norse creation bears a strong resemblance to the time scale in its metaphors. The creation of earth contrasts a dark, frozen world (the void) with a blazing, fiery world (creation). The rivers froze and sparks from the hot world melted them to form a giant called Ymir (an Aries celestial god) and the cow Audumbla (Taurus earth mother), who fed him with her milk. The first man was created by Audumbla licking salt into his form (Gemini). After a brief time, a set of giant brothers (Cancer) born of an evil thorn tree killed Ymir, and all but one were drowned in his blood. The surviving brother and his family were saved by climbing on a luor, variously described as a cradle, coffin, bier or ship (the flood). The brothers used Ymir's body to make the earth after carrying it to the centre of the world. The seas and lakes came from the blood, the earth from his flesh, the sky from his skull, supported at its corners by four dwarfs. The clouds came from his brains, and the stars and heavenly bodies from sparks from the hot world, and all were ordered by the gods, establishing days and years.

The anthropomorphic creation, with the cosmos being created from the body of the divine one, is similar to Iranian and Indian sources. The metempsychosis of giant, cow and then man is reminiscent of eastern and primitive creations. Jung quotes a Hindu creation myth:

> He (Atman) was as big as a man and woman joined together; he divided himself into two, and thus husband and wife were born. . . He joined himself to her, and thus men were born. She thought: 'How should he lie with me after having produced me? I will hide myself'. She became a cow, he became a bull; they joined and cattle were born. She became a mare, he a stallion; she became a she-ass, he an ass; they joined and the hoofed animals were born. Thus he created everything down to the ants, male and female. . . Then he knew: 'I am this creation, for I produced it all from myself'. Such was creation. He who possesses this knowledge creates his own being in that creation.[33]

The evolution of the myth is a transformative symbol of psychic processes in humanity. For Snorri (c.1179-1241), the writer of the Edda and the foremost Norse mythologer, creation was merely the first step towards Ragnarok.[34]

At the centre of the Norse world was the Yggdrasil tree, the tree of fate where the gods hold council every day to determine the welfare of the universe. Beneath it the well of fate Uroarbrunnr conceived the female fates who laid down the courses of men's and women's lives for all time. The tree rises to the sky, its branches cover the whole world. Its three roots reach down to the world of death, Hel, to the world of the frost-giants and to the world of men. It is on this tree Odin hanged himself, questing for wisdom, and upon it depends the very essence of the world. But, by the time it reaches its full growth, it has already begun decaying. The fate of the Yggdrasil tree is the fate of the world.

Flood Legends

Flood legends exist in virtually every culture and are so

pervasive that they have given rise to cults of universal destruction by water. The best known in the west is the biblical great flood of Noah and the ark in Genesis. Following is a list of many cultures which have a deluge legend:

1. Biblical Flood of Noah and his Ark
2. Greek legend of Deucalian and Phyrra
3. Babylonian and Sumerian Utnapishtim in the Gilgamesh Epic
4. Chaldean records
5. North Syrian Sisthes
6. Hindu Puranos of Satyavarata; Rig-Vedas; Satapatha Brahmana; four in the Upangas; three in the Matsya Purana
7. Icelandic Eddas of Bergelmir
8. Siberian shaman rituals
9. Norse epics
10. Welsh ballads of Dwyfan and Dwyfach
11. African Masai
12. American Indians, especially Minabozho of the Algonquins
13. Tarascan Indians of Central America
14. Guatemalan Nala and Nata
15. Toltec giant Shelua
16. Hottentots
17. Australian Aborigines
18. Fiji Islanders
19. Eskimos
20. Malays
21. Samoans
22. Burmese
23. Cambodians
24. Maori warriors
25. Dyaks of Borneo
26. Chinese
27. Arawakans of Guyana, Northern Brazil and Columbia
28. Phoenician cosmology of Sanchuniathon
29. Cushites
30. Iranian hero Yima in the Zend-Avesta
31. Thessalian Cerambos
32. Cos Island hero Merops
33. Aztec codex Chimalpopoca of Nata and Nena
34. Central American Popul Vuh
35. Chibchas of Bogota
36. Mandan Indians of North America
37. Iroquois, Chicksaws, Sioux and Okanagaus of America
38. Nicaraguans
39. Pima Indian tribe

Flood legends are similar in structure, and often contain the theme that representative species are collected and saved from a world-wide catastrophe with the assistance of a god. Fig. 9 shows the many places on earth where such legends have existed and affected virtually every culture before the present.

Memories of the world before a cataclysm emphasize a great, corrupt power of technology as a worldwide phenomenon. Legends describe gigantic shining metal cities reaching up to the sky, vast harvest lands stretching beyond the horizon. Blur-fast metal birds streaked overhead, spewing out flames, and men rode spaceships to the realm of the gods, the stars. Mass religious spectacles attended by millions of people vied with dissolute orgies involving whole cities. Humanity knew all there was to know, but it had fallen into devilish ways and ignorantly destroyed itself in a burst of fire and brimstone. The corruption of spiritual decline was attended by a proliferation of base and exploitative kings who shackled humanity in their greed. Propriety was thrown to the winds, and populaces indulged in endless intoxicated revels of Dionysiac frenzy, everyone following the uninhibited pursuit of gross material wealth. Those that had the wealth were forced to invent progressively more brutal ways to dispossess the masses and nations of underprivileged who created the wealth. There was continuous warfare between hopelessly decadent nations of rapists and developing nations with violent and corrupt leadership trying to regain their sovereignty.

The downfall of a world age was attended by aerial combat between warmongering silver birds and dragons breathing thunderbolts upon helpless populations. Hideous explosions created quasi-suns which burned all those within sight, followed by years of impenetrable darkness. Poisonous vapours filled the air, choking the life out of all vegetation and life. The carnage was only terminated when the gods arose in fury and initiated a total conflagration which was so powerful that it altered the course of the earth and the planets in the sky. The evil ended only when the entire world consumed itself.

Visions of the end of the world were passed on through the rites of elders as they huddled in fear and horror in their places of relative safety. The *"Edens"* where the survivors of the holocaust gathered were remote places, protected by

Fig. 9: Map of Cataclysm and Flood Legends
The world map shows those cultures and their locations which have flood legends (O symbol) or legends of cyclic cataclysms (● symbol). Such legends are common to the entire world. The A symbol shows the suggested locations for Atlantis.

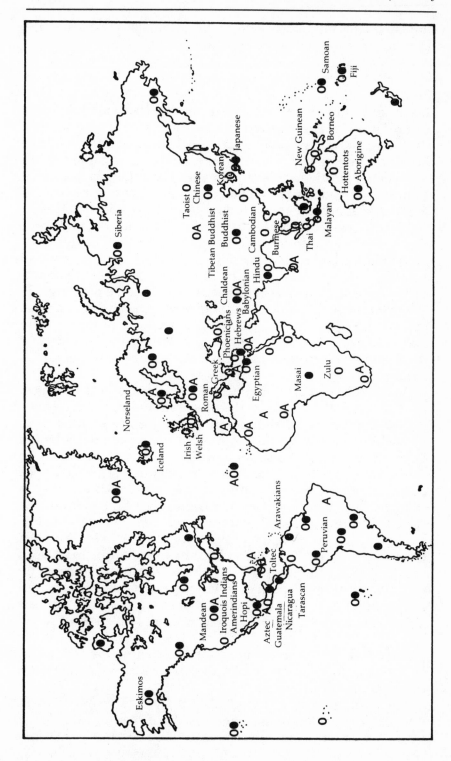

impenetrable mountain ranges or impassable deserts, and survival of the enlightened few implied isolation.

Atlantis

Myths depicting floods, cataclysms or the destruction by water or fire of a highly advanced civilization which has conquered the entire known world all point to Atlantis. Atlantis, so-called because European and Asiatic legends place its capital to the West while North and South American legends place it to the East, was assumed to be the acme of civilization of a previous world age which existed in the middle of the Atlantic Ocean.

Atlantis was considered to be the home of the gods, the Garden of Eden, Mount Meru, Paradise and the "golden age" of humanity before the present era. While the existence of Atlantis is not accepted by the scientific or historical establishment, there has been serious study of the possibility in an estimated 20,000 books. All proof is circumstantial, as it must be by definition because Atlantis is a decimated former world age civilization. The sheer number of commentators proves that the principle of a previous golden age is ingrained in human nature.

One of the earliest references to Atlantis is also the most persuasive. Plato described the physical design, history, laws, agricultural practices, shortcomings and virtues of Atlantis in "Timaeus". The destruction of Atlantis is partially described in "Critias", but the manuscript ends in mid-sentence.

According to Plato, the story of Atlantis was told to the grandfather of Critias by the revered sage of Athens, Solon (640-558 BC), who had heard it from Egyptian priests at the sacred centre of Sais. Solon dated the fall of Atlantis approximately 9000 years previously. (In the middle of the tenth millennium BC.) Since Plato, many attempts have been made to locate the exact site of Atlantis and to trace its effects on the mainstream of human mythologies, customs, art and architecture. The belief of Rudolf Steiner and the Theosophists is that Atlantis is the spiritual predecessor of the present world age.

According to various commentators, Atlantis was destroyed:
– as a result of comets bombarding the earth and great floods (Ignatius Donnelly);
– by a volcano which exploded at the Cycladic island of Thera in 1600 BC (Galanopoulos and Professor Marinatos);
– for no apparent geophysical reason but because of its decay

(Lewis Spence);

– by the earth capturing a satellite Luna (Hoerbiger's Cosmogonic Theory and H. S. Bellamy);

– through axis shifts (Immanuel Velikovsky).

No one theory is conclusive because all traces of such an ancient civilization have been either covered up by later humanity or integrated into the art and culture of early cultures. Proof of the existence of Atlantis, as well as the even earlier legendary civilizations of Lemuria and Mu in art, architecture and language, are compelling but fantastic. Desmond Lee, translator of Timaeus, avoids the issue by considering Plato the inventor of science fiction – and presents Atlantis as a construction of the imagination of all advanced material civilizations.

Atlantis-lore often supports eternal recurrence, as in *"The Secret Doctrine"* and *"Isis Unveiled"* by Madame Blavatsky, the founder of the Theosophical Society in 1875. Believers in great cycles of history accept the myth of Atlantis as proof of their hypotheses. An important assumption follows from the circularity of world ages: the destruction of Atlantis was not just the end of a former world age but a collective memory of the last recurrent world cycle. The doctrine of eternal recurrence implies an exact repetition of all events within each cycle and an Atlantean cataclysm caused by unrighteous avarice and power correlates with the present state of the world cycle, as we approach the end of a world age. The Atlantis myths of many ancient civilizations corroborate the idea of recurrent history, including traces such as the ceremonial ball courts of the Mayans which evoke the major stadia of modern societies.

Plato's description of the capital of Atlantis corresponds in many details to the organization and geography of New York City, although it must be understood that terms used in the fourth century BC must be updated. In Timaeus, one of the priests of Sais told Solon,

> There is a story which even you have preserved, that once upon a time Phaethon, the son of Helios, having yoked the steeds in his father's chariot, because he was not able to drive them in the path of his father, burnt up all that was upon the earth, and was himself destroyed by a thunder-bolt.[35]

The story is a prologue to a detailed description of Atlantis, but is symbolically the attempt by the child of the sun god Helios (humanity) to yoke father's steeds (nuclear energy similar to that of the sun?), and being unable to control them, destroys the earth. Most commentators have seen this episode as a metaphor for the deviation of planets from their courses in the heavens during a periodic conflagration of earth. The priest differentiates conflagrations caused and related to cosmic phenomena, for which it is disastrous to be upon mountains and dry, lofty places but safe to be near sea-level and low-lying land, and the floods, when it is best to be high and not to be low. He implies that because of the location and special features of Egypt, both types of cataclysm have spared the sacred land. The elderly priest chastised the young Solon by telling him that history as kept by other civilizations records only letters of State, while in Egypt the records of previous great ages are recorded in the temples.

> . . . when the stream from heaven descends like a pestilence, and leaves only those of you who are destitute of letters and education; and thus you have to begin all over again as children, and know nothing of what happened in ancient times, either among us or yourselves. As for those genealogies of yours which you have recounted to us, Solon, they are no better than the tales of children; for, in the first place, you remember one deluge only, whereas there were many before that; and, in the next place, you do not know that there dwelt in your land the fairest and noblest race of men which ever lived, of whom you and your whole city are but a seed or remnant.[36]

If a catastrophe occurred to modern civilization tomorrow, the primary record of extensive information of previous ages would be carried by books and in computers, both immediately expendable and likely to disappear first. There are no monuments to carry modern knowledge, and even the most rudimentary attempts are miserable failures. An example is the plaque designed for the Mariner 10 and 11 spacecraft, which is incomprehensible to the average human. A prototype was presented to a seminar of top scientists and only one could understand it at all. To modern society, history is very vague and the ability to transmit knowledge beyond a breakdown of civilization is virtually nonexistent.

Plato's detailed description of Atlantis in Critias can be compared to a view of modern New York City and the United States as described by a primitive person, although it could apply in a collective sense to any major city in the modern world. The following parallels are interesting and striking. The phrases in brackets denote modern parallels.

"He himself, as he was a god, found no difficulty in making special arrangements for the centre island, bringing two streams of water under the earth, which he caused to ascend as springs, one of warm water and the other of cold." (*The ancient Greeks could not have known of hot-and-cold running water.*)

". . . they dug out of the earth whatever was to be found there, mineral as well as metal, and that which is now only a name, and was then something more than a name – orichalcum – was dug out of the earth in many parts of the island." (*Orichalcum has confused scholars, but it is mentioned later in the commentary that the temples were all made of this wonderful and valuable substance, which is clearly aluminum!*)

Then follows a long segment describing the multitude of animals, plants, flowers and fruits which grew on Atlantis.

"First of all they bridged over the zones of the sea which surrounded the ancient metropolis, and made a passage into and out of the royal palace; and then they began to build the palace in the habitation of the god and their ancestors. This they continued to ornament in successive generations, every king surpassing the one who came before him to the utmost of his power, until they made the building a marvel to behold for size and beauty." (*An apt description of a modern city.*)

". . . constructing bridges of such a width as would leave a passage for a single trireme to pass out of one into another, and roofed them over; and there was a way underneath for the ships." (*Bridges link Manhattan Island to the mainland of New Jersey, New York and Long Island.*)

"Here, too, was Poseidon's own temple, of a stadium in length and half a stadium in width, and of a proportionate height, having a sort of barbaric splendour." (*One of many large sports stadia in New York.*)

"In the interior of the temple. . . adorned everywhere with gold and silver and orichalcum; all the other parts of the walls and pillars and floor they lined with orichalcum." (*Orichalcum, or aluminum is everywhere in the modern city, anodized to look like silver or gold.*)

"In both of the two islands formed by the zones; and in the centre of the larger of the two there was a racecourse of a stadium in width, and in length allowed to extend all round the island, for horses to race in. Also there were guard-houses at intervals for the body-guards." (*The horses race at the racetracks on Long Island, larger than Manhattan, and the horses pulling chariots are automobiles travelling around Long Island and Manhattan on expressways, with the toll gates being guard-houses.*)

The farmlands of the great plains are in rectangular grids like the midwest, and the surrounding mountains, celebrated for their number, size and beauty, are like the Rocky Mountains in the western United States.

Plato described the structure of government, where areas of the country are proportionally represented and have required military service. The leaders of the country proper are required to give a portion of their earnings to furnish war-chariots, so as to make up a total of ten thousand of them and thousands of ships to sail the seas. The rulers met every five or six years to consult about the laws. The general structure of Atlantis sounds very like modern democratic government, down to elections held at regular times. The traditions of the country are very noble and aspirations high, but the vast power carried by the citizenry led them to overvalue the material world. Their divinity began to fade.

> . . . then, they being unable to bear their fortune, became unseemly, and to him who had an eye to see, they began to appear base, and had lost the fairest of their precious gifts; but to those who had no eye to see the true happiness, they still appeared glorious and blessed at the very time when they were filled with unrighteous avarice and power. Zeus, the god of gods, who rules with law, and is able to see into such things, perceiving that an honorable race was in a most wretched state, and wanting to inflict punishment on them, that they might be chastened and improved, collected all the gods into his most holy habitation, which, being placed in the centre of the world, see all things that partake of generation. And when he had called them together he spake as follows. . .

Here Plato's story ends abruptly. In Plato's tales there are no goblins, no tales of giants – it is a reasonable tale of people who built cities and ships and farm the land – exactly like the modern world does. Atlantis is the end of the last world age.

Donnelly was a very thorough commentator on Atlantean matters, presenting an extensive historical and scientific theory of the existence of Atlantis. He called it an *"antediluvian"* world meaning "before the flood," and he parallels Atlantis with the Garden of Eden, the Garden of the Hesperides, the Elysian Fields, the Navel of the Earth, the Asgard of the Eddas and the Mount Olympus of the Greeks – a symbol of the universal memory of a great land where early humanity dwelt in peace and happiness. Donnelly divided the early history of the world into a stage before and after the deluge, but does not recognize that the world of Atlantis was his world.

The psychic prophet Edgar Cayce regularly mentioned Atlantis in his Life Readings as a great civilization destroyed by world-wide catastrophe. He stated that the lowland plains of

Atlantis were located in what is now the eastern seaboard of the United States. He even predicted that evidence for Atlantis would be found in 1968-1969 off the coast of America. Charles Berlitz and others did discover man-made structures near Bimini off the coast of Miami at the time predicted by Cayce – the remains of huge stone buildings, gigantic steps, a causeway and even a circular formation of forty-four marble columns. Although photographed, the finds were not recovered.[37]

Evidence For Atlantis

Many aspects of civilization could hold traces of ancient Atlantis, such as modern alphabets and languages, the cultivation of vegetables and the domestication and raising of animals unknown to the Greeks. Domestication is a mysterious process which is not well understood today. There is a proliferation of terms in Plato's story which describe technological achievements unheard of until recent history, such as the mariner's compass, the magnet, gunpowder, navigation skills and devices, paper and silk.

Donnelly said that the Greeks associated the origin of astronomy with Atlas and Hercules, who were Atlantean kings or heroes. The Egyptians regarded Taut, Thoth, or At-hotes as the originator of astronomy and the alphabet.[38] All these influences parallel the many books which attempt to verify the existence of Atlantis on iconographic grounds, especially through the similarities of artifacts from the Mayan, Aztec, Toltec, North American Indian, and many other civilizations.

There have been numerous volcanoes in the past fifty thousand years which could have been the source of the Atlantis myth, and enough of them to justify the idea of periodic destructions.

The Greek island of Thera (Santorini) was the site of a volcanic explosion somewhere between 1600 BC and 1400 BC. Professor Marinatos of the Greek Department of Antiquities has proposed Thera as the site of Atlantis, but the evidence for a civilization as grand and technologically proficient as the myths is inconclusive, resting as it does on magnificent wall paintings and frescos and little more.[39] More recently, Jacques Cousteau made an exploration of Santorini in 1976, finding traces of two volcanic explosions, one of them in 2500 BC.

Otto Muck's "*The Secret of Atlantis*" (1976) presents the most recent scientific evidence for the existence of Atlantis. He states that the Thera volcano is certainly later than the story of Plato, and that it must have been one of the outposts of the Atlantean empire, as are the traces found in the Bahamanian and Caribbean waters. He includes testimony from the Soviet scientist N. F. Zhirov from his book Atlantis, stating that a large landmass dropped out of the bottom of the mid-Atlantic ridge in recent geological times. Muck's conclusion is that Asteroid A plunged into the area of the so-called Bermuda Triangle in 8498 BC and destroyed in one brief day an ancient civilization and a majority of the world's population. He adduces evidence in the realms of anthropology, calendrical systems, climatic phenomena, astronomy, architecture, archaeology and many other fields. As a scientist of great repute and technological ability, the book is a very convincing presentation of evidence.

Another way to look at the Atlantis phenomenon is that illustrated by Lewis Spence in "Will Europe Follow Atlantis?", which compares the social and moral conditions in the modern world with that of the reputed Atlantis. Again he draws on a wide variety of mythological material and makes the parallels between Atlantis and our present day quite reasonable.

Finally, the work of Immanuel Velikovsky is evidence for cyclical cataclysms more than for the existence of Atlantis. His books "Worlds in Collision" (1950), "Ages in Chaos" (1952) and "Earth in Upheaval" (1955), all present the idea that there have been many axis shifts of earth, caused by collisions with asteroids or comets which affected life, and bring evidence from widely diverse fields. His central theme is that the cataclysm is described in detail in the Biblical story of the Exodus.

The reason why images of floods, cataclysms and Atlantis have taken such a deep hold on the imagination of humanity is that we possess memory of the actual event, programmed into our genetic code, through the resonance of the patterns of Time. The Age of Humanity always ends and begins with cataclysms, and these definitive shock points in time are the collective property of all humanity. H. S. Bellamy's "The Atlantis Myth" correlates the destruction of Babylon in the Book of Revelations with references from the books of Ezekiel, Isaiah, Jeremiah about Babylon and concludes that they refer to Atlantis. The images of the Tower of Babylon and its confusion of tongues, the vice and depravity, and the collapse of civilized values are consonant with our modern world.

★Chapter Three★
★Eternal Recurrence★

Eternal Recurrence. The Stoics. Jesus, Vico, Nietzsche, Pythagoras and Haldane. Sentiment du deja-vu. Plato's Myth of Er. Catastrophe Theory. The schools of Gurdjieff, Ouspensky and Collin. The Theory of Celestial Influence. Time and the new physics. Measure, meditation and maya. Spengler and the Mathematics of History. What is memory? Sheldrake's New Science of Life. The wedding of astrology and biology.

> For the earth once more begets what it's begotten from of old.
> Goethe

Cyclic history leads naturally to the concept of eternal recurrence – the exact repetition of events in time. Recurrence is experienced in the phenomenon of the *sentiment du deja-vu*, which is the feeling of having been somewhere before, experienced a particular situation before, or known someone before; a strange feeling of familiarity which remains unsatisfied regardless of attempts to trace the feeling to its source. Scents, sights, tastes or other sensations open floodgates into previous experiences. Such feelings happen to everyone at some time in life, and many people are besieged with constant access to such "other worlds".

Recurrence is an ancient idea symbolized by the ouroburos snake biting its tail, or the serpent (an image of time) spiralling around the world egg. (See Fig. 5) In modern physics it is accepted that the curvature of time is a property of a cyclic universe and that repetition occurs at many levels of reality. Molecules break down into their component atoms (die) and reassemble into new molecules, the equivalent of creating a new molecular body. Cells in the body die and are replaced daily, with the complete cellular body being replaced continuously. The variation from body to body is so slight that it apparently recurs just as it was before and carries the exact same habits, form, constitution and health. The mechanism of such astonishing continuity is recurrence, described in *"A New Model of the Universe"* by P. D. Ouspensky, *"The Theory of Celestial Influence"* by Rodney Collin and *"Living Time"* by Maurice Nicoll.

Ouspensky illustrates recurrence by a cyclic wave for each day, a sequence of such waves making a year, which is itself one wave within the lifetime of seventy-odd years, which is a wave within the time of all humanity. When seen end-on, each cycle is a circle, but when seen side-on, from a higher dimension, is a continuous wave, like the solar system seen in its time dimension. (Fig. 10) Each wave seems to be independent of the whole when seen as a circle, yet is a whole in itself and parallels the waves below and above it. The basic nature of sine curves is to appear as circles seen from a higher dimension of existence.

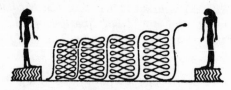

Fig. 10: *Temporal Waves and Successive Lives*
An Egyptian image of the snake of time contorting into a series of individual spirals within a larger spiral, a symbol of the repetitive nature of time and its relevance to human existence. *(Nicol, Living Time)*

A point contains an infinite number of points. A line contains an infinite number of points bounded by a beginning and end. The circumference of a circle contains an infinite number of points without a beginning or end. A plane contains infinite lines and a solid contains an infinite number of planes contained within its periphery. When the transition to higher dimensions is made, each moment of time contains an infinite number of possibilities. As a plane contains an infinity of lines, a moment of time contains an infinity of histories and futures. All lines in a plane are there awaiting discovery, and in time all possible histories are also there.

Pythagoras taught *eternal recurrence*.[40] Eudemus envisaged a complete return in every detail and identified two kinds of recurrence: one is "repetition in time" of the natural order of things such as the seasons, day and night, produced by cycles of the sun, moon, earth and the planets; the second is "repetition in eternity" in which identical things exist in a number of existences.

Plato's *"Phaedo"* refers to the triple repetition of lives. Knowledge is recollection, implying a previous time in which that which is recollected was learned. The soul must have had a previous existence in the same body – a proof of the immortality of the soul.

> Now into the same place from which each Soul cometh, she returneth not again until ten thousand years have been accomplished; for sooner is no Soul fledged with wings, save the Soul of him who hath sought after True Wisdom without deceit, or hath loved his comrade in the bonds of Wisdom. The Souls of such men, when the third course of a thousand years is finished, if they have chosen this life three times in order, being fledged with wings do then depart.

Plato implies that the Soul incarnates many times with periods of thousands of years in between, and that hundreds of lives are lived, each three times, and that True Wisdom is the only escape from recurrence.

The Stoics believed man to be a microcosm of a Universal Being which periodically reincarnates into a world governed by cycles.[41] After the destruction of each world, individual souls return to the divine home from which they emanated. Cosmic life is an infinite series of exactly similar world cycles, populated by the same souls.

The New Testament contains references that Jesus taught recurrence. His crucifixion and rebirth was a return after three cosmic days. Christ spoke of recurrence: "Ye shall see the Son of man ascend up where he was before,"[42] and, "I will come again, and receive you unto myself."[43] The church later eliminated references to recurrence, but the Gnostics retained them. The *"Treatise on Resurrection"* states: "Do not suppose that resurrection is an apparition. It is not an apparition; rather it is something real. Instead one ought to maintain that the world is an apparition, rather than resurrection."[44] Resurrection is the moment of enlightenment, revealing what truly exists and a migration (metabole = change, transition) into newness, a secret teaching transmitted directly to the disciples. In the *"Wisdom of Jesus Christ"* the disciples gathered on a mountain after Jesus's death, when he appeared, smiled and offered to teach them the "secrets (mysteria) of the holy plan" of the universe and its destiny.[45]

In medieval times many philosophers who accepted cyclical world ages also supported recurrence, such as Clement of Alexandria (c. AD 150-220), Arnobius (280-340), and Joachim of Floris (1145-1202). G. B. Vico put forward a scheme of cyclic civilization in his "*Scienza Nuova*" (1725).

Nietzsche accepted eternal recurrence because of the necessity for a finite number of centres of force which;

> In infinite time would realize every possible combination an infinite number of times. Since between every combination and every other combination all other possible combinations would have to take place, and each combination conditions the entire sequence of combinations, a circular movement of absolutely identical series is thus demonstrated: the world as a circular movement that has already repeated itself infinitely often and plays its game ad infinitum.[46]

Nietzsche saw recurrence as a means for transcending cause and effect and liberating the soul.

> This world: as force throughout, as a play of forces and waves of forces, at the same time one and many, increasing here and at the same time decreasing there; a sea of forced flowing and rushing together, eternally changing, eternally flooding back, with tremendous years of recurrence, with an ebb and flood of its forms;
> . . . this my Dionysian world of the eternally self-creating, the eternally self-destroying, this mystery world of the twofold voluptuous delight, my 'beyond good and evil', without goal, unless the joy of the circle is itself a goal; without will, unless a ring feels good will toward itself.[47]

If the logic and sentiment of modern civilization opposes the idea of eternal recurrence, Pythagoras, Plato, Aristotle, Jesus and Nietzsche are formidable references to its reality. The recurrent nature of subatomic phenomena weighs heavily in favour of a recurrent model of reality, and it is impossible to ignore the implications of the concept. J. B. S. Haldane wrote that "there must be a general recurrence of events" because "everything must recur".[48]

The only time track known is the one along which one's life is lived; one possible realization among an infinity of possibilities. Following another track would make a different person living another life. Most people never consider that there are other possibilities because they limit their awareness to only one. The present moment contains an infinity of possibilities and histories. There is an already existent All in eternity, available at any moment to any individual. Ouspensky said,

Time does not exist! There exists no perpetual and eternal appearance and disappearance of phenonema, no ceaselessly flowing fountain of ever-appearing and ever-vanishing events. Everything exists always! There is only one eternal present, the Eternal Now, which the weak and limited human mind can never grasp and conceive.[49]

While the world contains infinite possibilities, the mind only follows one. All possibilities are actualized, but one does not see and know them, only the actuality as lived.

Not only is it impossible for things to be other than they are, it is even impossible that the initial situation of the universe could have been other than what it was. No matter what we are doing at a given moment, it is the only thing that was ever possible for us to be doing at that moment.[50]

Ouspensky hypothesized a fifth dimension, *eternity*, as a further dimension of time, which contains all possibilities of historical time as one discrete entity which recurs infinitely. The universe perpetually recurs within eternity. To understand eternity is to discover the evolution of the universe within. The temporal universe is a mental process, not a sensible object. The universe is available equally to everyone.

Ouspensky applied the principles of eternal recurrence to individual life. Life is a circular process. At the moment of death incomplete life energies disseminate and pass outside of linear time only to reassemble again at the original conception instant in the womb of the same mother, impregnated by the same father, and at the same time. The unique set of circumstances which define "a life" can go nowhere else in the universe of space and time but back to their original beginning to start all over again. Life recurs in time as a loop and is repeated infinitely.

Plato observed in the Myth of Er that, although souls have totally open choice, most souls out of force of habit return to repeat the experiences of the previous life.[51] The impure soul passes through the river of forgetting, the River Lethe, and in its new life, a repetition of the last life, cannot remember what it was, or why many events of life seem familiar. The Orphic mysteries initiated the soul to remember by drinking the cold water of the Lake of Memory. The choice, if indeed there is choice, lies in this life, because this life is a synthesis and summation of all lives. Only by remembering the personal past, which is the past of all individuals and of the universe, can one ascend to enlightenment and be free from the endless wheel of rebirth. Collin soberly stated that it takes full recognition of the futility of recurrence before the task of penetrating consciously into the unknown and unimaginable dimensions which lie beyond will be undertaken.

"The Theory of Celestial Influence" shows that time perception is relative to the length of the lifetime of the perceiver. The word *"cosmos"* describes self-evolving wholes which are complete in themselves and divine images of the universe. Cosmoses exist throughout the universe, greater cosmoses reflecting greater degrees of consciousness and intelligence and giving birth to smaller cosmoses. The hierarchy of the chain of cosmoses is: the Universe (the Absolute), galaxy, solar system, sun, earth, nature, humanity, an individual human, the cell, molecule and an electron. (Table 1 and Figure 11) The differentiation of level from level is determined by the relative dimension of each cosmos, based upon the length of their duration.

> Entry into each new dimension represents movement in a new direction. A point of no dimensions, such as the point of a pencil or lighted cigarette in the dark, when moved, traces a line. A line – the spokes of a bicycle-wheel or crayon, for example, when spun or moved at right angles to itself (or a disk spun on its axis) traces a plane. A solid, such as a man, when extended into the past and future, traces a lifetime. A lifetime, extended at right angles to itself, brings us to the idea of parallel times, of time-repetition or eternity outside of time. The totality of such repetitions, projected in yet another direction, implies an absolute whole, the realisation of all possibilities, everything existing everywhere.[52]

The point has no dimensions, a line one, a plane two, a solid three, a lifetime four, a life repeating eternally five, and All in six dimensions. The dimensions in each successive cosmos slide along a scale. A man perceives a cell as a point of no dimensions, while to nature man is a point, and to the sun the earth is a point. The lifetime of a cell is a solid to man, as it is his body, just as the lifetime of nature is a solid relative to earth. The human is made up of the lifetimes of his cells, as humanity is made up of the solid of all men and women in history. "Remembering his life as a whole, man sees himself as Nature sees him. Thus, memory, for man, is the key to perceiving

Table 1   Collin's Table of Times and Cosmoses

Each level of existence in the universe is considered an organism in its own right, with a lifetime of relative stages like all other organisms. Each organism, from the Electron to the Milky Way is governed by the same mathematical laws, as the table shows.

TABLE OF TIMES AND COSMOSES

(From Collin,
The Theory of Celestial Influence)

Cosmos	Moment of Recognition	Breath	Minute	Hour	Day	Week	Month	Tear	Lifetime
Electron	—	—	—	—	—	—	—	—	$1/1500$ s.
Molecule × 28,000	—	—	—	—	$1/1500$ s.	$1/300$ s.	$1/50$ s.	$1/4$ s.	18 sec.
Blood-Cell × 4,800	—	$1/1500$ s.	$1/90$ s.	$2/3$ s.	18 sec.	$1\frac{3}{4}$ m.	7 min.	$1\frac{1}{2}$ hr.	6 days
Man × 28,000	$1/30$ s.	3 sec.	1 min.	1 hr.	1 day	7 days	29 days	1 year	76 y.
Nature × 365	$1/4$ hour	1 day	18 days	$3\frac{1}{4}$ y.	76 y.	537 y.	2150 y.	25,800 y.	$2\frac{1}{4}$ mn.y.
Earth × 7,800	$3\frac{1}{8}$ days	1 year	18 years	1075 y.	25,800 y.	187,000 y.	750,000 y.	$9\frac{1}{3}$ mn.y.	750 mn.y.
Sun × 100,000	75 years	7000 y.	135,000 y.	8 mn.y.	200 mn.y.			—	5.6^{12} y.
Milky Way	$7\frac{1}{2}$ mn.y.	700 mn.y.	13,500 mn.y.	—	—		—	—	5.6^{17} y.

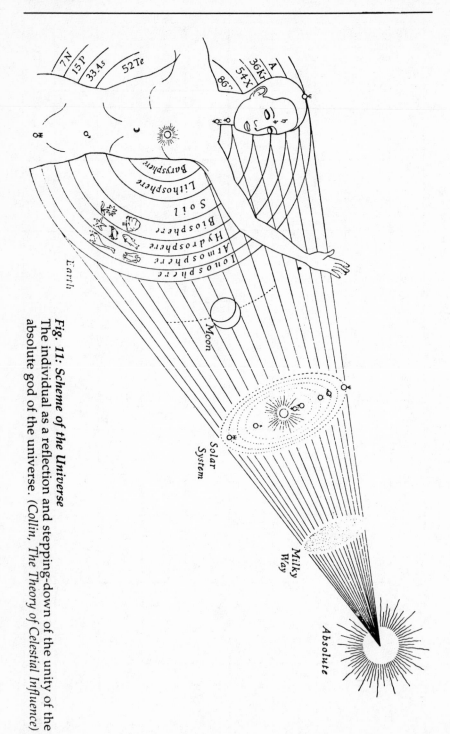

Fig. 11: *Scheme of the Universe*
The individual as a reflection and stepping-down of the unity of the absolute god of the universe. (Collin, *The Theory of Celestial Influence*)

himself and his surroundings as they are perceived by a higher cosmos."[53] Every cosmos is linked to every other by relative size and time sense as determined by the length of life. The scales of forms from electrons to galaxies are in this way reconciled into a perfect whole rather than occupying incommensurable niches as in contemporary science.

All living beings are conceived, born, mature and die in time, and in this sense all cosmoses are alive and live their own lives in their own relative time. Just because a galaxy has a vastly greater duration does not mean that it is not alive. After all, we are composed of atoms which resemble galaxies and we are alive. All dimensions are interdependent and mathematically connected. The key is that time is created by the period of rotation about the vital centre of a greater world. Kepler recognised in his Third Law that the relation between distances from the sun (line) and periods of rotation about the sun (time) is the relation between square roots and cube roots. Since all cosmoses are built on the same general plan, and since the relation between cosmoses now appears to be similar to the relation between dimensions within a cosmos, the connection is made. Linear space develops by cubes as time develops by squares, as Table 1 shows.[54]

Human perception is usually limited to three dimensions out of the many available. Three primary principles govern the relationships between cosmoses. The "law of three" relates each cosmos:

(a) to its past (the cosmos next smaller) by attraction,
(b) its future (the cosmos next larger) by radiation, and
(c) to its present (itself) by time, which combines the effect of receiving the past and projecting to the future.

The relations between the three are exponential powers of ten. A perceiver can only understand the cosmoses above and below with any clarity. Beyond these limits only those who manifest transcendent (beyond time) reality have access. For example, humans have awareness of their cellular body, their own existence as a human and a general awareness of Nature as a whole, although the centre is individual ego-existence rather than either the body or Nature. It is only the exceptional being who is able to extend awareness into the molecular world or electronic world in the microcosm, or earth, the sun or the galaxy in the macrocosm.

Collin describes the relationship as that between a breath, a day and a life. A breath is 1/28,000th of a day (three seconds), a day is the present, and a life is about 28,000 days (77 years). As nature is the next higher level of perception, a day for a man must be a breath for nature, and the life of the Earth equivalent to a breath of the galaxy, and similarly other cosmoses may be related to each other. The relativity of time allows the human to relate to and understand the entire universe.

The Darwinian Cataclysm

Cyclical cataclysms and the evolution of life on the earth are inseparable systems, but have received little support from scientists since Darwin. In 1849 the anthropologist d'Orbigny stated:

> A 'first creation' appeared after the Silurian Age. After its total annihilation by some geological cause and after the passage of a considerable span of time, a second creation took place at the Devonian stage. Thereafter twenty-seven successive creations repopulated the entire earth anew with plants and animals, geological upheavals having each time destroyed all living nature. These are certain but incomprehensible facts.[55]

D'Orbigny believed that since there was positive proof of successive geological periods punctuated by cataclysms, and that identical species existed in these periods, there must have been extinctions followed by the re-creation of species. Even now there is an astonishing lack of solid evidence to corroborate the evolutionary theory of Darwin. The idea of a gradual, step-by-step evolution is obsolete because there are no traces of the intermediate forms of any species, and if there is no proof, how can the hypothesis be maintained? As the anthropologist Hoffman states, the terrible catastrophes which happened in previous ages were not gradual, but the work of a moment. Animals and plants died out suddenly as the conditions required for their existence ceased to exist.

The great scientist Georges Cuvier (1769-1832) classified the animal and plant kingdoms on the same principles used up to the present day, and held that the various species and types of animals do not exist independently, but are closely interrelated. "Every living organism forms a whole. No part can change without changes in the other parts."[56] Cuvier proposed a static order of species, each relegated to a specific time and place, each wiped out in turn by a catastrophe. Floods, volcanoes and earthquakes on a worldwide scale destroyed the land and remade the whole. Entire races disappeared, leaving only traces.

Cuvier's successor Charles Lyell (1797-1849) postulated a Uniformitarian Theory which stated, first, that it was necessary to assume uniform natural laws in time and space. This is an a priori claim all scientists must make about the world – that nature acts in the future as it has acted in the past, and that it is not capricious. Secondly he stated the obvious, that geological processes are uniform through time. Lyell's two other laws were highly suspect and intended to finally disprove catastrophism. The third is that present processes alone were admissible to explain nature, and that geologic change is slow, gradual and steady. His fourth concept was that the earth has been the same since its creation. What is fascinating about Lyell is his view that "the fossil record is representative of only one part of a great year – a grand cycle that will occur again when the huge iguanadon might reappear in the woods, and the ichthyosaur in the sea, while the pterodactyl might flit again through umbrageous groves of fern trees."[57] Stephen Jay Gould of Harvard accepts that the catastrophists took the literal view, saw the direction of history and were right.

Louis Agassiz (1807-1873) accepted Cuvier and catastrophism and annotated Lyell, accepting that the "summation of present causes over geologic time cannot account for the magnitude of some past events".[58]

Darwin's *"Origin of Species"* of 1859 spelled the decline of the catastrophist view of history, even though his strongest champions, Professor Gray, Thomas Huxley and Haeckel, refused to accept the idea of natural selection – that the fittest survive. Today, one hundred and twenty years later, proof is unobtainable and evolutionary theory is under even greater pressure than in Darwin's time because the fossil line consists for the most part of gaps. Nonetheless, Darwin's unworkable theory is still accepted by the majority.

The death-knell of cyclic reality was the acceptance of the linear Darwinian view of evolution as a development of successive organisms, each one better adapted to its environment, culminating in humanity as the apex of the evolutionary scale. *Natural Selection* is the mechanism by which evolution acts – the *"survival of the fittest"* means that the fittest of each generation tend to survive to transmit survival traits to their offspring. Characteristics which are not survival-proven are gradually eliminated from the inherited pattern of the species.

Proof for Darwinian evolution is fragmentary and contradictory at best, primarily in the case of humanity, where there should be traces of a succession of intermediate beings connecting the higher primate apes to modern homo sapiens sapiens. As is well known, no such "missing links" have ever been found. The gaps in the fossil strata from which the proof is taken are so large as to totally refute the theory. Charles Fort spent a lifetime collecting and publishing data which are inexplicable to science, and had a unique and amusing criticism of Darwinism,

> As for Darwinism:
> The fittest survive.
> What is meant by the fittest?
> Not the strongest; not the cleverest – weakness and stupidity everywhere survive.
> There is no way of determining fitness except in that a thing does survive. "Fitness," then, is only another name for "survival."
> Darwinism: That survivors survive.
>
> How do geologists determine the age of rocks? By the fossils in them. And how do they determine the age of fossils? By the rocks they are in.[59]

The fossil record does not validate Darwin, and on the contrary shows fossils with no significant change over 10 million years.[60] An alternative is "punctuated equilibrium", where well-defined groups of creatures adapt sporadically interspersed with long periods of little or no change. Niches in the sequence of organisms are filled by other beings adapting to the niche, and once in its niche, the organism does not change. The obvious analogy is to the structure of the atomic shells. When an electron is knocked out of its position in an inner ring, another electron from the next ring out moves into its place – but the overall structure of the atom remains the same. The implication is that the sequence of life forms is set, and that development fills up the available categories, an idea which sounds like metempsychosis.

Genetic code is a record of all past reproductions. The great problem is that the programme of the present-day organism resembles a text, proof-read and corrected for two billion years, continually improving, refining and completing itself, gradually eliminating all imperfections, but without an author. Natural selection may choose only among organisms in existence. It appears that each molecule was specifically engineered, and even the sophisticated modern genetic technology is far away from understanding the origin of the process of life in time.

The dangerous modern scientific techniques of genetic engineering use the common bacterium e. coli as raw material. The fact that such a non- specific organism has the capability to approximate human genetic information poses an interesting point. Every life form on earth uses that same basic genetic structure. The differences are the result of differential utilization of the base coding sequence in time. Just as in physics all particles are composed of the same set of four quarks in their three modes ($4 \times 3 = 12$), so the genetic code uses the four acid bases in their three forms (also $4 \times 3 = 12$ combinations).

The parallel to the four elements in three modes of astrology is clear. Genetic code resonates with the movements of the planetary bodies and its formal pattern existed in an energetic pattern from the beginning of earth's history, and is in turn derived from the information carried by the planets. The form of a solar system determines the form of life in residence there.

The idea, common to the esoteric view of creation, such as that of the Theosophists, Alice Bailey, Steiner and the Eastern religions, that before incarnating in the human body the soul passes through planetary existences is formally correct. It is implied that:
  – the code was fully operational at the start
  – the code did not evolve
  – all life forms have the same source
  – there is a spiritual and physical link between all beings throughout the universe

The Divine Plot uses astrological language to describe the pattern in time which guides development in physical, emotional (astral), mental, spiritual and cosmic realms, which satisfies the requirements of prevailing theories of evolution. The major problem is the definition of terms, because those used by previous cultures have been inadvertently re-discovered by modern science and renamed. A primary example is that an idea previously called *"reincarnation"* has been renamed *"genetics"*.

Catastrophe Theory

The most recent advances in astronomy imply that our cosmology is based on *catastrophe*. Physicists accept the Big Bang theory of creation, and similar ideas are being applied to genetics and evolutionary processes. The change in species is not caused by external influences such as natural selection, but by catastrophes. The genetic code from which we are created is virtually the same as that of apes – biochemical comparison of the forty-four proteins and enzymes common to both chimpanzees and human beings to show them to be 99% identical – thus bringing into question the mechanism of how we separated from apes, if that is indeed what happened. The genes of humans and chimps are as similar as the genes of sibling species of other organisms, so much so that it requires biochemical analysis to tell them apart.[61]

The radiation that accompanies comets, earthquakes or the proliferation of nuclear weapons could be the required catastrophic agent of largescale biological change. Variety may not be produced by random variations, but can by circumstances as exist today in the world. "Numerous catastrophes or bursts of effective radiation must have taken place in the geological past in order to change so radically the living forms on earth, as the record of fossils embedded in lava and sediment bears witness."[62]

The similarity of species in early life may even be linked to the concept that evolution works backwards from humanity to the other animals.

> Nature's favourite form seems to be that of the circle. In the same way that a straight line is an optical illusion and becomes a segment or arc of a circle in the context of space; that matter, seen closely, resolves into orbiting electrical charges; that space and time are governed by the spherical properties of the universe; that the galaxies rotate in stately waltzes in a universe which itself, no doubt, spins as it expands; so man's life and social forms follow circular principles. The cycles of birth and death; of the disintegration into the earth and the arising of new life from the earth; the rise and fall of dynasties, of nations, of civilizations, of species all tend to support this view. Why should the development of man alone in the universe follow a straight path from slightly differentiated living matter to miraculously complex intelligent forms and proceed forever in a linear manner to further and further progress? Is it not more probable that his destiny, like that of everything else, is to follow a circular course, and that as he approaches an apogee, the forces of life will spin him back to his beginnings?[63]

The theory of catastrophism is a "controversial new way of thinking about change – change in a course of events, change in an object's shape, change in a system's behaviour, change in ideas themselves".[64] Professor Rene Thom of France's Institute for Advanced Scientific Studies proposed a mathematical explanation of the processes of change. While science can explain gradual change, it has never been able to describe spontaneous change, where discontinuity is the rule. Changes of form (in processes as well as in objects) are real, and the aim of science is to grasp the universal "ceaseless creation, evolution and destruction of forms".[65] Number has two functions, and the mathematics and geometry of catastrophe theory are qualitative rather than quantitative, which allows a description of the similarities between tree branching patterns, a river system and a nerve cell. Thom believes that the qualitative features of all natural processes are recurrent, an assumption not shared by science generally. Thom recognises the inherent stability of physical systems which continuously pursue a process of change throughout their lives. He compares the genetic legacy of each individual with its necessary parallel in the ecological stability of the species.

Invoking Lyell, scientists assume that two experiments can produce the same quantitative results, but they cannot, because the circumstances can never be exactly reproduced, nor can external influences be eliminated. The earth moves hundreds of thousands of miles through space and time every day in the movement of the solar system through time. Reproducability is a central fallacy of modern science, and Thom's goal is to describe qualitatively repeatable observations and through them the origin of forms, which process he calls "*morphogenesis*", the same term later used by Sheldrake.

Morphogenesis includes "mind" in its frame of reference as the most complex system − by definition, because it must be at least one degree more complex than that which it perceives or imagines. Our concepts are mathematical models or topological maps of universal processes, which we use to shape our world. Catastrophe theory is a way of leaving behind the static reality of Newton and entering the relativistic world beyond, which Thom calls "the landscapes of change".

C. H. Waddington, a paleontologist, embryologist, geneticist and evolutionist, realized in investigating the development of species through time that the contours of the landscape of change are multidimensional. Biochemistry alone cannot explain morphogenesis − he wanted a theory which would topologically describe biological forms. Thom at that time (1962) was developing a model which created a mathematical "cross-section in time" of an integrated process. All genetically governed beings follow the same stable pathways and "every organism's form represents a partial record of the processes of development and metabolism".[66]

Thom formulated seven elementary catastrophes and many mini-catastrophes inherent in every system, any of which could potentially incite the whole system to jump from one state to another. The great conceptual leap is that different systems, at different scales, could have similar processes of change but different sets of causes. Basic structural geometric patterns recur in many processes in nature. Sudden and forced systemic change happens in atomic structure when electrons are knocked out of inner electron rings and outer electrons rapidly jump from ring to ring to fill up the missing inner spaces. Packets of energy (quanta) exhibit similar qualities of rapid change when stressed instead of smoothly changing nature through the spectrum of energy.[67]

Catastrophe Theory is a paradigm which may be applied to many areas, such as biology, sociology, psychology, behaviour, mechanics, politics, economics and other processes. "The old idea of Man, the microcosm, mirroring world, the macrocosm, retains all its force."[68] The inclusion of these ideas with astrology, metaphysics and psychology yields The Divine Plot.

The Changing Scientific View

Sir William Ramsay related perception to time and eternity. As we undergo mental transformations, we imagine worlds – that is to say, we construct mental cosmologies.[69] The universe is in the mind. According to the level at which the universe is perceived, greater and greater dimensions of actualization become available. There are recurrent mental cycles and recurrent universes. Our universes are successive layers of perception reached during the inner journey reflecting successive layers of what we perceive to be the physical world. The only obstacles to transcending the temporal universe are within us.

A new understanding of the world is coming into being which was foreshadowed in eastern religion and western mysticism. Since the time of Newton, the scientific method has been to maintain an empirical approach to the universe, verified by repeatable experiments, evaluated statistically. Science requires objective observers and the separation of the object or event observed from the whole within which it exists. It is now clear that there is no such thing as an objective observer because the observer is inseparable from what is being observed. Nothing can be isolated from the whole in the way required by science. The light required to observe subatomic events itself alters the structure and nature of the events. The presence of a measuring device itself alters what is being measured.

Heisenberg realized that the observer alters the observed by the act of observation and the degree of alteration is affected by the consciousness of the observer. Mind can and does affect space, and also time, because the space-time continuum is a product of the mind which perceives it. The traditional view of the world as a *"great machine"* is changing to the world as a *"great thought"*. Scientific laws that describe events in the large-scale macro-world seem not to adapt and work in the micro-world. Scientists can predict the behaviour of groups of particles or events, but not one particle and its movements. Either the macro-world has different laws than the micro-world, or science is making a profound mistake in transition. Scientists align themselves with either the statistical quantum mechanical view of reality or the causal reality of Einstein, but the true state of affairs includes both, and must be able to describe both.

Scientists searching for successive generations of elementary particles believing that their mechanisms determine the nature of the universe are only belatedly discovering that matter is ultimately composed of patterns of energetic events. The universe cannot be broken down into isolated parts, but must be understood as a whole. The relative perspective which enlivens each cosmos provides such a unification missing from even the New Physics.

Particles are patterns of energy in constant movement, interaction and transformation, and the universe is a web of relations rather than an accumulation of particles. Previously matter and mind have been treated as mutually exclusive, rather than integrated as in eastern religions or western mysticism. Mind can affect space and time, and in a very basic way the whole space-time continuum is a product of the mind which perceives it, a concept which has led to great confusion inside and outside science.

Measure, Meditation and Maya

For the Holy One hath weighed the world (aeon) and with measure hath he measured the times, and by numbers he hath numbered the seasons, neither will he rest nor stir until the number be fulfilled.
Esdras Gospel, Nag Hammadi Texts[70]

David Bohm worked with Einstein and states that to take any

physical theory as an absolute is to fragment knowledge about the universe because the mere act of so doing differentiates one from the universe. The solution is for the observer and the observed to become "merging and interpenetrating aspects of one whole reality, which is indivisible and unanalysable."[71] The world must be viewed in terms of the universal flux of events and processes. The nature of the world is historical process. The world must be seen as a whole in which the observer occupies the central place amidst the formation and dissolution of energy and life. The search is for formative causes or overall patterns of reality, the structure and order which underlies what is, in distinction to the atomistic and fragmentary view of the modern sciences, empirical psychology and biology, where a mechanistic rationale for life is sought in the structure and function of DNA molecules.

> Thus we arrive at the very odd result that in the study of life and mind, which are just the fields in which formative cause acting in undivided and unbroken flowing movement is most evident to experience and observation, there is now the strongest belief in the fragmentary approach to reality.[72]

The fragmentation has contributed to social, political, economic, ecological and psychological crises in individuals and society. Even holistic principles are being treated as absolute knowledge rather than as theories of perception.

Bohm states that notions of measure play a key role in determining world views. Instead of the modern definition of measure as comparison to an external standard unit, measure has a deeper significance as an indicator of conformity to harmonious reality. Measure means, in a deeper sense, the proportion or ratio acting in universal relationships. To understand ratio is to understand the innermost beauty of something. The words medicine, moderation and meditation all have the Latin root which means "to measure". A meditator is led to a quieting process whereby fragmentation is lessened and unification encouraged. Inner measure is necessary in healthy, happy and spiritual life. Measure in Greece and Rome was the underlying harmony of the world as expressed in music, art and architecture. The notion of measure as human quality was expressed by Pythagoras as *"man is the measure of all things"*.

In the West, measure has been desacralised by a science and technology dependent on measurement, while the Eastern focus is on religion and philosophy directed toward the immeasurable. The idea that only what is measurable is real is a fallacy, but measure can help bring about order and harmony when treated by the wise. The Sanskrit word meaning "measure" is the root of *"maya"*, the illusion of reality. Balance between East and West, religion and science, lies with the integration of opposite and contradictory ways of experience. Bohm beautifully states that the original and creative insight within the field of measure is the action of the immeasurable.[73]

It is important to distinguish between number as quantity and as Platonic idea – two oranges is a measurement of quantity, while the action of the number two as duality is immeasurable. Numbers are meaningful carriers of patterns and proportions, rather than being purely and simply quantities of objects. The Greeks had a word for the two equivalent aspects of time: *"chronos"* is objective and quantitative, while *"kairos"* is subjective and qualitative.[74]

Number is a device used to organise the world. In school the dates of events are often given more significance than events themselves. The sequence of history is controlled by the significance of number presented as quantity. In the West history is thought of as linear and has no rhythm or proportion, but in the East history is thought of as circular, recurrent and relative, as we have seen.

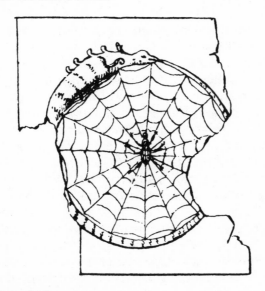

Fig. 12: Web of Maya
Maya, the eternal weaver of the illusory world of the senses, encircled by the Uroboros serpent of cyclic time. *(Brahmanic fragment from Jung, Psychology and Alchemy)*

Spengler mentions the opposition, which has rarely been noted, between "chronological" and "mathematical" number. In the time scale to be presented, number is the guiding force in history, but it is not related except correlatively to the "years" BC and AD to which we attach events. It was in AD 525 that Dionysius Exiguus proposed the AD sequence, and as recently as 1681 Brossuet suggested the idea of BC years. The accepted system of identifying dates has not been in operation for long. Jewish years are measured relative to the lunar calendar, and Islamic years are measured from the Hegira of Mohammed in AD 622. The latent measurement of history enables the identification not only of what historical facts at a particular time "are" but what they signify, what they point to and how they relate harmonically to other facts and times.[75]

> The morphological relationships that inwardly bind the expression-forms of all branches of a Culture, beyond politics, to grasp the ultimate and fundamental ideas of Greeks, Arabians, Indians and Westerners in mathematics, the meaning of their early ornamentation, the basic forms of their architecture, philosophies, dramas and lyrics, their choice and development of great arts, the detail of their craftsmanship and choice of materials – let alone appreciate the decisive importance of these matters for the form-problems of history.[76]

There is no theory-enlightened technique of historical treatment beyond the realm of physical cause-and-effect, and physics has never addressed itself to history. By the standards of physicists or mathematicians, historians are careless about the way in which they assemble and order their material and pass on to interpretation. Kant restricted himself to establishing rules governing the relationship between human cognition and the world: for him, knowledge is mathematical knowledge. Kant never applied his categories of consciousness to the historical process, nor did Schopenhauer, who utilized the Kantian categories and spoke contemptuously of history. Both limited themselves to the understanding of cause and effect. Few of the great individuals of history have even attempted a synthesis such as Spengler proposes, although many would have liked to. Spengler identified other necessities, such as the "logic of space" which is the organic necessity of life, called Destiny, and the "logic of time" which suffuses mythological religions and artistic thought and constitutes the kernel of all history, but is unapproachable through Pure Reason. Spengler believed in 1926 that the theoretical formulation of these new logics was still to come. The Divine Plot is a attempt to apply a mathematical order to history which fits the conditions of Spengler.

The Form-Creating Mechanism

Our "being" exists through a series of events in life, changes of form and phase, yet we retain our identity, even though change is the essence of life. The historical process reflects a continual transmutation of Self as it seeks manifestation in the world. Adam and Eve in Eden are symbolic of the original male and female reality. They transform from mythological deities to god-heroes sired by the gods and humans, to heroes with god-like attributes, to hereditary kings and queens descended from the gods, to humans with heroic qualities, then finally to components of the individual. The theme of the world age is the awakening of individual consciousness and its differentiation from nature.

Everyone relives the historical process in life, but the question is how we can learn from the fact. We inherit many strands of ancient, primordial historical reality encapsulated in our body, emotions, mind and spirit. The instincts to hunt, kill and survive remain, and when suppressed are dangerous. In modern societies where the primitive has been outwardly eradicated, aggressive instincts find expression by breaking through in sport, war, pornography and vicarious cinematic violence. The barbarity of world wars, terrorism, religious fanaticism and racism are widespread examples. The urges result from hundreds of thousands of years of instinctive survival following millions of years of primate reality – the veneer of civilization is only a few scant thousand years old. Instincts precede individuality and are a base we all share, regardless of race, religion, nationality and sex. What differentiates us is the way in which we express our common heritage and our closeness to the origin.

The memory of past life is stored in the brain, heliacal genetic code, body substance, soul and spirit – at every level of interaction with the universe. Esoteric knowledge describes levels as "bodies" of increasing fineness and closeness to god. Every person has physical, emotional, mental and spiritual bodies. In each system the number of such bodies and the terms used to describe them change, but the principle is clear in all systems. As we age, we naturally transfer awareness to higher and finer bodies. Thus in gestation the physical body is created within the mother, in childhood the emotional body is created within the home and family system and in maturity the mental body is created within the world. If an individual is able to extend reality beyond the initial three bodies, a transpersonal or transcendent body is available. Each body encompasses the previous bodies as successive shells of reality. Our bodies may be represented as proportional interpenetrating circles and forming a link between heaven and earth. (Fig. 13)

The ascent through the bodies in life parallels the evolution of humanity. The earliest reality was physical; emotions evolved which differentiated humans from the animal world; mind evolved; and finally the realm of the spirit, out of which all arose, became the goal. All four bodies are inherent in us from the beginning. It is more a matter of utilizing each successive vehicle for experiencing the world than creating them. Complete reality is existence on all levels.

Exactly how and where memory is stored is not really known. There is increasing evidence that the brain is merely a receiving apparatus, rather than a receptacle for information. It is well known that humans use only a small proportion of the brain – less than ten percent. The use of the other ninety percent is unknown. That control resides in brain centres can be demonstrated when certain parts of the brain are damaged and an equivalent set of bodily functions are impaired, but if the damage occurs at an early enough age, other parts of the brain can take over the functions of the damaged part. A strict localization is impossible.

The biologist Rupert Sheldrake has proposed a *"A New Science of Life"* which supersedes the mechanistic view that genetic code is the primary form-creating and guiding mechanism for organic life. The hypothesis of formative causation states that every organism possesses a non-physical *morphogenetic* (form-creating) *field* which organizes the coming-into-being of developing biological systems.

> Specific morphogenetic fields are responsible for the characteristic form and organization of systems at all levels of complexity, not only in the realm of biology, but also in the realms of chemistry and physics.[77]

Morphogenetic fields are ordered patterns derived from the field of all past systems transmitted through a developing organism. Sheldrake likens genetic code to a computer program which requires the existence of a programmer, implying that physical and chemical interactions are structured in time and

Fig. 13: Fludd's Universal Spheres
A mathematical representation of the history of the microcosm,
shown as spheres of varying proportions in both humanity and the
solar system. *(Fludd, Utriusque cosmi historia)*

space. The "interactionist" theory postulates that properties of
mind are influenced by past mental states, rather than through
the physical storage of memory within the brain. Parallels to
Jung's collective unconscious are not lost on Sheldrake, and he
mentions that an inherited collective memory containing
archetypal forms could be valid.

Previous systems influence subsequent similar systems by
morphic resonance, acting through vibrational frequencies.
Systems select, out of a mixture of vibrations, the particular
frequencies they need.[78] All living systems, from atoms to
organisms, vibrate continually and have their own
characteristic vibrational rates and internal rhythms. Sheldrake
proposes that the spatio-temporal pattern of former systems

superimpose a characteristic vibrational structure onto present systems with a similar form. As resonance is non-energetic and energy-and mass-less, it could be "just as effective over ten thousand miles as over a yard, and over a century as an hour".[79] Physical form, character, instincts and learning processes could be influenced not only from the past, but from future systems which do not yet exist.

The principle of morphic resonance carried through the medium of time is central to the mechanism of The Divine Plot. The effect of all past systems creates a matrix from which individual forms, characteristics and ways of learning derive their initial creation. The gradation of time with an exponential time scale is the way to describe developmental stages of time for an individual, the collective, the physical universe as a whole and correlate them to stellar rhythms. The fact that Sheldrake proposes a non-physical resonance which nonetheless influences the development of all organisms refutes a primary objection of astrology. Scientists have rejected astrology because there is no physical or energetic way of explaining the mechanism by which it works. Astrology is a language by which morphic resonance can be decribed, and in turn is also a language which can be formally related to the structure of DNA and to planetary movements. All are patterns in time.

Sheldrake is concerned with the repetition of forms and patterns of organization and admits that the origin of these forms and patterns lies outside of the scope of "*A New Science of Life*", precisely the issue which is confronted by The Divine Plot. The eternal recurrence of the world can be applied to individual life.

★Chapter Four★
★Life★Time Astrology★

The spiral path of the sun and DNA. Biological time, metabolism and memory. Life★Time Astrology. The octaves of gestation, childhood and maturity. The process of life. The zodiac signs and life. The transcendent octave. Initiation. Death and the last judgement. The psychedelic experience. Interpretation of the horoscope. The deeper significance of astrology. The personal and collective unconscious. The eternal ovum. The individual recapitulates history. The acceleration of history. Henry Adams and H.G. Wells. Great scientists and logarithmic time. The divine proportion of time. The mathematical matrix of The Divine Plot.

> This life is the way, the longest sought after, the way to the incomprehensible, which we call divine. There is no other way.
> C. G. Jung[80]

The most ancient system for integrating the cosmos with the individual is astrology. Contemporary astrology is being restructured to include modern understanding of the universe, as described in *"The Round Art"* and *"Life★Time Astrology"*. The starting point is understanding the relativity of time which we experience every day.

Everyone knows that the earth orbits around the sun, a star suspended in space, and the moon orbits around the earth. Every year the earth returns to the same spot in its exorable path around the sun, just as every month the moon returns to its similar position in the sky. In reality, these statements are not true. The sun moves around its sun, the star Sirius, at more than three-quarters of a million kilometres per day, pulling the planets along with it. The planets do not move in circular orbits because they trace a spiral path around the moving sun – the inner planets spiral tightly and the outer planets tag along. (Fig.

14) Sirius, in its turn, orbits around the centre of the Milky Way galaxy, currently at 28 degrees of Sagittarius, in 250 million years and the entire flattened spiral galaxy itself moves through space. (Fig. 15) The simultaneous movements of earth, sun and galaxy combine to propel us through space (and time) at an astonishing rate. It is shocking to picture such great movement while the tea on the table maintains its apparent stillness.

The astrological horoscope is an angular slice through this spiralling circus at a specific time and place of birth. Everyone lives within the same spiral but from different relative vantage points. The spiral projects backward into the past and forward into the future.

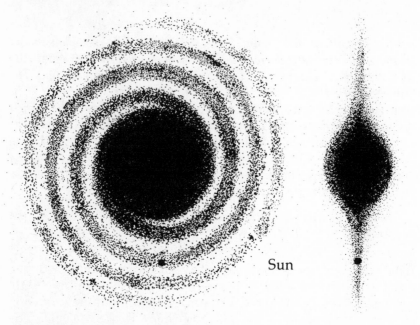

Sun

Fig. 15: The Sun in the Milky Way
The sun orbits around the star Sirius, which in turn orbits the galactic centre, currently in the zodiac sign Sagittarius. The sun is about two-thirds of the way from the centre to the periphery of the Milky Way.

Fig. 14: Spiral Solar System in Time
The sun's path is the central core around which the planets spiral through time. The earth is the third planet out from the sun, and each of its complete spirals is one year of time. An astrological horoscope is a slice through this spiralling circus taken at a place and angle reflecting a particular time and place of birth. The spiral extends backwards to creation and ahead into the future. *(Mann, Life★Time Astrology)*

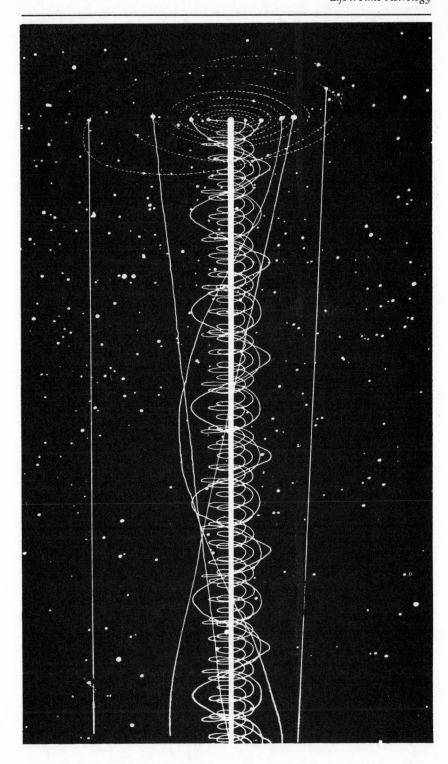

There is a formal connection between the movement of the solar system in time and space and the structure of the DNA molecule in which organic life is structured – both are spirals. Knowledge of life is encoded in DNA as it is encoded in the galactic model. In Fig. 12 the path of the sun is shown as a straight line, but when the path of earth is the central viewpoint, it is a spiral within the sun's apparent spiralling path. (Fig. 16) The form of the resultant double spiral is similar to the genetic code DNA which carries the mechanism of life and controls growth in time. The pattern of the solar system in time in the macrocosm reflects the pattern of the DNA molecule in the microcosm. In *"Cosmic Cybernetics"*, Dr Theodore Landscheit refers to remarks by the physicist Jacques Bergier:

> If Ducrocq, Hoyle, Narlikar and Costa de Beauregard are right, then the universe is just as well organized and functions just as precisely, as a DNA molecule in the nucleus of the cell. Just as one has succeeded in discovering the genetic code, one should also be able to find the astronomical code. The communication of information is not restricted to living organisms, it is also an integral part of the universe, just as matter and energy are.[81]

The DNA molecule bears the form pattern of every cell and the entire organism of which the cell is a component. When parents mate, the genetic code of their offspring is a combination of the separate genetic memories of the parents, half each. The "individual" is a set of characteristics defined by the gender, psychology, physical appearance and many other qualities, derived from the combined qualities of both parents, four grandparents, eight great-grandparents and so on. Through childhood experiences resonate with the basic genetic molecular coding. When the child becomes an adult and reproduces, the second generation offspring combines both the inherited characteristics of the grandparents and the experiential permutations derived from the parents' experiences. Every living being is affected by previous lifetimes stored in the genetic memory matrix common to all. The differences between individuals are due to varying emphasis within the same coding process.

The general characteristics of each species and the differences which distinguish individuals from one another are maintained through reproduction. For example, molecules are self-replicating. A molecule experiences a life cycle of conception, gestation, childhood, maturity and death, finally replicating copies to replace itself in its own image. Such efficient

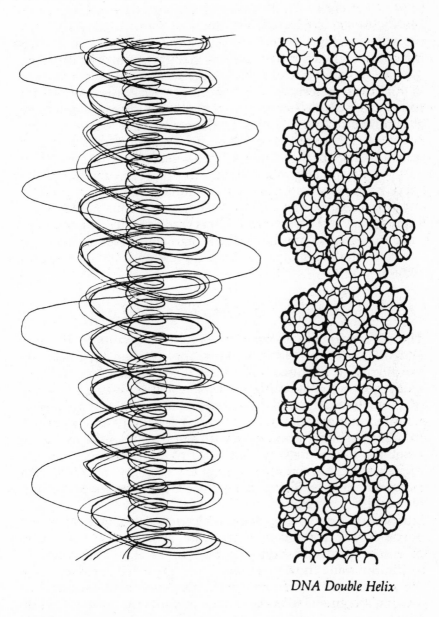

DNA Double Helix

Fig. 16: Double Spiral and DNA
On the left the spiralling Solar System is seen with the earth's spiral path as central, with the sun and inner planets spiralling around earth, and the planets further out from the earth enclosing the whole.

reproduction ensures the continuity of the organism – its continuing existence depends upon repetition in time. Molecules parent other molecules in their own image – molecules only make variations when errors occur. Molecules are composed of atoms, so the replication of a molecule is when a parent molecule organizes atoms in its own image, and when a molecule dies (changing form is death in the molecular world) it reverts back to free atoms. All the molecules in our entire molecular body replicate, yet it takes many cycles before there is any change apparent in the body as a whole. The eyes temporarily sag after a drinking bout, but recover twelve hours later. One continually dies and is recreated over and over again, being broken down into constituent atomic and molecular parts and reassembling again. Yet in the life of the species many generations of individuals repeat until there is any noticeable change. The spiralling of millions of electronic impulses around a strand of DNA is similar to the movement of the entire galactic mechanism through time. The question is, how can the cosmic process be understood and applied to personal life?

Astrology is Knowledge of Time

The experiments in *biological time* of Pierre Lecompte de Nouy (1883-1949) form the basis for the relationship between astrology and biology. During the First World War, de Nouy analyzed the rate at which wounds healed according to the age of the wounded, and discovered that metabolic processes, reflected in the rate at which the body consumes and processes oxygen in healing, slow down with age. The older the wounded man, the longer healing takes. De Nouy calculated that the impression of the passage of time for a twenty- and fifty-year old man would be four and six times faster than for a five-year old child.[82]

Biological time is the relationship between metabolism and perception. Metabolism is the rate at which an organism processes food and oxygen, based on relative body weight, respiration rate, food consumption and age. The perception of the passage of time is primarily determined by the number of images the brain receives in any given time period. When metabolism increases, the rate at which images are processed increases. If six images per second are normally processed, but in an excited state nine are processed, the brain overestimates duration and signals that one and one-half seconds have passed – it would feel like time is passing slowly. When metabolism decreases, only three images per second are received, and the brain underestimates the passage of time, because it seems that only one-half of a second has passed. As metabolic rate slows down, time appears to pass faster.[83]

At conception, metabolic rate is determined by the very fast "molecular" time scale of the ovum, while at death, metabolism ceases. As we age our metabolism gradually slows down, counterpointed by local and temporary modulations. This is why time seems to pass so slowly in childhood, but faster and faster as we age, until near death time passes so quickly that we cannot keep up with it. Youth and old age are characterized by fast and slow metabolic rates. Months in gestation seem like years in childhood and decades in maturity. Excitement and stimulation increase metabolism, temporarily inducing the time perception of youth, while boredom and depression decrease metabolism, like old age. Our time sense is continually modulated by internal and external conditions including diet, sensory imput, drugs, psychological states and physiological factors.

Metabolic rate is proportional among organisms of differing sizes. Rodney Collin found similar proportions between lifespan and breath for organisms at many different scales from cells through Man, Nature, Earth, Sun and the Galaxy, and found that each cosmos had a relative time sense. At each level of being, a lifetime seems to have the same length, whether a galaxy or an insect. A summer gnat has a lifetime of one day, but it lives its life 30,000 times faster than does a human. The gnat can only respond to information and perception at its accelerated time. Sound waves would be very slow pulses, relative to the gnat's time. In spatial terms, when a man shouts at the gnat from the length of the garden, for the gnat the voice will be coming from 1700 miles away. The gnat moves at a speed close to the limit of human perception, but the gnat sees a human as an immovable object. When a gnat is in a rainstorm, it perceives the particles of water moving at the same rate as humans perceive the advance of icebergs in the sea. Air would be liquid, and water would be solid.

A psychological factor which acts according to the same mathematics as metabolism in foreshortening time is memory. Each present perception is compared to the memory of all previous days of life. With each passing day more memories are added, and as we grow older the collection increases. Each day is related to the whole, yet contains the whole. For example, the first day of life is 1/1, or 100% of the whole, and influences registering then are very important as the women's movement has recognized. The second day of life is compared to memory of the first, making it 1/2 of the lifetime. The third day is 1/3, then 1/4, 1/5 and so on, until at one year old each day is 1/365th of the whole, and at thirty years old each day is only 1/10,000th of the whole. With age, each successive day is a smaller and smaller proportion of the whole life. As we age, time appears to contract, to compact and to pass more quickly. The mathematical expression describing the compaction of life in time is a logarithmic progression.

Life ★ Time Astrology

The lifetime of a human ovum is one lunar month, and the average lifetime of the cellular body is one thousand lunar months, or 77 years. The timescale of the ovum is one thousand times faster than the timescale of a person at 77 years old, and the lifetime of the ovum is one thousandth that of the cellular body.

A lifetime can be subdivided using a logarithmic scale to the base ten with the lunar month unit. The sequence 1, 2, 3, 4 is expressed 1, 10, 100, 1000 in a logarithmic scale. The intermediate divisions occur at ten lunar months after conception (nine calendar months), at birth, and one hundred lunar months after conception (seven years old), when the personality is formed and childhood is generally considered to be complete. The divisions create three developmental "octaves" of life – *Gestation*, *Childhood* and *Maturity* – which are unequal in calendar time but perceptually equal.

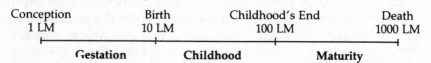

Conception	Birth	Childhood's End	Death
1 LM	10 LM	100 LM	1000 LM
Gestation	Childhood		Maturity

In *Gestation* the physical *Body* is created within the mother; during *Childhood* the *Personality* is created within the home and family system; and during *Maturity* the *Soul* is created in the world. Soul is the total of moments of self-consciousness in the lifetime and the ability to utilize the finest energy levels derived from experiencing life as a whole. Each successive octave occupies ten times more calendar time, but the same quantum of energy and growth is put into each octave. As one ages, time seems to contract, compact and accelerate.

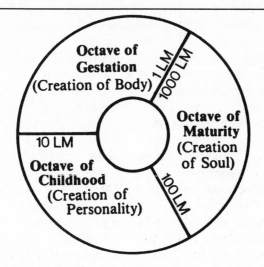

Fig. 17: Astrological Octaves
Gestation technically begins 1 lunar month after conception, when
the fertilized ovum has attached itself to the uterine wall; 10 lunar
months is birth; 100 lunar months the end of childhood at about
seven years old; and 1000 lunar months after conception, at about 77
years, is the average age of death. Note that conception and death
coincide – beginning and end are the same.

When the logarithmically graded time scale is wrapped
around a circle, conception coincides with death, closing the
circle. (Fig. 17) At conception the soul enters the space-time
continuum and the spiralling solar system, leading to the
creation of the astrological pattern which resonates with the
genetic code as derived from its morphogenetic fields. The
pattern activated at conception, of which the genetic code is the
physical manifestation, determines the form of life in time,
which is all potential – none of its actuality has been realized.

The life energy enters into the space-time continuum where it
becomes subject to more rigid laws than in its previous domain
of spirit, which signals an incarnation – birth onto the cross of
matter and the wheel of karma. At the moment of death the life
is all actual, all its potential has been utilized, and the identical
code registers as a last judgement, flashing before the dying. All
events in life are stages in the transformation of potential into
actual reality.

The log time scale is superimposed upon the horoscope and
further subdivided into twelve developmental stages,
equivalent to the twelve *houses*, as the pattern of life. The
positions of the planets describe:

– events in life occurring at specific times from conception to old age,

– archetypal and individual psychological mechanisms which determine character and behaviour,

– influential individuals in life and their equivalent inner mechanisms,

– bodily glands, organ systems and the times of their release.

Integrating biological time with astrology creates a revolutionary picture of the whole life, based on mathematically derived principles; a valuable tool in psychotherapy, healing, psychiatry, the raising of children, in relationships, executive placement, work on the self and individual awareness for personal growth.

The patterns and sub-patterns of life may be reconstructed using the log time scale. The path around the periphery of the horoscope circle symbolizes the events and mechanisms of life activated at spiritual, psychological, emotional and biological levels. The events of gestation, from the mother's point of view, and the long forgotten events of early childhood may be reconstructed, together with the people who participated in or caused them. Both outer environment and inner psychology are shown in the horoscope in symbolic form – the greatest barrier in astrology being the interpretation and translation of symbols into words. Life is cyclical and knowing the origin of behaviour patterns is a great help in understanding the present and future. Life★Time Astrology is an analytical tool and also a way for making future projections.

The *Signs of the Zodiac* are symbols of a twelve-fold process of months in the year and developmental stages in life. The interpretation of the astrological horoscope is a description of your lifetime from conception to death, following the sequence of Houses numbered from one to twelve in counter-clockwise direction. The sequence of houses is archetypal when the first sign Aries coincides with the First house. (Fig. 18) Table 2 shows the signs of the zodiac, their equivalent houses and seasons of the year, and the general characteristics which define them.

Life★Time Astrology describes life from beginning to end:

– *Gestation* is the creation of a *physical body* within the mother; a recapitulation of the entire evolutionary process from a one-celled ovum to homo sapiens; the initial relationship between parents; the nature of the sexual act of conception; gestation itself shows the creative mechanism;

—*Childhood* is the creation of an *emotional body* in the family system and shows the personality determined by the birth process; components (subpersonalities) shown by people present at birth and during early family life;

—*Maturity* is the creation of a *mental body* within the world and shows when one is educated, finds life work, produces a family and lives the remainder of life.

—*Transcendence* is the creation of a *transpersonal* or *spiritual body* outside time and is a higher octave of gestation, a knowing and experiential return to the collective unconscious.

Table 2   The Zodiac Signs

♈ *Aries the Ram*   Cardinal   Masculine Fire Sign   00° – 30°
21 March to 20 April   Germinating time; unfolding energy. Self
assertion; initiatory energy; adventure; daring; impatience; the
personality.

♉ *Taurus the Bull*   Fixed   Feminine   Earth Sign   30° – 60°
20 April to 21 May   Invigoration and strengthening; form creation;
preservation. Physical world; matter; fertility; security; finances;
stewardship; form; endurance.

♊ *Gemini the Twins*   Mutable   Masculine Air Sign   60° – 90°
21 May to 22 June   Diversity; multiplication; vitality; adaptability.
Instinctive mind; imitation; communication; duality; versatility; mobility;
facility.

♋ *Cancer the Crab*   Cardinal   Feminine   Water Sign   90° – 120°
22 June to 23 July   Mothering; fecundation; fertilization. Feeling;
emotions; mother; home and family; the unconscious; dreams; protective
urge.

♌ *Leo the Lion*   Fixed   Masculine Fire Sign   120° – 150°
23 July to 24 August   Ripening; summer heat; full energy; extraversion;
harvest. Self expression; personal love; games; pleasure; ruling; vanity;
arrogance.

♍ *Virgo the Virgin*   Mutable   Feminine   Earth Sign   150° – 180°
24 August to 23 September   Ripe fruit; orderly storage and collection;
selection. Discrimination; work; perfectionism; health & hygiene;
analysis; prudence; diet.

♎ *Libra the Balance*   Cardinal   Masculine Air Sign   180° – 210°
23 September to 24 October   Balance & adjustment; thanksgiving; social
equilibration. Partnership; marriage; public relations; enemies;
persuasion; sublimation; yielding.

♏ *Scorpio the Scorpion*   Fixed   Feminine   Water Sign   210° – 240°
24 October to 23 November   Vegetation death; seedlife; survival;
endurance. Death & regeneration; passion; separation; others; losses;
inheritance; metaphysical.

♐ *Sagittarius the Centaur*   Mutable   Masculine Fire Sign   240° – 270°
23 November to 22 December   Hibernation; advent; inner life;
meditation; expansion. Realization; higher mind; religion & philosophy;
sport; freedom; action; rebirth.

♑ *Capricorn the Goat*   Cardinal   Feminine   Earth Sign   270° – 300°
22 December to 20 January   Preservation; patience; reality; self-
concentration. Perfected matter; ego objectives; organisation; power;
success; society; government.

♒ *Aquarius the Waterbearer*   Fixed   Masculine Air Sign   300° – 330°
20 January to 19 February   Waiting; fasting; Lent; observation;
planning; abstraction. Social consciousness; humanitarian; collective;
progressive; cold; altruism; utopian.

♓ *Pisces the Fishes*   Mutable   Feminine   Water Sign   330° – 360°(0°)
19 February to 21 March   Swelling seed; purifying rain; serenity;
potential. Sensitivity; receptivity; self-sacrifice; psychic; karma; seclusion;
hospital; dreaming.

Table 2   The Zodiac Signs

Each zodiac sign describes the qualities of a thirty degree segment
of the ecliptic, a third of a yearly season, and other qualities
commensurate with its time of the year. (From Mann, *Life ★ Time
Astrology*)

Fig. 18: Zodiac with LTS

The scale of times in life may be superimposed upon the birth
horoscope with the birth point in any of the twelve signs. Here the
alignment is archetypal, as the sign Aries is aligned with the birth
moment. Although the house developmental stages are shown as
equal twelfths of the circle, due to the elliptical geometry and orbit of
the earth, the actual horoscope houses are never exactly equal, but
larger or smaller according to the length of time one takes to
experience the house.

The horoscope is the unfolding of life from its potential pattern.

The times of the beginning and end of the twelve houses in life are determined mathematically. They have an archetypal timing based on the average lifetime, but for every individual unique times are determined by the place, date and time of birth. The ages at which the houses begin closely match the developmental phases identified by the psychologist Piaget and the stages in the evolution of consciousness as described by Ken Wilber in *"Up From Eden"*. In each house all previous development is assimilated and integrated to higher levels of awareness and consciousness, and psychic energy is transferred to ever higher levels. Due to the mathematics of the logarithmic time scale, the duration of each house is almost equivalent to the entire preceding time from conception to the beginning of that house. Although each house is almost twice as long as its predecessor, it takes the same time to experience each one in turn. For example, the six year time during which one experiences primary education in the 5th house from seven years old to thirteen is almost equal to the entire preceding time back to conception.

The Process of Life

The Life★Time Astrology time scale corresponds to and may be the root of the general house attributions of traditional astrology. Traditional astrology is restricted to perceptive character study or the investigation of psychological mechanisms in individuals, but the whole remains an enigma. The leap to a logarithmic biological time scale is like the change from the static Newtonian world view to Einsteinian relativity. As such it is important to understand the process of the time scale.

First, a logarithmic scale is unique because it does not begin with zero, but one. As soon as unity is reached, it can be seen to contain another smaller-scale whole. In the smaller numbers log scales approach but never reach zero, a fact which evokes the mystery of creation: the cellular body is created from the unitarian ovum and sperm. It could not have been created from nothing, unless one accepts a Biblical spontaneous creation. The mathematical properties of logarithms are critical in The Divine Plot.

All ova exist in the mother in potentia from seven weeks after she herself was conceived, derived from her extra chromosome, passed down directly from her mother, all the way back in history to the first ovum. Each ovum is directly connected to the first life and is therefore eternal. During gestation the ovum repeats the metamorphosis of all life through the evolutionary scale, which is therefore the collective property of all humans. We carry the history of life within every cell in our bodies.

While the horoscope is a circle, it must be understood as a spiral. When the horoscope circle is extended along its time axis, like the solar system through time, it generates a cylinder, with the centre of the horoscope as a central axis. The spiritual ascent spirals around the periphery of the cylinder, moving around the circle at the same time. Fig. 19 shows the *Spiral of Life*. The horoscope is a slice through the cylinder at the time of birth, although theoretically the slice can be (and is) taken by astrologers at any point. As one ages, the cylinder fills up with experiences. The present moment is the surface of the cylinder at any given moment in time.

Planetary spiral movements animate the inside of the cylinder of life. In addition to the lifelong process around the spiral path, whenever a planet returns to the same position in the cylinder it occupied at birth, an event of the nature of the planet is activated, much like a combination safe when the correct combination of numbers are dialled opens a specific tumbler. Each planet has a specific period of revolution, and combinations continuously occur.

Traditional astrology accepts the Ascendant, the sign of the zodiac on the eastern horizon at birth, as the starting point of life. In Life★Time Astrology the birth moment does not begin life, because conception point is moment of creation. The beginning of the 9th house and the sign Sagittarius is the conception-creation point in individual life.

Each house is a developmental stage of individual life which resonates with an equivalent evolutionary stage, as will be seen in Chapters Four and Five. (Traditional interpretations are given in brackets after the house and sign designation.)

The Octave of Gestation

The Octave of Gestation begins with conception on the 9th cusp and ends at birth on the Ascendant (1st cusp), during which time the body is created within the mother. During gestation the foetus repeats the entire evolutionary process from a one-celled ovum to being fully human at birth. Hereditary characteristics from the parents combine to determine the qualities, shape and health of the body. In gestation influences

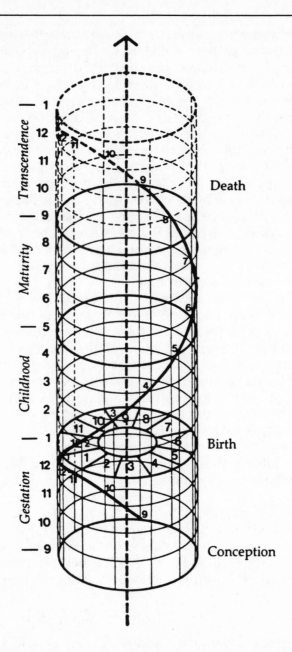

Fig. 19: Spiral of Life
When the two-dimensional horoscope is extended along its time axis,
the life may be seen as a cylinder, with conception at the bottom and
transcendence at the top. As one ages, the cylinder fills up with
memories. The rising surface of experience within the cylinder is the
present moment of consciousness.

are transmitted through the mother to the developing child and are carried somatically, within the physical body.

9th House   *Sagittarius the Centaur*

Conception until 7 weeks after conception
(Higher mind, meditation, religion and law, long journeys, foreign influences, philosophy, psychology, initiation, self realization.)

The 9th cusp is the sexual act of conception, which begins with the long journey of millions of sperms to the ripe ovum and culminates in fertilization. The first lunar month after conception is a compacted pattern at a molecular time scale of the entire life of the cellular body while being attached to the wall of the uterus. The three main body systems are present as spiral germ layers of the embryo. The embryo develops in parallel with the early phases of evolution, retaining memory of these stages in the structure of the brain. The mother does not yet know that she is pregnant and gradually discovers that there is a creative energy within her.

10th House   *Capricorn the Goat*

7 weeks until 12 weeks after conception
(Perfected matter, concrete relationships, organization, father, public affairs, fame and fortune, ambition, aspirations, pragmatism.)

According to Buddhists and Hindus, at forty-nine days after conception the soul enters the physical matrix. The embryo becomes a foetus, and sex and physical appearance are determined as the physical body takes form through its skeletal system. The cusp of the 10th house is when the mother realizes she is pregnant and the quality of her acceptance of that fact, as well as the reactions of others, particularly the father. The level of spiritual awareness of the mother is a gauge of the consciousness of the child. The parents' ability to organize the physical world during pregnancy, to communicate the coming of the child, and to concretize parental relationships all affect the stability of the child.

11th House   *Aquarius the Waterbearer*

12 weeks until 28 weeks after conception
(Altruism, selflessness, humanitarianism, idealism, planning, friends, group relationships, social matters, abstraction.)

In the midstage of gestation before the mother gains weight and appears pregnant, she concentrates upon the coming child becoming abstract and detached from the outside world. She plans and speculates about the future and idealizes the entire process. Her concentration is upon someone other than herself and she tends to attract others who have had children before. Often the mother will join birthing classes or women's groups.

12th House   *Pisces the Fishes*

28 weeks after conception until birth
(Self-sacrifice, extreme receptivity, psychic activity, sensitivity, karma, destiny, escapism, institutions, isolation, loneliness.)

The mother begins to gain weight, primarily water, which restricts her mobility, makes her much more susceptible to external influences and increases the psychic contact with the child within as well as with others. As the reality of the birth nears, deep self-sacrificial feelings become stronger, until the birth itself, when mother relies upon her own instincts in the life and death process.

The Octave of Childhood

The Octave of Childhood is from birth until about seven years old, when the personality is created within the home and family system. Planets in childhood are mechanisms of behaviour learned from or projected onto parents, family, brothers and sisters, and others who affect the development of the personality. Personality is an emotional body composed of instincts, feelings and values. Childhood is related to the early development of consciousness when humanity was still integral to the natural world.

Ascendant (ASC)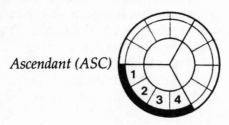

Ascendant

Birth

The birth process is symbolic of the origin of the personality and its expression. An easy birth promotes self-expression, while a long labour is an inhibited personality. People present at birth are prototypes of sub-personalities and their relationship to the complex of personality. Historically the ascendant is the first consciousness in early prehistory.

1st House   *Aries the Ram*

Birth until seven months old
(Self-assertion, the personality, shape and appearance of the physical body, early family environment, independence, selfishness)

The newborn child bonds with the mother for her support, protection and nurturing. Virtually all energy is directed to getting needs met and asserting the personality within the family. Children perceive all others as extensions of themselves.

2nd House   *Taurus the Bull*

Seven months until one year eight months old
(Physicality, undifferentiated matter, pure substance, the senses, perception, security, property)

The child discovers its body as an object among other objects and learns to use the senses to explore the physical world upon weaning from the mother.

3rd House   *Gemini the Twins*

One year eight months until three years six months old
(Instinctive mind, communication, movement, adaptability, mimicry, siblings, diversity, short journeys)

Walking and talking provide greater freedom and mobility, and lessen dependence upon others. The necessity to communicate by observing and copying others creates a duality through the identification with others as an extension of oneself.

4th House   *Cancer the Crab*

Three years six months until seven years old
(Parents and the mother, family, feelings, home life, receptivity, heredity, intuition, the psychic world, personal life, belonging)

Emotional responses to the ability to communicate are formed within the family system, and parental relationships begin to be comprehensible. The feelings of family, belonging and the acceptance of the parents is primary to establish security.

The Octave of Maturity

The third Octave of Maturity is when the body and the personality are combined, integrated and projected into the world to work out one's various possibilities. The soul is rediscovered through self-consciousness and the function of life in spiritual, family and occupational objectives in maturity, culminating in a mental body or philosophy of life. The developments of maturity parallel the creation of civilization and individuality in history.

5th House   *Leo the Lion*

Seven years until thirteen years old
(Self-consciousness, creativity, pride, affections, love of the self and others, acting, confidence, education, publications, speculation)

Primary school is the first detachment from the family structure where one learns how to make relationships and to satisfy the need to be loved in the world. Games provide a way to relate to others, and the ability to accept and make rules is a basis for being able to structure life.

6th House   *Virgo the Virgin*

Thirteen years until twenty-three years and five months old
(Differentiated matter, distillation, discrimination, puberty, diet and health, secondary education, work, service)

Physical and mental growth dominate adolescence and the youth must take responsibility for decisions in school and at work. Many binding choices are made and the rules of the society are confronted and learned.

7th House   *Libra the Scales*

Twenty-three years five months until forty-two years old
(Sublimation of self, balance, partnership, the public, obligations, enemies, justice, communal and business relationships, sociability)

Balance is sought between oneself and others, inner and outer realities embodied in permanent relationships in the world which are a summation of all earlier conditions. Family is created, a reputation gained and a sense of permanence is sustained.

8th House   *Scorpio the Scorpion*

Forty-two years old until death
(Life processes, karma, separation, death, regeneration, occultism, metaphysical beliefs, shared resources, legacies, perversity)

After mid-life crisis there is a gradual separation from the world, an increased reliance upon others and a tendency to produce works and adopt views which carry influence beyond the physical world. Energy declines, health deteriorates and the senses gradually weaken. Time sense becomes highly compacted and time passes incredibly rapidly.

The Transcendent Octave

How can a man be born when he is old? Can he enter a second time into his mother's womb and be born? Jesus answered, "Truly, truly, I say to you, unless one is born of water and the spirit, he cannot enter the kingdom".

John 3:4-5[84]

The fourth octave beyond the three of the physical world is an octave of transcendence and transpersonal reality. Most individuals are quite asleep and mechanical in only understanding their being in a linear, physical, finite lifespan. For most, life begins at birth and ends at death. But it is possible to extend reality beyond the confines of the physical body.

The foundation of the fourth octave, a higher spirit of transcendence, is in gestation, when the collective unconscious creation of a body occurs within the mother. The influences of gestation parallel the transcendent reality, not as repetitive events, but with a similarity of meaning. The way in which one's mother realizes that she is creating life within her and responds to the process is the prototype of the way in which one realizes and accepts spiritual life. If one's mother revels in creation, one would feel elated in the realm of the spirit. Access to the transcendent realm occurs through *"initiation"* which involves experiencing the death/conception point as access to the transpersonal reality of creation.

Originally initiation was a symbolic transition from childhood to maturity. The women's mysteries concerned the sacred knowledge of conception and childbirth, signalled by the first menstruation. Life★Time˙Astrology is based on the resonance between gestation and initiation. The medieval *"Axiom of Maria"* described the process: "One becomes two, two becomes three, and out of the third comes the one as the fourth".[85] Jung related this to the discovery of the natural history of the psyche within everyone. Transcendence starts with a return to the beginning.

In Gnostic alchemy, heaven and earth have a womb-like shape.[86] The alchemical process is shown in *"Alchemy"* by Johannes Fabricius not as the transmutation of gold, but as a transformation of the psyche. Jung discovered parallels between the process of psychic growth and the visions of the alchemists. Fabricius shows that alchemical diagrams which seem like bewildering dreamscapes are accurate diagrams of the processes of conception, fertilization, meiosis and mitosis, up to the moment of birth. (Fig. 20) The process by which we are created is the recapitulation of the evolution of the spirit since its incarnation in matter, and reliving the process is realization.

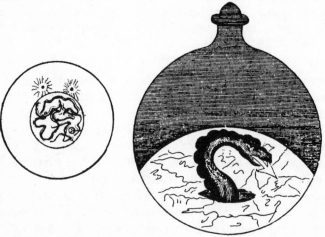

Fig. 20: Alchemy and Mitosis
The action of the snake within the alchemical retort echoes the action of mitosis, when genetic material separates and rejoins to create new life during conception. *(Rosarium)*

Many primitive legends and folklore carry the belief that at the moment of death one's entire life flashes instantly before the mind's eye. The phenomenon, known as *"panoramic memory"*, is being studied in near death experiences.[87] With the last registration of the life pattern at death, life is actual and all its potential has been realized. All life is continually available except that we lose sight of the whole while it is happening.

The remembrance of life at the moment of death is the *last judgement* of religion.[88] The weighing of the soul at the moment of death in the underworld is a powerful archetypal image. (Fig. 21) The last judgement is an assessment of the value of life to the soul as a determining factor for its next incarnation, similar to the process in operation in the quest for transpersonal reality. The factual material, the content of life (the prime material of the alchemists), must be understood so that it can be transmuted to a higher level. The death of the former reality is a requirement for the transcendent process to ensue. Death signals not just the extinction of the physical body, but a transmission of life energy beyond individuality into the "realm of the mothers", of Goethe's Faust.

Fig. 21: The Last Judgement
The panorama of the Last Judgement in Egyptian symbolism shows the soul being weighed against a feather and the sequence of archetypal images within the self along the top.

Each of the four houses of gestation has a higher manifestation in the transcendent octave.

Higher Conception Point   9th Cusp

The conception as shown by the 9th cusp in the horoscope

describes the way in which the mother and father join to produce the child as a metaphor for the differentiation and then integration of the female and male components of the psyche, called by Jung the "anima" and "animus". The parents attitude to the conception is reflected in the nature of the conjunction within the psyche in creative action.

Higher 9th House   *Sagittarius*

The hormonal changes within the mother echo the transition through the early stages of multicellular, invertebrate and vertebrate reality. The way in which the mother realizes the creative, spiritual Self within parallels the journey of discovery of the higher self within.

Higher 10th House   *Capricorn*

After the recognition of the birth, the parents organize the physical world and make the coming of the child known. Higher perceptions must be structured and integrated into the Self in the world on a practical level.

Higher 11th House   *Aquarius*

The idealism of mother is transmuted to the way in which the higher Self projects itself to the world of media, groups, circles of friends and organizations beyond the self-oriented personal level. Utopian aims and idealistic pursuits alter prevailing social systems.

Higher 12th House   *Pisces*

The mother sacrifices her own existence as she carries her child prior to birth, and the enlightened Self must give itself totally to the whole, dissolve into the void, in order to achieve final unity with the realm of pure spirit.

While the transcendent octave may be seen as a return to the beginning, the centre of the horoscope is also the transcendent centre of the Self, always available. The eternal presence of the transcendent is the energy driving the process around the horoscope of life stages.

There are two integrated ways to circuit the horoscope. (Fig. 22) The traditional cycle is from Ascendant (1st cusp) to

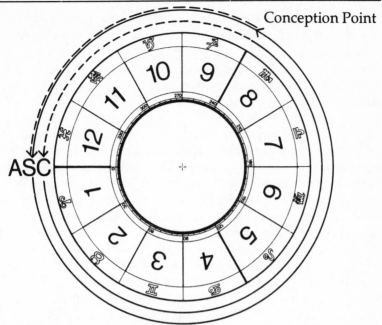

Conception Point

ASC

Fig. 22: Two Paths Around the Horoscope
The traditional circuit begins and ends with the Ascendant, with death as the 8th house and the houses 9th–12th being higher mind. Life★Time Astrology cycles from conception at the 9th cusp around to death, also at the same point, and an overlap octave where the prototype of the transpersonal realm is gestation.

Ascendant, which does not include gestation because there is no explicit time scale, but does attribute "higher mind" to the 9th through 12th houses. Life★Time Astrology cycles from 9th cusp/conception to 9th cusp/death or initiation, which, being biologically organized, includes gestation and integrates the higher octave as an overlap of gestation. Beginning life at birth requires gestation to provide collective roots, and the overlap is essential for describing the transpersonal. The mechanism is much like the four seasons where, although the year begins with the spring growth, the seeds have been stored the previous autumn.

Life history is recorded and stored logarithmically in a code based on metabolism, therefore any action or influence which affects metabolic rate is potential access to individual and collective life history. Emotional states increase metabolism, as in childhood, and when in the throes of intense emotion, we are childlike. In contrast, depression decreases metabolism, as in old age, and the depressive feels prematurely old and tired.

Psychological states are stored at their appropriate age in life experience. When a developmental stage becomes a barrier, we tend to regress back into previous states which were more comfortable. Thus there is a counterclockwise movement in time, and a clockwise movement back to the source in gestation. The entire process revolves around the centre of the horoscope and the psyche.

Psychotropic drugs alter time sense by affecting metabolism, and create apparent time-travel back into life.[89] LSD increases molecular metabolism – the subject seems to become younger. Parental identities are projected onto whoever is nearby and critical events of childhood are transcribed into the local environment. The adult subject acts as a young child, backtracking the process of growing up. As the effect of the psychedelic becomes stronger, earlier and earlier circumstances and modes of perception begin to register. As the child learned to walk and communicate, the feeling is that those abilities are being lost, until eventually the helplessness of the newborn infant is experienced. Visual phenomena, familiar to the adult, are scrutinized as if for the first time and the process of coming into contact with and using the senses is intensified.

If the dosage is sufficiently high, the subject passes through birth in reverse. The compression into a protective yet terrifyingly claustrophobic space within the mother is attended by those influences which accompanied the original birth. When born by traumatic surgical delivery, the trauma is re-enacted, as in Janov's "*Primal Scream Therapy*". As the birth moment signalled the creation of the personality, a way of seeing oneself, the reversed psychedelic experience is an elimination of personality and the entrance into the womb. Once within the womb the "objective" outside world vanishes and is replaced by the incredibly vivid psychic tapestry of intrauterine life. Direct perception is replaced by psychic contact, and the mundane realities of family life are replaced by a transit of the collective unconscious. As gestation repeats the evolutionary process, the psychedelic experience is travelling back in time.

When the subject takes a particularly potent dosage, the journey may extend all the way back to the time of the registration of the MC, when the soul/ego entered the physical matrix and the embryo became human for the first time. The process is commonly known as "ego-loss". An earlier stage is the 9th house, during which the various brain structures are formed as vestiges of primary evolutionary forms. The hallucinated journey back through the primary states is sometimes horrifying − it is experienced like the Bardo states described so vividly in Tibetan Buddhist texts. Quite literally the subject experiences unfamiliar life-forms in the primordial world of saurians, the primeval swamp and still earlier, the pre-planetary existence of earth material. The final stage of the psychedelic experience is a return to the burst of energy at conception which echoes the Big Bang and is called the *White Light* in Buddhism. Although the White Light is unity, wholeness and pure bliss, the wanderer gradually feels the impulsion of incarnation, begins to seek a womb, and the experience is repeated back, a recreation of the life and a return to reality.

The psychedelic experience is no less than a journey back through the space-time process of life and parallels the perceptions of millennia of mystics and seers as an investigation of the origin of the psyche.

Life★Time Interpretation

The positions of planets in the horoscope show when formative influences register. They can be evenly spaced around the horoscope, clustered, randomly scattered or concentrated, just as in life. Some develop early, peak in secondary school and then lead quite mechanical lives after that time, while others do not really develop until their thirties or forties. The process is the same for everyone, drawing as it does on the same bank of archetypal behaviour patterns and events, but it is experienced from different relative viewpoints. Each individual has a unique history and developmental pattern, creating a viewpoint carried by a life story.

An example of Life★Time interpretation is the horoscope of the astronaut Neil Armstrong. (Fig. 23) The inner ring shows the planets, house and sign cusps and personal points dated in log time. Armstrong has the Moon in Sagittarius, governing long journeys, at the age of 38 years 6 months, the exact time when he became the first man on the moon. The significance of his achievement may be seen on deeper levels by the planets which aspect the Moon at earlier ages. Aspects are geometrical relationships between planets which connect dates, qualities and psychological mechanisms around the circle. The stabilizing trine (120 degrees) to the Node (association) in Aries (self-assertion) in the 12th house occurs near the end of gestation when he was assertive in his mother's womb − a

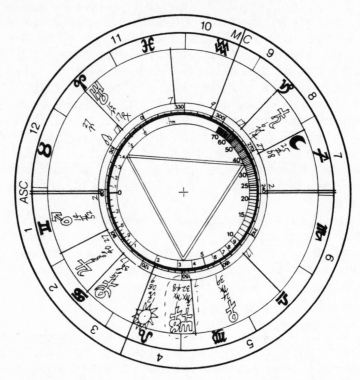

Fig. 23: Neil Armstrong
When the horoscope of Neil Armstrong is dated using the inner
wheel, it may be clearly seen that the Moon in Sagittarius (the sign of
long journeys) registers when Armstrong went to the Moon, and that
a previous experience of floating in a weightless capsule occurred
when he was gestating, as indicated by a trine aspect from the moon
to the Node in the 12th house.

precursor of the weightlessness of the spacecraft. The trine to
Mercury (communication) and Neptune (sensitivity and ESP)
in Virgo (precise work) in the 4th house (home and family)
indicate the importance to Armstrong of communication back
to earth by radio (Moon/Mercury aspect) and the psychic
experiments (Moon/Neptune) which were performed on the
spaceflight. The tensioning square to Venus shows separation
from children and loved ones. The horoscope shows both the
external circumstances and the inner psychological
mechanisms which parallel each other. A complete astrological
reading is much more complex and comprehensive than this
short example, and describes a lifetime in great depth.

Archetypal Astrology

A more profound mechanism lies under the seemingly innocuous surface of astrology. The signs symbolize deep primeval impulses which come into play within the psyche but are not adequately expressed in outer life.[90] The meglomaniac qualities ascribed to the sun-sign Leo do not really do justice to the feeling of primal awareness that the lion carries, the power, regal spendour and pure consciousness of the king of beasts. It is the rare moments when the archetypes are lived that life is most vital, but paradoxically it is usually moments when civilization is bypassed that they occur. The more effectively the cultural surface is shed, the more vital one is and the more alive one feels.

Everyone carries archetypal qualities, certain ways of behaving, thinking, feeling and responding to the spiritual impulse which lie beneath the civilized facade of modern humanity and are so strong that they never lose their potency. The behaviour of humanity is deeply ingrained, as if pre-arranged. No therapy can hope to pacify or eliminate the primitive that lies sleeping within for long. Whether it is sexuality, hunger or power which brings out one's inner King Kong, the veneer of civilization just barely keeps real being in check. People are differentiated by the way in which they choose to hold, act out, rationalize or suppress the ancient essence carried within the soul.

> . . . for in me the most dangerous native tendencies have been subdued, civilized, purified, applied and compelled to good and great ends, by dint of a character sprung from somewhere else. My ego – a balancing trick, only just achieved.[91]

The metaphor of the world as a stage, with women and men as mere players, has a ring of truth. Transcendent experiences show that even the most profound or natural human is shallow and mechanical in comparison to the energy and pure being which lie beyond personal characteristics. True reality emerges in "peak" experiences, pain, extreme hunger, love-making or death.

The great significance and power of astrology lies in its appeal to many cultures throughout history, even now, when one would think that the scientific tide would sweep it away. The ability to remain in contact with the primal life is paramount when society has imprisoned itself. It is impossible to break out or to remain trapped anymore.

Psychotherapy, astrology and other techniques of liberation

can do no more than provide a catalyst for allowing inner reality to manifest in life through initiating a dialogue with the symbols of freedom.

The Eternal Ovum

Life is lived in time. We may transcend time in spiritual or meditative experiences, but only temporarily. As a fourth dimension beyond the three spatial dimensions of the physical world, time contains all space, and by extension, all material reality.

Life★Time Astrology shows that an individual life signified by the horoscope is a recapitulation of all life in the universe. The progress of spirit and soul through earthly incarnation is the descent of unity and its entrance into physical form. The Creation of physical form has been repeated in every being from the dawn of time and the process is embodied within form itself.

The lunar month unit of Life★Time Astrology corresponds to the lifetime of the ovum. The common thought that the ovum is "created" each month in a fertile woman is not dissimilar to Aristotle's belief that the human embryo develops out of an admixture of menstrual blood and male seminal fluid, with the male merely providing the stimulus to growth to the already developed embryo. It was not until 1827 that the ovum was discovered and seen by the biologist Karl Ernst von Baer. The ovum is not created each month any more than menstruation is an expulsion of an ovum. All the ova which a woman brings to fruition are present seven weeks after her own conception. The ovaries contain more than a quarter million immature cells, one or more of which ripen each month within alternate ovaries.[92] The ripened human cell was first seen in 1930, and the events of the first seven days were not understood until the 1950's. It was only in the 1960's that the intricate cell structures which shape heredity had been partially understood.

The ova originate not in the mother, but in the extra chromosome which women possess from their own conception. In this sense the ovum is eternal. But it can only be so because it is impossible for life to be created from nothing. Being eternal, the ovum carries the memory and structure of all previous life within it, ready to provide information when required. Every ovum is similar to the ovum which created the first life, recurring an almost infinite number of times in the past, and carrying all its predecessors within it.

Each cell contains genetic material sufficient to build and monitor all genetic structure in the body. The 100,000 genes which describe and create a specific cell are only one one-hundredth of the genetic material. The other 99% are for "regulation". The parallel between the brain and the genetic code, each using a tiny fragment of its capacity to create and maintain life, leads one to suspect that the remainder is devoted to the whole of life and all history, which is carried within.

Freud hypothesized that ontogeny (the life of the individual) recapitulates phylogeny (the life of the species). The experience of childhood is similar to the mythological reality of humanity thousands of years ago, after the emergence of consciousness. Individual life reactivates patterns established millennia ago. The deeper instincts of sexuality, hunger, sleep and anger originate before consciousness and are not learned from parents, but are contained within the psyche. Jung identified two types of inherited characteristics as a *"personal unconscious"* which contains all memories derived from childhood, and a *"collective unconscious"* shared with all other humans. Everyone is influenced by both levels of reality, in varying degrees.

The principle of recapitulation is central to depth and transpersonal psychology, and Life ★ Time Astrology.

I. The *Octave of Gestation* from conception to birth reflects the time from Creation to the origin of consciousness, and is the collective unconscious. During this time we repeat the process from fertilized ovum to birth and all influences registering are stored somatically within the physical body as instincts.

II. The *Octave of Childhood* from birth to seven reflects the mythological time of human pre-history, from when humanity first became conscious until the emergence of the first historical individuals, and is the personal unconscious. All familial influences are carried in an emotional body.

III. The *Octave of Maturity* from seven until death is analogous to the development of civilization in history, from the first historical individuals to the realization of the renaissance. Influences derived from the educational life process are stored in the mental body as a world view.

IV. The *Octave of Transcendence* is the higher level of creative being which reflects gestation but lies outside of individual time. The historical parallel is the age when humanity realizes its existence and function within the cosmos. The search for the origin of life is carried in the spiritual body as transcendence.

Each successive developmental stage in life becomes longer and longer, taking almost as long as the entire preceding time back to conception. In history, each successive stage is shorter than its predecessor. When the life of an individual is compared to all history, the direction of expansion and contraction is reversed. (Fig. 24) Individual developmental stages increase with time and collective developmental stages decrease with time. The two opposite flows of time mutually compensate the historical perspective of time. If the time sense for the individual and species both compacted in the same direction in time, the result would be cumulative, exaggerated and much more noticeable than they are. Since they flow in different directions, they have compensatory flows, which accounts for the fact that although most people recognise a variation in the flow of time, very few would actually posit it as a natural law, and fewer as a central mechanism of the universe.

Once history, both individually and for the species, is understood as being exponential and circular instead of additive and linear, a unique and profound picture emerges. Historically it is easy to find cultures which espouse both systems of grading history. Buddhist and Hindu cycles of great ages decrease in length towards the present as examples of the first, and the Precession of the Equinoxes of 25,000 years in the Platonic Year is an example of the second.

Hindu and Buddhist world ages decrease successively according to the ratio 4:3:2:1. The belief that each age reflects the same events as the former but in less time indicates a progressive deterioration. The length of life decreases as does the quality of life. The Chinese also had theories of a fall from a "Golden Age" recorded in the "Record of Rites" of Li Chi in AD 100 and, before that, by Huai Nan Tzu in 200 BC.[93] There are significant advantages and logic to both linear and exponential systems of describing history – The Divine Plot includes them both.

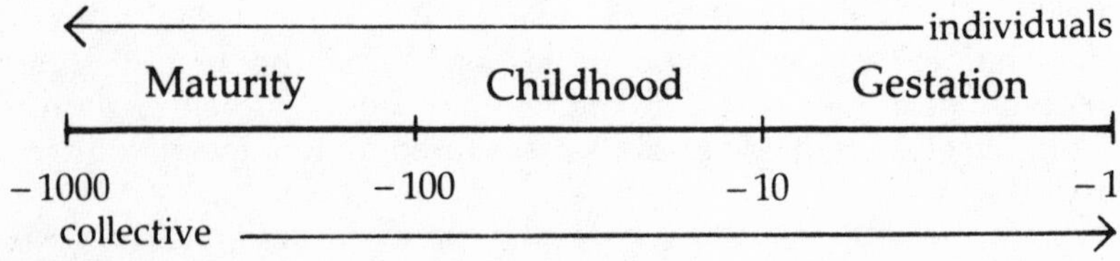

Fig. 24: *Differential Time Contraction*
Individual and collective life compacts perceptually in different directions. The human develops rapidly in gestation and slows down with age, while history develops slowly at first and accelerates through time. The proportion is the same in both directions, creating a balance between individual and collective which focuses upon an eternal present moment.

The Acceleration of History

It seems that the universe develops at a constant rate, but this is not the case. The turn-of-the-century historian Henry Adams studied the relationship between science and social history, being familiar with electromagnetism, the laws of thermodynamics, the then recent discovery of radioactivity and the dilemma of Michelson and Morley's time equations, as well as the pace of modern history. Adams plotted the rising curves of scientific discovery rates, coal output, steam power, mechanical and electrical usage and many others, and said, "Any schoolboy could plot such curves and see that arithmetical ratios were useless; the curves followed the old familiar law of squares".[94] The curves rise more steeply as they ascend from the base line of time. (Fig. 25)

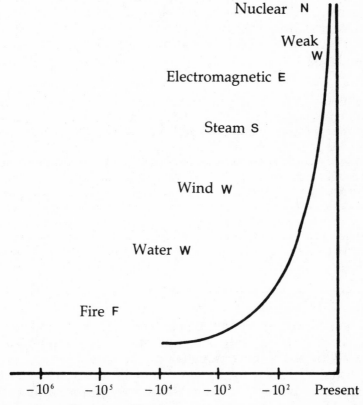

Fig. 25: The Acceleration of Time
When graphs illustrating the exponential increase in energy sources, the discovery of elements, in agricultural and industrial output are combined they generate the curved Law of Acceleration of Henry Adams.

The logarithmic time base line of Adams' chart gives equal space to the last millennium as to the preceding 10,000 years. It not only serves geometrical convenience, but also reflects the compression of the past in memory. "Acceleration is the law of history."[95] Conclusions drawn from statistics on energy use and changes in phase in history related to thermodynamics indicated that at a constant logarithmic progression, humanity would reach a limit of possibilities by the year 2025, by Adams' most optimistic projection.

Adams likened the life of humanity to the passage of a comet which traverses the infinite without origin or end. Occasionally it is attracted to an object of curiosity lying in its path, which forces it to greatly condense its velocity as it curves past, implying that evolution has already passed its perihelion and is moving retrograde already. According to Adams, by 2025 humanity will have overbalanced its ability to integrate by an increased ability to disintegrate.

H. G. Wells voiced similar ideas just before the first nuclear bomb tests:

> Events now follow one another in an entire untrustworthy sequence. Spread out and examine the pattern of events and you will find yourself face to face with a new scheme of being, hitherto unimaginable by the human mind. This new cold glare mocks and dazzles the human intelligence, no matter how this intelligence under its cold urgency contrives to seek some way out or round or through the impasse. The writer has come to believe that the congruence of the mind, which man has attributed to the secular process, is not really there at all. The two processes have run parallel for what we call Eternity and now abruptly they swing off at a tangent from one another – just as a comet at its perihelion hangs portentous in the heavens for a season and then rushes away for ages, or forever.[96]

The world is accelerating past its breaking point.

Events in the modern world verify these eighty- and fifty-year old predictions. Shortages of food, energy and natural resources, coupled with an exponential increase in population have followed the most negative predictions.

Hermann Kahn and The Hudson Institute predicted logarithmic increases "In the Year 2000" for measuring Gross National product projections; Postwar Economy Growth; Rate of Increase of Energy in Particle Accelerators; GNP Extrapolations; Populations; Total GNP; Individual Country Production; Population from 8000 BC to AD 2000; GNP per capita; Population per GNP; United States GNP per capita;

Japanese GNP per capita; and many others.

Bertalanffy, the founder of General Systems Theory, gives exponential growth as a basic law of nature. The great eras in the earth's prehistory are all shorter than their predecessors. The time scale of evolution is not a clock marked by equal intervals, but more like a stone falling to the ground.

J. G. Bennett, in *"The Dramatic Universe: History"*, confronts the problem of historical time scales, presenting accelerated progress as an idea no one doubts. "Statistics show that the output of science and technology has for a long time been increasing at an accelerated pace. Moreover, accelerated progress seems to be a law of nature."[97] Bennett constructed a graph of the logarithmic nature of the great eras.[98] He calls acceleration "objective eschatology," but runs into a problem when he carries his time scale any nearer the present than 100,000 BC. His mathematics prevents measurements except those remote from the present. In the larger sense, the rate of development went out of control 100,000 years ago. Humanity's entire existence occurs within a mere hyphen of nature. Bennett does allow, however, that the acceleration must continue into historical time – even through to the present, stating that, "We should expect the completion of the eighth (and last) Era within the next half-million years and perhaps very much sooner".[99]

The concept of an exponential (logarithmic) spiral of life and time is not new. As well as by Descartes in 1638, exponential time has been proposed by Bernoulli, the biologist J. B. S. Haldane and even Charles Darwin.

The exponential spiral governs the growth pattern of the nautilus, many varieties of shells, flowers, trees, and even galaxies.[100] Organisms which utilize the divine proportion in its natural form continue to grow and expand while maintaining the same shape, making its name of "spira mirabilis" appropriate.

Many great scientists and thinkers have used logarithmic scales in the attempt to describe the natural world. Hans Kalmus proposed a logarithmic scale to study the numbers characteristic of generations of various levels of organization from virus to man through the geologic ages. Rolland Fisher used a logarithmic spiral of "biological time" for describing increasingly rapid events in learning processes through time.[101] J. B. S. Haldane observed that since the existence of humanity the natural evolutionary rate has increased exponentially, a frequency of change which affects the length of generations and could be a factor in the extinction of species.[102] Nigel Calder graded history from Creation to AD 2000 with a log scale because: it allowed great spans of magnitude to be collated; proportional scales are more relevant than linear yearly scales alone; the detail available is greater the closer one approaches the present; in terms of human population it compensates for the rapid increase in growth; and brain size is proportional to lengths of time and lifetime.[103]

None of these theories takes full creative advantage of a log scale applied to individual and collective history.

The Divine Proportion of Time

> Wherefore He resolved to have a moving image of eternity, and when He set in order the heaven, He made this image eternal but moving according to number, while eternity itself rests in unity: and this image He called Time.
>
> Plato[104]

The two most important proportions used in The Divine Plot are the *golden section* and the *logarithmic scale*. According to Pythagorean number symbolism the golden section is five-based, the number of creation, and the logarithmic scale is ten-based, the number of diversity and completion.

The golden section proportion is the ratio "phi" (1.618:1), derived from the projection of a half-diagonal of a square. Kepler called it the *"divine proportion"* because it is pleasing when used either mathematically or aesthetically, and he used phi to describe planetary orbits. The phi proportion generates an additive and geometric series where each successive number is the sum of the two previous numbers and is the product of the previous number multiplied by 1.618.

The golden section is the geometric basis of the pentagram and pentagon worshipped by the Pythagoreans and later by magicians and mystics of the middle ages and the renaissance. The pentagon is a regular five-sided figure which, when its sides are extended, forms the pentagram star – both yield many phi relationships. Fig. 26 shows the pentagram and the geometric technique discovered by Albrecht Durer for constructing a pentagon from a hexagon.

The golden section is a linear, planar and spatial proportion. Lines may be divided into segments proportioned by phi; planes may be divided into golden rectangles as in painting; and in architecture and sculpture phi may be used to define the internal and external proportions of buildings or sculptures.

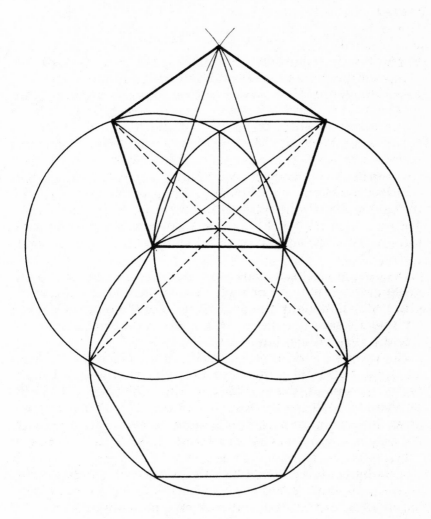

Fig. 26: Durer Pentagram and The Golden Section
Phi proportions derive from the pentagram, and Durer's solution
with only a straightedge and compass is a very elegant way of
constructing a regular pentagram. The Golden Section was used in
much sacred architecture from Egypt to the Renaissance.

What is the equivalent of the phi proportion for time? The proportion which governs the growth of nature, civilizations and individual men through time is the logarithmic proportion, base ten. The base ten logarithm constitutes the golden section of time.

"Ten represents the ten in one, ten integrated by one."[105]

In the Buddhist Hwa-yen Sutra, Fa-tzang characterized two aspects of the enlightened condition by the numbers one and ten. One is the *Unus Mundus* (One World), unity and all-embracing Self, and ten is the form in which unity may be experienced in the multiplicity of existence, a pervading continuous identity. Marie Louise von Franz interprets numerological correspondences psychologically in an attempt to explain the paradoxical multiplicity and unity of the Self which denotes psychic wholeness, because numbers form the midpoint between the spiritual and the material (extrasensory). The log progression 1, 10, 100 and 1000 embodies the operative force which is the emanation of a divine dynamic which creates matter.[106]

Egyptian sacred scientists attributed the number ten to the synthesis, the origin of phenomenal nature and also its aim.[107]

In Platonic thought, the Sixth Ennead of Plotinus proposes a ten-fold division of existents, within which every element of the world is divided into ten genera.[108]

The mystical and numerological Hebrew Qabbalah is based on the Tree of Life of ten sephira, where Kether the Crown (unity) emanates the qualities of the Universe, eventually received by Malkuth the Earth (multiplicity). "Planetary lives are composed of ten dreams of a hundred years each, and each solar life is a thousand years; therefore is it said that a thousand years are in the sight of God as one day."[109]

Alchemical Table 3 shows the process of multiplicatio, whereby the base material is converted into the divine gold by factors of ten, called true sun-making and moon-making.

The Incas created a sophisticated mathematics which used rope-adding devices utilizing base ten logarithms.

As we have seen earlier, *"The Round Art"* and *"Life★Time Astrology"* describe an integration of the work of de Nouy, who identified the base ten log sequence as the proportion of biological time governing growth and metabolic processes in humans and Rodney Collin, who utilized the base ten log sequence 1, 10, 100 and 1000 as divisions of lunar months defining the developmental stages of human life. The time

Lapidis multiplicativa Auri.

$$
\text{Proje\&io}
\begin{cases}
\text{I.} & 1000 \\
\text{I I.} & 10000 \\
\text{I I I.} & 100000 \\
\text{I V.} & 1000000 \\
\text{V.} & 10000000 \\
\text{V I.} & 100000000 \\
\text{V I I.} & 1000000000 \\
\text{V I I I.} & 10000000000 \\
\text{I X.} & 100000000000 \\
\text{X.} & 1000000000000 \\
\text{X I.} & 10000000000000 \\
\text{X I I.} & 100000000000000 \\
\end{cases}
$$

Centum milliones millionum tingunt.

Table 3   Lapidus multiplicativa Auri

An ancient alchemical formula shows that the final stage of the transformation involves multiplication by factors of ten to produce the 'golden stone'. "And if one part of it (the stone) in the first place converts with its bodies a hundred parts: in the second it converts a thousand, in the third ten thousand, in the fourth a hundred thousand, in the fifth a million, into the true sun-making and moon-making." (*Philosophia reformata*, Frankfurt, 1622.)

sequence of life is modified by the mathematical proportion of metabolism and memory and their effect upon perception. The logarithmic-lunar sequence of biological mechanisms and perception is integrated with the linear-yearly sequence of astrological signs, mathematically describing the combination of linear and circular, additive and exponential realities, which together determine perceptual space-time. The same circular matrix is used for both systems, reflecting the circular, repetitive and recurrent mechanisms which operate in the year, in ones life and in all life.

The three necessary criteria for a mathematical matrix for The Divine Plot are:

1. An **Additive** scale of cyclic recurrent years independent of subjective time values, measured in seconds, minutes, hours, days, calendar months or astrological signs, equinoxes and solstices, years, millennia and precessional cycles of 25,000 years.
2. A **Geometric** scale of base ten logarithms, reflecting the subjective compaction of biological time and memory as humans, humanity, civilizations, nature and the universe develop through their life cycles.
3. A **Circular** matrix around which the additive and geometric systems may be placed, so that the beginning and end of cycles coincide, satisfying the necessity of recurrent lives, ages, civilizations, world ages and universes.

★Chapter Five★
★The World Age★

The length and divisions of the World Age. The transmigration of souls. The fifty-year unit. Egyptian, Sumerian, Greek and African Sirius myths. Chakras and history. The astrological structure of history. The Time Scale. The Octave of Mythology: Aries, Taurus, Gemini and Cancer. The Octave of Civilization: Leo, Virgo, Libra and Scorpio. The Octave of Realization: Sagittarius, Capricorn, Aquarius and Pisces. The End of the World Age. Panoramic Memory. Historical Shock Points. The Tibetan Bardo states between lives. Media, fashion and unconsciousness. The Last Judgement of History. Higher octave Aries, Taurus and Gemini. Disidentification is liberation.

> For the Holy One hath weighed the world and with measure hath he measured the times, and by numbers he hath numbered the seasons, neither will he rest nor stir until the number be fulfilled.[110]

The cycle of a World Age parallels an individual life. The consensus among anthropologists is that humans became conscious about 50,000 years ago at the time human pigmentation occurred.[111] Richard Leakey states that homo sapiens sapiens is 50,000 years old.[112] At that time the supremacy of the Neanderthalers came to an end as the more advanced Cro-magnons eradicated them over the next 15,000 years. The transition is interesting because there exist no earlier traces of the Cro-magnons, from whom all modern humanity developed. The "missing link" is still missing. The conquering Cro-magnons interbred with the beetle-browed, hairy, short, stocky and immensely powerful Neanderthalers, creating intermediate characteristics which still remain in the present homo sapiens sapiens stock. Their brain capacity was nearly the same, but the Neanderthalers were closer to proto-primates in habit, appearance and social structure, while the mysterious Cro-magnon was virtually identical to modern humans of the twentieth century. The situation is reminiscent of Creation as described in the apocryphal scriptures, where the sister and first wife of Adam, Lillith, created a race of half-humans by mating with degenerate angels.

The World Age of humanity began 50,000 years ago, but its duration must be determined. Projections relating to population explosion, the inability of humanity to distribute the food necessary to feed the world, the threat of destruction from nuclear energy and weapons, and ecological collapse all seem to focus around the year 2000. It is also a common target date for the "end of the world" as predicted by many prophets including Nostradamus and the raving Jehovah's Witnesses.

The Jewish Jubilee Cycle is 50,000 years and added importance was given to the year AD 1000 as the beginning of the last thousand-year Jubilee Year, which would make AD 2000 the changeover of world ages. These cycles are repetitive and the end of one age is the beginning of the next. Jose Arguelles chooses the end of this century as the "end of history" and the beginning of "post-history", which begins with a quantum leap into the next level of planetary consciousness.

The astronomical-astrological mechanism of the precession of equinoxes also corresponds to the duration of about 50,000 years as two equinoctial cycles – a night and day of creation similar to the night and day of Brahma.

If 50,000 years is the duration of the World Age from the origin of consciousness to the end of its cycle of manifestation, by applying base ten logarithms, the unit of measurement is determined to be one-thousandth of the duration, or fifty years. Fifty years in history is equivalent to a lunar month in individual life, just as 50,000 years is equivalent to 1000 lunar months (seventy-seven years). The feminine lunar unit in individual life is balanced by the masculine solar unit in collective life. The last fifty year period represents the death experience of humanity, the "last judgement", a compacted reliving of the entire life cycle and an ovum seed time of the next world age. The beginning of the last judgement is fifty years before AD 2000, or AD 1950, just after the explosion of the atomic bombs at Hiroshima and Nagasaki, the year of the first hydrogen bomb tests and the the proliferation and testing of such weapons in the atmosphere and underground. The coherent ecological system of planet received a shock which signals the "death" of the world age. As has been mentioned previously, it is estimated that population living between 1950 and 2000 is approximately the same as the number of people who have lived in the last 50,000 years.[113] Everyone alive during the whole world age is returning to experience the end and the beginning of a new age.

The limits of the world age of 48,000 BC and AD 1950 are graded by an astrological sequence from Aries to Pisces. The same log sequence divides history as individual life, but in the reverse direction in time.

1	10	100	1000
−50yrs	−500yrs	−5000yrs	−50,000yrs
AD 1950	AD 1500	3000 BC	48,000 BC

The intermediate dates occur at 5000 years and 500 years before AD 2000, which places them at 3000 BC and AD 1500, equivalent to the beginning of Leo and Sagittarius.

About 48,000 BC humanity became conscious and self-assertive, but was immersed in the unconscious. Beings wandered in an undifferentiated state inseparable from the natural world around them, and reality was collective and mythological. They worshipped the gods of heaven, earth, sky and sea.

Five thousand years ago, about 3000 BC, humanity became individual and self-conscious. Many early cultures dated the Great Flood at about 3000 BC, also the time of the "eras of creation". The Jews and Christians believed that the world was created in 3761 BC. The first legendary Pharaoh Menes was believed to have existed at about 3200 BC. The original Chinese Emperor Tai Hao existed about 2850 BC. The beginning of the Kali Yuga (Era of Darkness) was computed by the Indian Brahmins as 3102 BC. It also signalled the beginning of the Bronze Age and the first use of water power.[114] It was the time of formation of the great ancient civilizations of Babylonia, China, Egypt and Sumeria. About 3000 BC the first individuals were recognized and monotheism reigned. Between 3000 BC and AD 1500 the classical civilizations of Egypt, Greece, Rome and China, guided by powerful rulers, determined the development of humanity. By the middle ages the great civilizations had interbred, spread and disintegrated, which led to the dark ages of feudalism, monasticism, crusades, magic and the great plagues.

Five hundred years ago, around AD 1500, is the Renaissance and the realization of the self. The death, destruction and decay of classical reality gradually transformed into the Renaissance, the age of humanism. The Enlightenment coincided with the discovery and colonization of the New World, the circumnavigation of the globe, trade routes to India and China, the final fall of Constantinople, the beginning of the reformation of the Church, all abetted by Renaissance individuals transforming government, religion, art, architecture, drama, literature, science and statesmanship.

From the reawakening in AD 1500 until the destruction in AD 1950, humanity grew and matured. The renaissance provided intellectual and scientific tools for the incredible expansion of the Industrial Revolution and the twin bastions of modern society; capitalism and socialism, the dominant national and international control systems. From their idealistic foundation both systems steadily gained power until their clash in the wantonly destructive World Wars of the twentieth century. The promise of technology and sophisticated politics turned poisonous, contaminating psychology, science and the environment, bringing about with astonishing rapidity the End of a World Age.

The final "panoramic memory" of the last fifty years of the 20th century is a repetition of the three stages of the World Age, compacted so densely that it is hardly recognizable. Every person in the entire world age has a representative present in the year 2000. The concept seems outrageous, but it must be remembered that the whole world 10,000 years ago had only about five million people: the present population of London could have more than populated the world.[115]

According to the Pythagorean doctrines of "transmigration" and "metempsychosis", there are a quantum of souls which continually and in succession animate all living beings. Upon each conception the soul enters a body, and upon death leaves it – the soul is the vehicle upon which the impressions of many lifetimes are registered. The Pythagoreans believed that the animal characteristics of zodiac signs represent a sequence of identities through which the soul progresses towards becoming divine. The quality of a lifetime determines the next incarnation in either an ascension to higher life forms, or if the life is degenerate, a descending scale down through the lower life forms. The soul travels outside of time, reentering space-time upon reincarnation in either future or past, relative to the last incarnation.

Every individual living in the World Age is animated by a soul which approaches the last judgement. The type of reality manifested during all recurrences into the temporal continuum – barbarian and cultured, primitive and modern, male and female, spiritual and atheistic – is accumulated and repeated in the company of all other souls, which gives each soul the opportunity to be present at the final moment of death and rebirth of the world soul of which each individual soul is a manifestation. A vision in Revelations is descriptive of this state:

> And I saw the dead, small and great, stand before God, and the books were opened: and another book was opened, which is the book of life, and the dead were judged out of those things which were written in the books, according to their works. And the sea gave up the dead which were in it; and death and hell gave up the dead which were in them: and they were judged every one according to their works. And death and hell were cast into the lake of fire. This is the second death. And whosoever was not found written in the book of life was cast into the lake of fire.[116]

Christianity absorbed and integrated the ancient doctrines of reincarnation, manifesting in the Last Judgement.

Alternatively, the end of a World Age is an opportunity to raise spiritual consciousness to a higher level, to discover the planetary logos and to make an evolutionary quantum leap to a single social super-organism.[117]

The Symbolism of Fifty

> I am the master. The steep mountains of the earth are shaken violently from their peaks to their foundations.
> In my right hand I hold the disk of fire. In my left hand I hold the disk that slays.
> I hold the raised weapon of my divinity, the fifty-spoked solar wheel.[118]
>
> An ancient Chaldean magical invocation

The duration of a World Age of humanity of 50,000 years uses a base unit of fifty years, which can be supported in many ways.[119]

– 50,000 years ago humanity harnessed fire.
– 5000 years ago was the Bronze Age and the use of water power
– 50 years ago we entered the Atomic Age after Hiroshima

The symbolism of the number fifty and its factors of ten pervades nature and myth. Five was the magical number sacred to the Pythagoreans. The pentagram is the classical magical number of protection and invocation. Brahma is fifty cosmic years old in the present age. The innermost five electron rings contain a maximum of fifty electrons. There are 50,000,000,000 cells in the brain.

The number fifty appears in many measurements and proportions embodied in the Great Pyramid. The Pyramid Inch, upon which the entire system of Egyptian cosmic geometry is based, is 1/500,000,000th of the earth's diameter. The King's Chamber is set upon the 50th course of stones, and contains 100 facing stones. The Queen's Chamber is set on the 25th course (5x5). The two chambers refer to the two precessional cycles in a world age. (Fig. 31)

The Egyptians possessed sublime and accurate astronomical information and integrated it into their culture. The cosmic archaeologist Schwaller de Lubicz recognized that monuments of ancient Egypt, when interpreted in terms of number, cycles and hierarchy, provide insight into higher realms. "Egypt organised and administered her civilization upon this knowledge; it is this that accounts for the structure of her system of calendars, the changes in emphasis in her symbolism, the ascendance of one Neter (power) over another and the shifts of the theological hegemony of her various religious centres."[120] De Lubicz made observations which lead to an integration between the spatial proportion systems of the monuments of Egypt and the temporal mechanisms of the calendar, and which are central to The Divine Plot.

The great calendrical mystery is that the cycles of the sun and moon are incommensurable. The solar year of 365.24 days cannot be evenly divided by the length of the month, whether the lunar month (when the moon returns to the same zodiacal position each cycle) of 27.3 days, or the lunation cycle (the time from one new moon and the next) of 29.5307 days. Schwaller de Lubicz noted that the Egyptians based their lunar calendar on periods of twenty-five years, which correspond to 309 lunar months. A double cycle, which would express the Golden Section, comprises fifty years; 618 = (phi-1)x1000. It is interesting that this is the cycle given by the African Dogon as the orbit of the invisible companion star of Sirius, upon which the whole of Dogon astronomy is based.[121] It appears that the number five is the basis of Egyptian symbolism, architecture and religion, of their calendar and astronomy as well – the long searched after mathematical missing link between Pythagorean number symbolism and astronomy. The integration of the Golden Section phi, a cycle of fifty years, the lunar calendar and astrological-astronomical correlations is the essence of The Divine Plot.

The Egyptians worshipped the Dog star Sirius, which they believed to be a greater sun than the sun, as central to their religion of reincarnation. The heliacal (with the sun) rising of Sirius was celebrated with a fifty-day season at the beginning of their year, an evocation of Creation. Modern astronomy has revealed that Sirius is the greater sun around which the sun and solar system orbits. Sirius is a double star with one vast low-density star and one smaller, extremely dense star which orbits in a period of fifty years. Its structure looks similar to the nucleus of an atom with its positron and neutron. Rodney Collin proposed that Sirius filled in the gap in cosmoses between the Solar System and the Milky Way, as the distance of the Sun to Sirius is one million times the distance from the Earth to the Sun, falling naturally into the scale of cosmic relationships he proposed in the "Theory of Celestial Influence".

The religion of the African Dogon is based on the fifty-year cycle of Sirius B in its revolution around Sirius.[122] Many mythological parallels show that knowledge of Sirius was widespread in ancient times, beyond the Dogon and the Egyptians. Spiritual and oracular centres such as Thebes, Miletus, Dodona, Delos, Delphi, Mount Ararat and Metsamor were astronomically oriented and the basis of their mysteries was calendrical, mathematical, mythological and astrological. The myth of Jason and the fifty Argonauts, the landing of Noah's Ark on Ararat, and the entire geographical structure of religion in the ancient Mediterranean world is reflected in the stars and constellations.

The major star of the constellation Argo is Canopus, which means the pilot. The Sumerians identified the star with the amphibious descendant of the gods Oannes in the Sumerian flood legend – a proto-Noah who assisted humanity and was the Jehovah of the Hebrews. (Fig. 27) Canopus is correlated with Egyptian, Sumerian, Babylonian, Hebrew and Greek legends of the great flood, religious centres of these cultures and the very creation of humanity. Deucalion is the Greek Noah, associated with the central Delphic cults of Apollo, which controlled music, art, philosophy, astronomy, astrology, mathematics, medicine and science. A large boat was used in the Delphic mystery ceremonies, and at Delphi is an omphalos, a navel of the world. (See Fig. 7) Dionysiac cults were celebrated every five years. The near eastern religious belief that Noah landed on Ararat parallels the Greeks belief Deucalion landed

Fig. 27: Sumerian Fish God Oannes
The Sumerian forerunner of Noah is both a celestial god who brought life to earth, and a fish-tailed amphibious daemon from the unconscious.

at Delphi.[123] Temple's conclusion is that these myths refer to beings from Sirius who fertilized earth in prehistory, although they point numerically to the mathematics of The Divine Plot.

Legends associated by Temple with the mysteries of Greek and mid-eastern culture are crammed with the symbolic number fifty:

- the heroes of Anu were the fifty Anunnaki or assembly of gods, of which seven are underworld gods and as such determined destiny[124];
- there were fifty Danaids, Pallantids and Nereids, and fifty maidens of the Celtic Bran[125];
- the dog of the underworld Cerberus, associated with the Egyptian Anubis, the devourer of souls and god of time, and had fifty heads[126];
- the Sumerian god Marduk had fifty names[127];
- Actaeon and the fifty hounds of Hades, the underworld[128];
- Thespius had fifty daughters by a celestial union who were priestesses of the moon, and Hercules impregnated them all in one night or seven nights[129];
- Gilgamesh, the Babylonian solar god, had fifty companions[130].

The White Goddess' fifty moon goddesses are related to the fifty lunations between Olympiads, in turn reflecting ancient esoteric fifty-year, fifty-month and fifty-day sequences. The fifty-month sequence is also connected with the reign of a sacred king.

- the sacred king Lycaon caused the flood and had fifty sons[131]
- the myth of the fifty-month stag hunt[132];
- the fifty-oared ship of Orestes[133];
- the primeval earth goddess Gaia had fifty bones, referred by Graves to Stonehenge[134];
- the fifty stones of Deukalion (Noah);

The recently discovered asteroid Chiron, named after the Greek god of healing, has a fifty-year cycle. All these are astronomically based myths utilizing the numbers fifty and one hundred, which are the basis of the time scale.

Prototypes for the fifty-year cycle occur in Hebrew mysticism. "And ye shall hallow the fiftieth year."[135] The Hebrew year was originally divided into seven fifty-day periods, with seven plus seven plus one bringing them to 365 days. There were seven times seven years in the Jubilee Cycle, plus one year making a Jubilee year every fifty years, and seven seven-thousand year cycles culminating in the Jubilee period of one thousand years, making a 50,000 year cycle. The larger cycles were celebrated each year in the seven weeks of the Passover

Feast of Weeks (Shovus), when Moses received the Ten Commandments on Mt. Sinai, described in the first five holy books of the Bible, the Pentateuch. The Canaanite calendar was also based on seven cycles of fifty days. Obviously, the dating of Easter as fifty days after Pentacost, when the Holy Spirit descended as tongues of fire, reasserts the symbolism.

In traditional Indian teaching, the chakras are force centres in the human body represented by mandalas in the form of flowers, each petal showing a correspondent harmonic frequency and mystic sound. The Svadhisthana or sacral chakra has five petals and the Manipura or solar plexus chakra has ten petals. In the five lower chakras there are forty-eight petals; when these are added to the two-petalled lotus of the Ajna (brow) chakra, fifty arises as the number of the perfected personality. (Fig. 28) The Sahasrara or crown chakra is the throne of spiritual dominion which heralds the point in evolution when incarnation no longer exists, and has one thousand petals. In Buddhism it symbolizes the Bodhisattva who vows to reincarnate until all sentient beings have reached perfection.[136] The product of the two is 50,000.

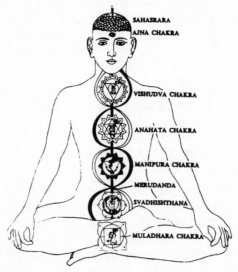

Fig. 28: Chakras
The chakras are energy centres in the form of flowers. In the five lower chakras there are forty-eight petals, which when added to the Ajna chakra of two petals make a total of 50 petals, symbolic of the perfected personality. The 1000-petalled Crown chakra heralds the ascendancy over personality in Buddhahood. The product of the two is 50,000.

There are fifty numbered sections of Plato's Timeus. There are fifty Knights of the Round Table who were members of the Brotherhood of the Knights of the Holy Grail.[137]

The references to the number fifty in the preceding myths and legends all concern aspects of The Divine Plot — the time and nature of Creation; the relation between the lunar unit of human life and the fifty-year unit of humanity; the relationship between humanity and the gods; the mythological origin of the universal cycle; the organization of cycles and cosmoses; and the origin of humanity.

The Astrological Structure of the World Age

Each successive octave of the Time Scale is one-tenth the duration of the preceding octave, yet carries ten times the density of people, information and energy.

Table 4   Logarithmic World Age

Zodiac Sign	Beginning Time	Function
0 Aries	48,000 BC (−50,000yrs) *Self-Assertion*	Fire — Consciousness
0 Leo	3000 BC (−5000yrs) *Self-Consciousness*	Water — Great Flood
0 Sagittarius	AD 1500 (−500yrs) *Self-Realization*	Pestilence — Black Death
0 Aries	AD 1950 (−50yrs)	Fire — Atomic Bomb

In each octave humanity expresses more sophisticated development, higher levels of consciousness and more individuation. The transition times between octaves are *"shock-points"* at which human development changes dramatically, often in concert with drastic changes in environment. The idea of gradual evolution with periodical cataclysms, "punctuated equilibrium," is the most likely explanation of the evolutionary process. The sequence of fire, water and pestilential shock-points evokes the plagues of Revelations, with the World Age beginning and ending with a trial by fire, initially the discovery of fire, and finally the atomic bomb. In each octave a new level of reality emerges.

The Time Scale of the historical World Age has an astrological structure subdivided into twelve developmental stages. The zodiacal signs are a progression of developmental phases with the advantage of allowing geometric relationships between signs. The rhythms are in two-, three-, four- and six-fold like the aspects in the horoscope in connecting events in life at various ages, the internal zodiacal geometry connects events at different times in history by parallels of meaning. The set of internal harmonies and rhythms provides the main integration mechanism in history, as it does in astrology. This approach to history reflects the emphasis of the new physics on the "web of relations" of history rather than particles embedded within, i.e. events, of history. The astrological parallel also brings the stages of history into relationship with the progression of seasons in the year through the solar cycle, with the natural unfolding of the growth cycle, and with the stages of development of consciousness in the individual.

A circular mechanism exists in the working of all natural systems. As Thomas Mann observed,

> For distance in a straight line has no mystery. The mystery is in the sphere. But the sphere consists in correspondence and reintegration; it is a doubled half that becomes one, that is made by joining an upper and a lower half, a heavenly and an earthly hemisphere, which complement each other in a whole, in such a manner that what is above is also below; and what happened in the earthly repeats itself in the heavenly sphere and contrariwise. This complementary interchange of two halves which together form a whole and a closed sphere is equivalent to actual change – that is, revolution. The sphere rolls – that lies in the nature of spheres. Bottom is soon top and top bottom, in so far as one can talk of top and bottom in such a connection. Not only do the heavenly and the earthly recognise themselves in each other, but, thanks to the revolution of the sphere, the heavenly can turn into the earthly, the earthly into the heavenly, from which it is clear that gods can become men and on the other hand men can become gods.[138]

The spring sign Aries symbolizes the birth moment and the initial assertion of personality at the dawn of consciousness from 48,000 BC to 26,000 BC. Table 5 shows the Time Scale divided into twelve parts related to the zodiac signs, the seasons and times in history. The logarithmic contraction from sign to sign makes each sign slightly more than half the preceding sign, a compaction offset by an increased density of population, evolutionary rate and events toward the present.

Astrological rhythms are keys to historical principles which correlate the events, movements, civilizations and individuals which combine to form the whole historical process.

The most basic rhythm is the binary alternation of masculine-patriarchal and feminine-matriarchal signs through the zodiac. Through the Time Scale there is a continual shift between the causal, masculine, left-brain view which is linear and mechanistic, and the acausal, feminine, right-brain view which is circular and synchronistic. In the historical process the fluctuations are indicated by patriarchal societies changing into matriarchal societies, open to closed value systems, and other bipolar social phenomena. Pairs of opposites keep short-term balance in the system. The ordered scheme of a powerful and cultured civilization is predicated upon the chaos out of which it emerged, and its fall is a precondition for its successors.

Oppositions act across the circle as polarities at opposite times, yet carry great attraction, like the attractive fusion and repellent fission forces in the atomic nucleus.

The four elements Fire, Earth, Air and Water occur three times in sequence in the zodiac, once within each octave of the Time Scale, creating a similarity in inner structure. For Plato the elements are a mathematical system of successively greater densities underlying Nature, and for Robert Fludd the elements are proportional to each other as they ascend from earth. The physicist Heisenberg stated: "in all elementary processes, from which all natural phenomena evolve, four different groups are to be distinguished."[139] The elements can be understood in a number of ways. In the classical meaning, fire is energy, earth is matter, air is mind and water is emotion. According to the psychology of Jung, fire is the intuitive function, earth the sensation function, air the thinking function and water the feeling function. In the context of physics, fire is the energy which motivates the universe, earth the particle nature of reality, water the wave nature of reality and air the complementarity between particle and wave. Similar ordering principles operate in the physical sciences as in historical processes.

The elements describe similarity of focus in each octave. The fire signs Aries, Leo and Sagittarius indicate initiative, creativity, pure energy, spiritual impulse and concentration upon Self. The earth signs Taurus, Virgo and Capricorn indicate the descent of spirit into matter (mother, matrix), physicality, tangibility and experience of sensation. The air signs Gemini, Libra and Aquarius combine and mediate between heaven and earth, between energy and matter, creating communication, balance and abstraction through ideas. The concluding water signs Cancer, Scorpio and Pisces end each octave as a dissolution of barriers, the accumulation and synthesis of previous developments and the emergence of feelings about the action of the cycle which ends and creates the possibility of the next, higher cycle.

The three historical times of each element show a three-phase development required to completely manifest the qualities indicated by the element within the World Age. Each element has a cardinal initiating phase, a fixed manifestation, and a mutable phase which synthesizes the elemental quality.

Astrology is quite complex to understand fully, as it deals with the complexity of human existence, but does provide a matrix, model and language of symbols which can assist the discovery of the whole within us all as represented by the historical process. The use of astrology also allows parallels to be drawn between an individual and the whole historical process of which everyone is a part and reflection.

The idea is similar to the workings of psychology, where the terminology identifying psychic processes is not intended to limit and define the individual, but rather to provide a set of terms which correlate individual behaviour with collective behaviour. Individuals create and define the process of history, while at another level they seem to be governed by history, mere cogs in a cosmic wheel, vehicles by which history enacts its unfolding, its becoming. History is often seen in symbolic form and the individuals within it as symbols. We seek our own personal and universal symbolism, the meaning of ourselves and our lives. The quest for meaning must proceed from the symbolic or ideal to the actual or real.

The Time Scale

The twelve signs in the Time Scale order the duration of the developmental stages, the compaction of events, understanding and population through history. Time periods in history contract in the same proportion as the house time periods expand in individual life. The resultant combination of the two temporal processes − the individual life experiencing longer and longer developmental stages, and the collective life compacting − are what make the flow of time seem to be constant. The sense of expansion in the inner world is balanced by the compaction of the outer world. We are affected to the extent that we identify with the outer world and its time or our inner world and its time. Time affects us profoundly, but its effects are altered by meditation, psychological states, drugs and many other ways. Consciousness exists in a balanced state (the Tao) where the two systems equilibrate, which is designated the "present". When the Time Scale is extended into the past to cycles longer than a World Age, time sense is expanded, while in the future cycles are shorter, and time is compacted more and more until the speed of light is approached. The movement of time into the future always balances a counter movement into the past. The present moment is powerful because it lies at the junction of past and future.

Table 5   The World Age

The time scale of the World Age of humanity describes the last fifty thousand years, from self-consciousness to the atom bomb. The table is shown schematically because of the intense compaction of information. The horizontal lines are shown in two places in the book. The left-hand column of Astrological Stages, Historical Events, Religions & Mysticism, and Works of Humanity are shown in detail in Chapter Five – The World Age. Aries to Cancer are on pages 132-3, Leo to Scorpio on pages 144-5 and Sagittarius to Pisces on pages 158-9. The central section shows the Stream of Civilizations, where the earliest civilizations coalesced from neolithic communities, advanced through their cycles, conquered rivals, joined and co-mingled to lead to the modern nations known today. Snake-like movements indicate conquests of other streams, and arrows indicate significant shock-points of change of status or direction. The right-hand section shows each of the seven planets as significators for each age. These are shown in detail in Chapter Seven – Reincarnation on pages 220-5. In the first four signs Aries-Cancer, pages 220-1, the planetary prototypes are gods and goddesses shown in four phases of development. The deities of many cultures are shown, while often they were known to many cultures simultaneously under a variety of names. From Leo to the end of Pisces, pages 222-5, the historical individuals emerge from legendary heroes, until the present, when heroes are manufactured instantly. Note that the lifetime of an individual is about one degree in Leo while it is more than the entire sign in Pisces. The later in history an individual exists, the more likely he or she are to influence more than one sign developmental stage. The Astrological Reincarnation Time Scale (Table 10 on pages 226-7) is a list of dates related to exact zodiac signs and degrees from which you can translate your horoscope into an exact age in history.

Table 5   The World Age

Signs		Historical Events Religion & Mysticism Works of Humanity
AD 1950		
Pisces	Institutionalism World Wars;chaos and collapse;isolationism	
AD 1910		
Aquarius	Scientific;Nationalism Socialism;idealism;science;evolution	*See* *p. 159*
AD 1840		
Capricorn	Industrial & national revolutions;capitalism Reformation	
AD 1720		
Sagittarius	Renaissance humanism Colonization;enlightenment;philosophy	
AD 1500		
Scorpio	Feudal;crusades;medieval;inquisition;magic Monasticism and Cathedrals	
AD 1100		
Libra	Dark Ages;Roman law;barbarians East-West synthetic religions & Islam	*See* *p. 145*
AD 400		
Virgo	Classicism;Greece & Rome Classical pantheons & Christianity	
800 BC		
Leo	Archaic hero-king religion & Hinduism Civilization;individuality;Egypt	
3000 BC		
Cancer	Neolithic grain goddess cults Religion;cities;nuclearfamily;Nippur	
7000 BC		
Gemini	Mesolithic tribal cults Language;villages;tanist	*See* *p. 133*
14,000 BC		
Taurus	Upper Paleolithic earth mother cults Earth Mother cults;fertility	
26,000 BC		
Aries	Paleolithic celestial cults Celestial cults;nomadic;consciousness	
48,000 BC		

Stream of History											Planetary Gods and Individuals						
South America	North America	Rome	Greece	Egypt	Russia	Persia	India	China and Japan			*Sun*	*Moon*	*Mercury*	*Venus*	*Mars*	*Jupiter*	*Saturn*

THE ATOMIC BOMB

Modern — United States — Colonization — Italian City States — Ottomans — Occupation — Chinese Revolution — Moghul Emperors

See p. 224   See p. 225

THE BLACK DEATH

Aztec — Norse — Mayan — Nazca — Olmec — Rome — Crete — Alexandrian — Old — New — Late — Babylonia — Ayyubids — Ming — Sung — Three Kingdoms

See p. 222   See p. 223

THE GREAT FLOOD

Nippur

Gravetian
Magdalenia
Salutrean
Upper Perigordian
Aurignacian — Ice Age / Ice Age / Ice Age
Perigordian
Mousterian

Plains Hunters — Neolithic — Mesolithic — Upper Paleolithic

Paleolithic
Old Stone Age

CONSCIOUSNESS

See p. 220   See p. 221

Each octave describes a developmental phase of history:

– First octave of self-assertion is mythological and instinctive, as the domain of the child.
– Second octave of self-consciousness is individualistic and civilized, as the domain of the adult.
– Third octave of self-realization is collective and conscious, as the domain of the parent.

The duration of every fourth sign decreases to one-tenth. Thus, of the fire signs, the cardinal Aries lasts 22,000 years, the fixed Leo 2200 years and the mutable Sagittarius lasts 220 years, yet the same number of people live during each sign. Developments happen at an accelerating pace.

The length of a human lifetime during the time scale occupies a full stop in the first octave, a tenth of a sign or so in the second octave and entire signs in the third octave, reflecting the increasing mathematical power of human perspective in nature. In the course of the Time Scale humanity goes from being totally dominated by natural rhythms and life, to having apparent control over the natural world.

Each sign is described with the following information:

– The *Historical Development* related to the time period, the advances of civilizations, the movements of people, the formation and dissolution of cultures and nations, and the important individuals who affect or are affected by the period. The description focuses on the evolution of consciousness within the historical process, both internal to individuals and external to populations.
– The *Great Works* of culture including literature, architecture, art, earth works, utilitarian or religious objects, inventions and discoveries, particularly those which are symbolic of the civilization of the time.
– The *Mythological and Religious perspective* from the first humans who worshipped gods of the sky, natural forces or the earth, through the descent of the gods. As humanity progresses the gods become intermediaries, the many gods united in monotheism, then godlike men and women, then a son of god is born on earth, then humans begin to believe that they themselves are gods on earth, until the end of the world age sees a lack of belief in god where material wealth, science, popular music, cinema and the artifacts of society become primary objects of worship and devotion.
– *Evolution of Consciousness* stage as described in "The Atman Project" by Ken Wilber.
– The equivalent *Astrological Sign* and its time period in Life ★ Time Astrology shows the parallel developmental stage in individual life, the mechanisms which function and the way in which life energy is transformed from stage to stage.

The intention is the creation of a higher understanding of the history of humanity and spiritual consciousness as a whole, unified and formally coherent. Throughout history individuals who have transcended time and history, influences which are particularly supportive of a spiritual overview of history are noted. In the following description of the World Age the focus is upon the astrological principles behind history, the mechanism rather than the fact.

The Octave of Mythology
(Aries-50,000 BC to Cancer-3000 BC)

The first octave of the World Age is the development of humanity in the mythological stage of evolution from the origin of consciousness in Aries at 48,000 BC until the recognition of individuality and the first historical individuals in 3000 BC at the end of Cancer.

Mythology is very difficult to order, being dreamlike and random in many respects. Its function is to transmit information carried down from archaic ages, before chronology existed, as oral traditions which were continually varied and distorted through constant retelling. Myths are passed through many generations and shifts of locale, and they absorb and transmit cultural and ahistorical models accepted by a society.

The original creation myths were attempts to understand roots combined with vague tribal histories – invasions, altered godheads, changed locations, the deeds of heroes and the respect of ancestors. One of the primary ways of subjugating conquered tribes was to dominate their mythology and alter the oral traditions through new names and hierarchies. The conquering gods became the fathers and mothers of the gods of the conquered people. For this reason Zeus had hundreds of progeny and was involved in virtually all the myths in the Greek domain during their dominant military power over many centuries. Myths contain a multitude of attributions and complex genealogies, all qualified by the timelessness of the mythological medium. Retrospective mythmaking produces situations where the more powerful and wide the realm of a god, the further back its legends go, until it approaches the Creator gods in power. The mythological substratum also carries the history of our instincts.

48000 BC

Aries to Cancer

7000 BC
Cancer
the Crab

City Religion
Feeling and Emotional
Matriarchal
Tigress-Euphrates
Nuclear Family Homes
Integration
Neolthic Societies
Cities and Nations
Mythological Religions

14000 BC
Gemini
the Twins

Tribal Language
Verbal
Patriarchal
Mediterranean
Instinctive Movement
Communication
Diversification
Music and Dance
Multi-god Cults

26000 BC
Taurus
the Bull

Earth Mother Fertility Cults
Physicality
Matriarchal
European
Fertility
Domestication of Animals
Possessions
Bull and Skull Cults
Tools

48000 BC
Aries
the Ram

Celestial Nomads
Self Consciousness
Patriarchal
African
Primitive
Self-Assertion
Hunting Bands
Celestial Cults
Weapons

3000 BC

Historical Events	The Gods	Works of Humanity

Historical Events		The Gods	Works of Humanity	
3000	3000 **The Great Flood**	Olympians	3000	Newgrange Ireland
	3000 Minoan civilization	Dionysians	3100	Cunieform
3500	3102 Death Krishan (Kali Yuga)	Home Gods	3500	Sumerian wheels
	3500 Founding of Ur	Grain Goddesses	3500	European megalithic graves
4060	3600 Taxes		3500	Mesopotamian writing
	3761 Hebrew Era of Creation		4000	Cretan pottery
4670	4000 Neolithic Greek city states			
	4004 Bishop Ussher's Creation			
5340	4500 Chinese civilization			
	5000 Nile valley farming			
6080	5800 Tigres-Euphrates settled			
	6000 Gold, Copper and Bronze worked		5900	Turkish Bull God temple
7000	6750 Catal Huyyuk		6000	Gold jewelry

Historical Events		The Gods
7000	7000 Jericho (1st City)	Titans
	8000 Copper Age	Kabiri
7800	Lake Dwellings	Hermaphrodites
	Domesticated animals	Twin Gods
8800	9000 Denmark hunters	Dioscuri
	Mesopotamia cultivated	
9900	Stone Age ends/Icecaps melt	
	10000 Neolithic humanity in Europe/Round stone huts	
11100	North American plains hunters	
	Introduction of pottery	
12400	Fishing cultures	
	Neolithic rock paintings	
14000	14000 Racial differences emerge	

Historical Events		The Gods
14000	15000 Microlithic tools	Earth Mothers
	Willendorf Venus figurine	Cyclopes
15400	18000 End of the Fifth Ice Age	Giants
	Grain planting in Africa	Grain Goddesses
17200	Herding animals	
	20000 America settled	
19100	Upper Paleolithic skull cults	
	Bow and Arrow huntings	
21200	22000 Landes Venus head	
	24000 Beginning Fifth Ice Age	
23500	Moravian Venus figurine	
	25000 Lascaux cave paintings	
26000	Clothing woven	

Historical Events		The Gods
26000	27000 Interglacial warmth	Creators
	N American migrations	Celestials
29000	30000 Ceramics	Primordials
	Trading routes established	Elementals
32000	34000 Last Neanderthalers	Asuras
	35000 Lunar calendar	
35500	Advanced hunters in Europe	
	End of Fourth Ice Age	
39300	4000 Blade tools	
	Seafaring cultures	
43000	End of the Old Stone Age	
	47000 Cave Bear cults	
48000	48000 Herbal medicines	

Aries   *(48,000 BC until 26,000 BC)*

Aries represents the birth of consciousness into the world age and self assertion, analogous to the earliest experiences after birth. The rise of consciousness creates the possibility of assertion in the instinctual world. The first true humans survived with and through consciousness, which differentiated them from the animals. As they were physically inferior to the carnivorous cave bears and lions, they relied on superior awareness for survival, banding together in small groups to improve their chances.

From about 48,000 to 35,000 BC, the primitive Neanderthalers, who had been dominant for the previous 120,000 years, were eradicated by the Cro- magnons. The Neanderthalers were short, stocky and beetle-browed, although with a brain size slightly larger than modern man. They survived during the previous Ice Ages by hunting and foraging, moving with climatic changes and creating a workable culture, evidence of which remains in the ochre-pigmentation used in burials, stone implements and cults of the cave bear. Cro-magnons were virtually identical to modern homo sapiens sapiens, yet anthropologists do not know from whence they came. They were supermen who eradicated the Neanderthalers so completely that there are only genetic traces left today. The new humans were highly adaptable, even changing physical appearance to cope with their environment.

The first calendars were developed by recording traces of the lunar cycles on bones as early as 35,000 years ago. The moon was magical and its disappearance for three days each cycle was a sacred time, when hunters did not go out and the danger from predators was greatest.

Food was gathered from near the habitation and eaten raw, and early humans preyed on and ate small animals, crustaceans and fish, as well as the meat from their hunts for game and woolly mammoths. They were omnivorous by necessity and sheltered in caves when they could oust the dangerous creatures which inhabited them naturally. Flint weapons improved until around 40,000 BC blades were made. Because of Ice Ages lasting until about 18,000 BC, yearly migration to find suitable weather and food sources was necessary. The most dreaded enemy was other humans and cannibalism was a usual practice because every available source of food and energy was greedily partaken. Survival was the total pursuit.

Aries was the primal time following a cataclysm when the

primary function was instinctive bonding with the world after the shock and loss of memory attending the end of the previous world age. Humans wandered aimlessly over the habitable areas of earth vaguely remembering a former utopia and its terrifying end, the dissociation of collapse, the darkening of the sun and the irrationality of natural forces caused by environmental breakdown. Many living things were annihilated and a feeling of desolation prevailed. The primary factors were the climate and the vagaries of nature which determined survival.

The mythology of these times concerned celestial dieties, Creator and Creatrix gods. The worship of the elements reflected a onesided reliance on divine beings – humans crouched in fear before Chaos, Wind, Air, Okeanos, and Chronos in his aspect as Time. Celestial sun and moon cults were primary – the sun was born every sunrise and died every sunset, and the uncertainty that he would return each day caused great fear and respect. Eventually sun worship was transferred to fire, its earthly surrogate. The deities Day, Night, Sky, Earth, Fire, Nature were absolute as they were beyond human control, even the fire in their caves. The feeding of the fire was a central ritual and its continuing light and heat the mainstay and protection against the elements and the predators. Celestial cults were complemented by those attached to the animals hunted or revered, such as cave bears or lions and the lesser animals. There were cult identifications of entire groups and for individuals.[140]

The earliest religion, Shamanism, enacted with the end of the last world age as an ecstatic process of returning symbolically to the death moment, and the shamans were individuals within whom the true beginning was perpetually re-enacted, intermediaries between the world of spirits and the tribe. The ritual production of fire in shamanic ceremonies represented the fire both at the end of the world and at the same time the birth of the world. The Vedas describe such a ceremony when all fires were extinguished and then rekindled on New Year's Day as a reenactment of the Cosmic night, corresponding to the fact that the New Year began on the first day of Aries on the spring equinox.[141]

Ken Wilber calls this stage *The Pleromatic Self* [142] where self and material cosmos are undifferentiated and there is a symbiotic relationship to the world. Feelings are oceanic and unconditioned in a paradise of innocence and ignorance. There is no conception of space, time or objects. Humans are at one with the world.

Aries time is analogous to the time from birth to seven months old, when the infant bonds to mother, learns to receive and focus light, differentiates nothing other than survival.

Taurus   (26,000 BC until 14,000 BC)

Taurus represents the creation, preservation and consolidation of form. The initial undifferentiated state of Aries led to worship of the Earth Mother and fertility goddesses, together with their related skull cults (connected with the opposing sign Scorpio). The coldest phase of the Ice Age began about 28,000 BC and the movement of mammoths south changed cultural patterns in many ways. Tusks and bones provided a new vocabulary of weapons and material for carving Venus figurines (c. 24,000 BC), and models for cave paintings at Lascaux (c. 26,000 BC) and other southern European sites.

Settlements were limited by the ice caps and traces have been found in Pennsylvania in North America (c. 19,000 BC), central and southern Africa, the southern parts of Europe, the middle east and Eastern Siberia, as well as in Southeast Asia, towards Australia. Groups of humans were small and widely spaced over the temperate zones of earth.

The stabilization of the weather at the end of the Ice Ages at about 18,000 BC allowed humanity to settle, which shifted the focus to the cave and engendered many changes in activities. Labour was divided into men hunting and protecting the tribe, while women tended the fire, cared for children and gathered foodstuffs. Women discovered that plants growing naturally around the home cave could be transplanted to a central location, easing the task of continually gathering foods further and further afield. The tiny nomadic units gradually enlarged, and as they settled down, animals which surrounded the settlement to graze were caught and penned. The herding and domestication of animals was a revolutionary change at about 18,000 BC. Cattle were used for their milk, offspring, meat and skins for clothing and tents, and eventually horses provided beasts of burden. Domestic animals made food available through the winter, which further deemphasized the hunting function.

Property could not be carried in the former nomadic stage, but here the concept of ownership or stewardship began. The shift in focus to the feminine domain of domestication, cooking, fertility and the increasing reliance upon the earth itself was reflected in the variety of artifacts found in the Aurignacian and Upper Perigordian eras.

The genesis from hunters to hunter-gatherers paralleled a shift in emphasis from celestial gods to earth goddesses and the resultant society was matriarchal. The earth was the womb and nourisher of plants and the final resting place of the dead, and woman was recognised as the creator and destroyer of life. Whereas in Aries reproduction was considered a magical act of the gods, now woman was impregnated by Wind and nourished by Rain, just as were the crops – woman was symbolic of fertility. The primary rituals were the plowing, planting or sowing of fields and the harvest and storage of the fruits of the fields. The old custom of the "bridal bed" in the field to encourage fruitfulness expresses the analogy in a clear form: to make the woman fruitful was to make the field fruitful. Sexual energy was transmuted to the service of cultivating and fructifying the earth.[143]

Mythologically the Bull, Great Mother and Earth Mother cults merged and diversified until the entire pantheon was feminine, i.e. Isis, Gaia, Mother Earth, Venus, Nature, the Fates, Neith, Astarte and many others. The great mother was a pregnant goddess without a face, or a bull with a lunar orb between its horns, or the anthropomorphic deities of these characteristics combined ad infinitum. (Fig. 29) The godhead was translated from heaven to the natural realm of earth. Cults venerating the body, skull cults, earth or mound burials were metaphors of the sowing the seed in planting, and moon phases were seen to coincide with menstrual cycles.

Fig. 29: Isis with Lunar Orb
The Egyptian goddess Isis shown with her cultic associations of fishtail, lunar orb headdress and ankh.

Wilber calls this the *Alimentary Uroboros*[144], when the primary structuring of the subjective self-sense is formed, albeit collective and archaic. People are dominated by visceral instincts and rudimentary emotional discharges, yet carried in the arms of the Great Mother. Reality is primary oral, and myths of being swallowed by whales and such originated at this stage.

Taurus is the time from seven months old to one year eight months, when the infant begins to discover physical sensation, tastes and begins to differentiate the body as a separate object within other objects.

Gemini   *(14,000 BC until 7000 BC)*

During Gemini time language was developed. Writing and numerals on cylindrical, spherical or conical clay shards in Iran indicated the first attempts to account for numbers of animals, loaves, etc. The singular functions of hunting, gathering and raising children diversified and became more complex as the declining emphasis on hunting brought men closer into the tribal fold and encouraged a wider development of skills which increased the quality of life and assured survival. About 12,000 BC the retreating glaciers caused a rise in sea level, flooded coastal areas and forced many tribes to develop seagoing crafts for fishing in addition to their natural food sources. Harpoons and fishhooks were found in Europe and Southern Africa as early as 9000 BC. An increase in the artistic merit of clay and ceramic pots, the diversity of cultivated grains and grasses, the variety of animals domesticated, all these meant a wider range of things to do and ways to express the self. In the western hemisphere hunters ranged over North America into South America, eliminating two thirds of all mammal species, stripping the continents of all but bison and llamas among large animals, and condemning the inhabitants to solely agrarian life until the present.

Words and sounds specific to the new activities arose, creating a multitude of variant languages. Communication was broadened by trade at market places, the herding of cattle, sea voyages and the multiple functions within each tribe. Instead of each individual duplicating the tasks and skills of all others, the various skills were spread throughout a tribe or an area, such that specialization became a positive survival characteristic. In addition to basic survival tasks certain families also functioned as priests, scribes, farmers, shepherds, weavers, hunters, toolmakers or builders.

The long-dominant matriarchal cults of the Taurean age were gradually replaced through the principle of the tanist.[145] Initially the power of the earth mother did not decline, but the role of her consorts, the male companions of the priestesses, changed. Originally he was chosen from the strongest, most intelligent and best bred to be king for a year, to mate with the priestesses, and then to be ritually sacrificed at year's end, only to be replaced by another consort. Gradually the term of the surrogate king was extended to two years or seven years, then two consorts alternated in the role, until finally the king was able to maintain parity with the Goddess, escaping the sacrifice altogether.

The mythologies of Gemini are epitomised by the family of Titans spawned by Uranus (sky) and Gaia (earth), and the many twin gods and goddesses who were companions of the earth mother – the dioscuri, the kabiri and the dactyloi – all of whom were intermediaries between the heavenly pantheon and mortals. Hermes predominated as the god of language, communication and the cult of the hermaphroditic gods. The godhead was gradually approaching humanity.

To Wilber this is the *Typhonic Self* [146], where the physical body is felt as separate from the physical world, leading to recognition, naming and communicating about the world. The world is ambivalent, potentially dangerous, and differentiating rapidly.

Gemini traditionally means instinctive mind, communication, movement, adaptability, brothers and sisters, short journeys, mimicry, multiplication and diversity. Gemini is the time from one year eight months old until three years six months old when a child learns to walk, speak and co-ordinate movements to objects. Speaking is an act of imitation which originates with naming and describing objects and actions. Words represent objects with a mental equivalent, a time Piaget calls the Pre-conceptual stage of concrete actions.[147] It is well known in psychology that when children at this stage cannot assimilate an object or action name, it is accommodated into fantasy and given a symbolic meaning. Reasoning proceeds slowly, with no comprehension of the whole, and each step is dualistic between assimilation and accommodation – fantasy is just as real as reality. The similarity between these developments and the myths of the Titans is striking.

Cancer   *(7000 BC until 3000 BC)*

Cancer begins with the creation of the first city Jericho about 7000 BC. The creation of market towns came about due to the revolution in agriculture, which freed the population from the bondage of food-producing occupations for the first time. In the fertile river valleys of the Tigress-Euphrates in Mesopotamia (c.6000 BC), the Nile in Egypt (c.5000 BC) and rice-growing valleys in China, societies emerged which differed dramatically from their predecessors because of the class system. With the decline of nomadic life the city provided a context for stabilization through record-keeping and the hereditary passing down of property and wealth. The institution of the nuclear family and intermarriage led rapidly to a hierarchy of families, the creation of a class system and specialization in society. The city structured itself around the occupations of administration, education and trades while the division of labour produced sophisticated alphabets, mathematics and calendars. The geographical segregation of city from countryside generated a congenital problem in future civilizations. The priests became separate and powerful in determining codes of conduct by equating agricultural functions with sacrifices and rituals through their control over the calendrical timing of festivals.[148] Although apparently modern, humanity was still in the grasp of the gods and goddesses. The gods controlled cities and protected them if given their sacrificial due. The agricultural influence swept into Europe at about the middle of the seventh millennium BC.

The technological advances which most enabled change were the invention of irrigation in the sixth millennium BC, of cloth in about 6500 BC, and the very important development of foundries in the fifth millennium BC, when copper and then bronze were made into plows and all other implements, particularly weapons. The earliest known foundries were in what is now Rumania, Bulgaria and Yugoslavia, but they spread very quickly. By now both men and women did agriculturally related work, with the men plowing and herding and the women spinning and weaving. The domestication of camels and donkeys as beasts of burden, and oxen as pullers of the plow were great leaps into the future, especially when around 3500 BC the wheel was invented in Sumeria. Dairy cattle were kept and the use of milk products was widespread. The surplus generated by these advances striated the community and created a greater emphasis upon warfare because those previously required to providing food were freed from those functions.

By 4500 the megalithic builders proliferated all over Europe, stone buildings were constructed for permanence, and by 4000 BC there were highly developed city-states and urban cultures.

Religion again became matriarchal and the Triple Goddess reigned over planting, the hearth and burial of the dead, all connected with the quality of home life and living conditions. As humanity became civilized, Dionysian orgies and ecstacies gave expression to the instinctive functions which were rapidly being suppressed, and the pantheon of Olympian gods ruled over the proliferating breadth of culture. The classic gods of all religions were father and mother to the myriad of creators, creatrix and nature spirits that preceded them. Temples began to appear housing the godhead for the exclusive use of the city and its inhabitants. The gods were subtly changing from nature deities to symbols of humanity's own collective power, as men began to believe that they were in the ascendancy over Nature. People worshipped hundreds of deities which symbolized the multiplying facets of their existence, and the resultant confusion gave rise to myths such as the Tower of Babel. Belief systems and languages were collected by the cities. The end of the Cancer time was signalled by the Great Flood of about 3000 BC.

To Wilber the *Membership Self* [149] evolved when, after the acquisition of language, a vastly extended emotional life emerged which was enabled by concepts of extended time and a sense of belonging to a tradition embodied by the parents. The emotional set is determined, choices must be made, and rules followed for the first time as a primary function is to reconstruct reality as it is perceived.

Cancer the Crab is traditionally attributed to home and family, the parents, particularly mother, fertilization and fecundation, heredity, conditions in old age, intuition and the psychic world. The Cancer time is from three years six months until seven years old when a child begins to realize the effect of its ability or inability to communicate and begins to look beyond imitation to create effects in others. Being a water sign, Cancer dissolves and assimilates the previous stages and channels them into a feeling tone or value, eventually seeing that the family is a structural system within which certain values and feelings are permitted and acceptable. Piaget calls this the Intuitive Stage, when thinking becomes dominated by immediate perceptions of the environment and children attempt to seek the reasons behind the beliefs and actions of family and self. The family system has a devastatingly dominant effect upon these patterns, just as society in those times was largely determined by the structure of the city. Although primarily feminine-dominant due to the powerful bonding influence with the mother in early childhood, at this time the question of male-female is asserted by the variable identification with either parent and their roles. The domestic situation of home and city, inside and outside, provides models for interpersonal relationships and hierarchical values for life.

The Octave of Civilization
(Leo-3000 BC to Scorpio-AD 1500)

3000 BC saw an important conjunction of influences: the approximate date of the Great Flood described in the mythologies of almost all early cultures and the emergence of the first individuals in history.

The Great Flood is both a real event which affected the world's populations and a metaphorical flood of diverse belief patterns, primitive languages, deities and animalistic tendencies which required a filtering process. There were widespread floods from 3300 BC until 2300 BC all over the world and a major flood occurred due to atmospheric warming in 2900 BC.[150] The flood is also symbolic of the necessity for unconscious, natural, animistic components of the psyche to be introduced into civilization. Certainly the rise of the individual in the second octave is the race of Noah and its offspring.

Before Leo polytheism of the gods dominated, as though humanity was immersed in the unconsciousness of childhood until this critical trial by water. The intuition that individuals are the representatives of the godhead on earth occurred at about 3000 BC,[151] which is also the time of the first great monotheistic religions. Each of these religions was founded by an individual who had direct experience of god. These great souls (mahatmas) carried the luminous thread of immortality into the Zistorical era. Tammuz, Osiris, Mithra, Bacchus, Apollo, Adonis, Balder, Orpheus, Krishna, Buddha, Jesus Christ, Quetzalcoatl, Viracocha and Hiawatha carry parallel strands of the soul into the second octave of the Time Scale.

The most critical development was the discovery of Time. Before Egypt humanity was ahistorical, like the lunar calendar a yearly repetition of seasons following each other eternally. The early cultures lived in an eternal present. The Greek Thucydides announced that no events of importance had occurred in the world before his time (400 BC). The Egyptians were a notable exception, believing the present to be a bridge between the whole worlds of past and future. The Egyptian religious practices of mummification and representing the soul as the "ka" figure were transcendental and showed a will to endure, to pass beyond time into eternity.

The primitives needed a perfecting touch, a second creation, to enable them to live as humans. The double task of separating humanity from the immortals and giving completion to mortals fell to Prometheus, the god who brought fire to mortals.

3000 BC	Leo to Scorpio

1100 AD **Scorpio** **the Scorpion**	The Dark Ages East-West Balance Patriarchal China and Islam Sublimation Law and Justice State-Religion Schism Zen Troubadours
400 AD **Libra** **the Scales**	The Middle Ages The Black Death Plagues Medieval Societies Matriarchal Medieval Europe Inquisition and Crusades Separation Feudal and Monastic Societies The Cathedrals
800 BC **Virgo** **the Virgin**	Classical Civilizations Discrimination and Rationalism Matriarchal Greek and Roman Distillation Classical Learning Culture Christianity and Buddhism Classical Architecture
3000 BC **Leo** **the Lion**	First Great Civilizations Self-Consciousness Patriarchal Babylonian and Egyptian Individuality Organizations Civilizations Monotheism and Divine Kings Temple Monuments

1500 AD

Historical Events	Religion & Mysticism	Works of Humanity

Block 1

	Historical Events	Religion & Mysticism	Works of Humanity
1500	1498 Da Gama to India	1490 Harmonia Mundi	1470 Mallory Morte d'Arthur
	1492 **Columbus discovers America**	1489 Malleus Malifocorum	1454 Gutenberg The Bible
1450	1453 Constantinople falls		1370 Chaucer Canterbury Tales
	1415 Battle of Agincourt	1370 Brethren of Common Life	1310 Dante Divine Comedy
1395	1348 **The Black Death** plague	1274 Mehlevi dervishes	1245 Westminster Abbey
	1307 Knights Templars massacred	1270 de Leon Zohar	1220 Toledo & Salisbury
1335	1280 Kubla Khan rules	1260 Siena	1200 Chinese paper money
	1255 Polos in China	1244 Cathars burned at Monsequr	1200 Tower clocks
1270	1215 **Magna Carta**	1226 Fransiscan Order	1163 Notre Dame Paris
	1214 Genghiz Khan in Peking	1215 Dominican Order	1150 Cambridge University
1190	1198 Innocent III Inquisition	1125 Cathars founded	1145 Chartres & Angkor Wat
	1147 2nd Crusade	1100 Buddhism revived in Tibet	1140 St Denis Paris
1100	1100 Jerusalem captured	1100 Knights Templars founded	1100 Chanson de Roland

---

Block 2

	Historical Events	Religion & Mysticism	Works of Humanity
1100	1096 European pestilence	1098 Chartres School	1090 St Marks Clock
	1096 Peoples Crusade	1090 Cistercian Order	
1020	1077 Henry IV Canossa Penance	1070 Kabbalistic mss.	1000 Chiming wheel clock
	1066 **Norman Invasion of England**	1057 College of Cardinals	963 al-Sufi, Fixed Stars
925	986 Eriksson in Nova Scotia	927 Bogomilism	813 Cluny Monastery
	982 Mayan Empire	750 Religion of Golden Elixir	790 Chitchen Itza
815	732 Battles of Poiters & Tours	700 Lindsfarne Gospel	760 Ellora Caves
	711 Moslems invade Spain	632 Koran	745 Han-Lin Academy
695	640 Surrender of Jerusalem	622 Mohammed's hegira	715 Medina Great Mosque
	592 Roman Plague	604 Gregorian Chant	547 St Vitale Ravenna
565	480 Huns invade India	529 Athenian Schools closed	532 St Sophia Turkey
	429 Vandals conquer N Africa	400 Augustine City of God	529 Code of Justinian
400	410 **Alaric sacks Rome**	400 Monasticism begins	

Block 3

	Historical Events	Religion & Mysticism	Works of Humanity
400	361 Julian Mithraism	350 Athanasian Creed	
	325 **Council of Nicea**	277 Mani crucified	244 Hermetic writings
260	164 Great Roman Plague	200 Christians persecuted	
	117 Greatest extent of Rome	150 Sepher Yetzira/Zohar	127 Almagest/Tetrabiblos
85	65 Britian invaded/Rome burns	100 Apocalypse of John	
0	0 **Birth of Jesus Christ**	60 Acts of the Apostles	10 Ovid Metamorphoses
110	51 Alexandrian library burned	33 The Crucifixion	
	264 Punic Wars	250 Code of Mani	228 Great Wall of China
320	325 Alexander in India	495 Temple of Jerusalem	432 Parthenon
	492 Battle of Marathon	500 Jainism	492 Kama Sutra
555	597 Babylonian captivity	563 Birth of Buddha	742 Sargon's Gate
	605' Chaldeans conquer Egypt		776 1st Olympic Games
800	749 **Rome founded**		8th Homer Illiad & Odyssey

Block 4

	Historical Events	Religion & Mysticism	Works of Humanity
800	820 Carthage built	810 I Ching	
	933 Kingdom of Israel	1000 Egyptian Bood of the Dead	
1095	1194 **Fall of Troy**	1000 Zoroastrianism	
	1362 Reign of Ikhnaton	1200 The Vedas	1250 The Lion Gate, Mycenae
1405	1500 Aryans descend into India	1300 Ten Commandments	1500 Karnac
	1600 Thera volcano	1362 Egyptian monotheism	2000 Avebury & Silbury Hill
1750	1650 Jewish Bondage in Egypt	1490 Genesis in the Torah	2100 Great Pyramid Giza
	1600 Babylon collapses		2170 Great Pyramid Giza
2130	1800 Bronze Age China		2250 Chinese almanac
	2200 Babylonia peaks		2500 Ur Laws
2545	2400 Golden Age of Ur		2600 Sumerian goat figure
	2875 Sargonunites Sumeria	2900 Rig Veda	2850 Stonehenge
3000	3000 Iron Age/Troy founded		

Leo   *(3000 BC to 800 BC)*

Both the first civilizations and the advent of monotheism
happened about 3000 BC. Early Sumerian civilization was a
collection of independent city-states in a tentative alliance, but
Egyptian civilization was unified and centralized from the start.
The invasion and amalgamation of Lower Egypt by Upper
Egypt was rapid and never subsequently threatened.

Egyptian civilization was derived from the Sumerian, but had
unique religious beliefs, architecture, administration and
writing. The primary difference between them was that
Sumerian gods were subservient to the city-states and stood as
much for them as for their natural prototypes, while in Egypt
the gods were supplemented by the worship of collective
human power made manifest through the pharaoh – they
believed the pharaoh to be god. The unification of Egypt
reflected the mythological relationship of Horus and Set. The
ritual murder of Osiris by Set and the revenge of Osiris' son
Horus originated in the death and rebirth of nature each year,
the cereals which the early Egyptians domesticated and the
animistic components in themselves they had conquered, but
the nature-myth was also adapted to political purposes.

What is interesting is that the myth of Horus-Set is also
symbolic of The Divine Plot. After killing Osiris (vegetation),
Set (Saturn or Time) cuts his body up into many pieces (the
stages of the time scale), each of which he scatters all over Egypt
(the world). The pieces are found and re-assembled by Osiris'
devoted sister and wife Isis. Osiris comes back to life and hands
his kingdom over to Horus, who has avenged him by killing
Set. Osiris has a height of 10 royal cubits, is the domesticator of
cereals and animals, and the parts of his body are the cities of
Egypt (each symbolic of an archetype) united by Egyptian
religion. Osiris became the god of the dead and weighs the soul
against a feather at the Last Judgement. The myth which is the
primary political force in Egypt describes the creation,
destruction and resurrection of the world age. Osiris was also
symbolic of the flooding of the Nile and the Great Flood. Osiris
was contained in a box similar to the ark of Noah, encased in the
trunk of a tree (the world tree). (Fig. 30) Plutarch states that,
"Of the stars, the Egyptians think that Sirius, the Dog Star, is
the star of Isis, because it is the bringer of water. They also hold
the Lion in honour and adorn the doorways of their shrines
with gaping lions' heads because the Nile overflows when for
the first time the Sun comes into conjunction with Leo".[152] Isis

Fig. 30: Osiris in the Tamarisk Tree
The Tamarisk Tree within which Osiris was buried is a reference to
the world tree, and as such is a centre of the world. *(de Lubicz, Sacred
Science)*

unites the parts of the divine world. The central myth brings
together many themes of The Divine Plot, including the 50-year
cycle of Sirius-Isis, the number 10 and Osiris, the astrological
sign of the Lion, the neters (archetypes), the numerical measure
of the sacred architecture of Egypt and its origin in astronomical
and astrological cycles, and the relevance of myth to reality.

Old Kingdom Egypt was a stable, thousand-year pharaonic
theocracy with an organized kingdom endowed with great
natural resources. The society was simultaneously materialistic
and desirous of eternal life, a unique combination. Previously
humanity lived in an eternal present, but the Egyptians
understood time and its mechanisms.

The step pyramid for the Pharaoh Zozer was built about 2650
BC by the architect Imhotep, the father of Egyptian
monumental architecture. Over the next two thousand years
the Egyptians continued to create massive pyramids,
culminating in the Great Pyramid (Fig. 31), supposedly built in
2170 BC. The lack of inscriptions makes its use as a burial
pyramid unlikely, but it was a complex and sophisticated
astronomical-astrological computer which measured time, a
standard for all measurements of length, acted as surveying
apparatus for land apportionment, an observatory for planetary

and stellar movements, and most interestingly of all, could have been a way of organizing Egyptian society. Schwaller de Lubicz reasoned that the smoothness and tight fit of the gigantic granite blocks was inconsistent with primitive technology – there had to be another explanation.[153] The descending passage, used for astronomical observations, was oriented to Alpha Draconis, the pole star in 2170 BC. Because the polar point moves about one degree every seventy years, it would have been necessary either to make a new pyramid every seventy-odd years or to change the orientation of the pyramid. Schwaller de Lubicz investigated many other Egyptian antiquities which integrated meaningful fragments from previous buildings, and deduced that the necessity to take the pyramid apart and shift its orientation every seventy years would have taken the entire population of Egypt, and would have provided a perfect task, organized by the Pharaoh and his Architect, for uniting and integrating the population. The building of the Temple is the metaphor of the masonic rites and mysteries of many ancient religions, and the Great Pyramid could have fulfilled this function. The movements of stone on stone through the generations would have worn down the surfaces of every stone until they fit as precisely as they do today. The pyramid was a manifestation of Egyptian knowledge of time and its symbolic and actual measurement. Victorian archaeologists developed elaborate histories based upon the measurements of the Great Pyramid.[154]

Both Sumerian-Akkadian and Egyptian civilizations underwent crises at about the same time in the 2200s BC when unitary political regimes collapsed under pressure from barbarians, but recovered to even greater strength, lasting until the ascendency of Rome two thousand years later. The expansion of both powerful civilizations was due to trade, and religion, language and writing were the tools by which they made their influence manifest. They taught the rest of the world.

Similarly, the Indus civilization sprouted, fully-formed from its birth in about 2500 BC, influenced by the Sumerians, but with unique elements, primarily a previously unknown script and an original and naturalistic art. The drainage, baths, water system and other public architecture of the civilization had a utilitarian quality much like the modern western standard, but with no known prototype.

Leo religious beliefs were monotheistic, where one being represents, or is, God on earth. Pharaoh descended from the

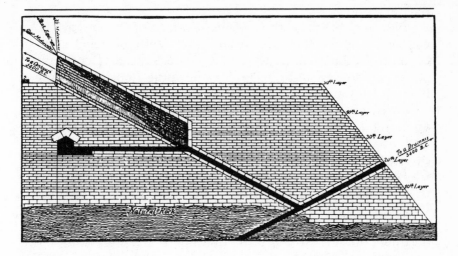

Fig. 31: The Great Pyramid
The Great Pyramid at Giza is astronomically oriented and shaped.
The descending passage aligns with the pole star – its angle is
identical to the angle of Giza from the equator. The King's Chamber
is set upon the 50th course of masonry and the Queen's Chamber
upon the 25th course, an obvious reference to equinoctial cycles and
world ages.

gods and his life was a complex ritual of identification with the
gods, providing for the people an image which they could see
and by which they could be totally directed. Pharaoh's life was
the yearly ritual, and the succession of pharaohs determined
Egyptian history. The king tables of Manetho were among the
first attempts to document a history in such a form.

The Assyrian, Akkadian, Babylonian, Chinese, Egyptian and
western Aegean empires were solar and masculine. Lion
images proliferated in their architecture, especially kingly
monuments and vestments. The pantheon of the Great
Goddess was subjugated by the hero-kings. The first historical
individuals were heroes, kings, warriors and prophets, and
their prime function was to structure civilization through laws.
They were divine and often took upon themselves the functions
of the creator. In Central America the Olmec civilization created
massive sacred architecture for the worship of a half-human
and half-panther god. The early phase flowered from 1150 BC,
and later affected the development of the Chavin culture in the
Andes. They were a thousand years behind the Indo-European
domestication of cereals, signalling a later shift from hunter-
gatherers.

Wilber calls this the *Mental-Egoic Self* [155] which is a consolidation of the life around ego, with parental contact becoming relationship. It is a self-conscious and conceptual stage of development which identifies outer models as higher-order personalities and breeds self-control and will-power.

Leo the Lion is associated with self-consciousness, love of self and others, creation, acting, confidence, education, speculation and game-playing and the exteriorization of the self, and its time is from seven years old to thirteen, leading up to puberty. Children begin to understand rules at this time, learn and invent games which transmit rules and their mechanisms. Piaget calls this the stage of concrete operations where physical actions are internalised as mental actions or operations, which become models for action ingrained in behaviour. The hierarchy of rules of games, school, society, religion and the culture are learned, digested and parallel the hierarchy of personal relations outside of the family. By the age of seven children are in primary school, where standards of behaviour and communication are programmed. As the child learns to exteriorise, new restrictions are presented and controls are more and more specific. The essence of all societies is a hierarchy of classes, elites and order of succession and education transmits the norm.

Virgo   (800 BC until AD 400)

Virgo is distillation, discrimination, the critical faculty and ordering processes. The consolidation of kingly Leo time set the stage for the classical civilizations of Greece and Rome, great cultural and political systems which synthesized many prevailing diverse tendencies and produced an amalgam which was then distilled. Their military organization conquered the entire known world – first by Alexander the Great in the 4th century BC and then by Julius Caesar in the 1st century BC – and provided such security and affluence for the population that creativity in science, philosophy, economics, politics, the arts and architecture was truly astonishing. The Greeks integrated a multitude of mythologies, religious beliefs and cultural identities within a common philosophy, language and governmental system.

During Virgo, cultures came into being where Homer synthesized previous mythologies, Pythagoras previous metaphysics, Socrates and Plato previous philosophies, Phidias previous sculptures, Herodatus previous histories and

Pericles former governmental systems. All acted within Greek ideals of concord and freedom. Specific ways of seeing and understanding the world of preceding ages were combined into an working whole which was extended throughout the vast empire. Technological advances and the increasing sophistication of the war-machine made the Greeks and Romans virtually invulnerable and when their classical way of life finally collapsed after 1200 years of domination, it happened primarily through internal chaos allied with religion.

The Greeks and Romans excelled at systematizing and assimilating the gods and heroes of the areas they conquered – foreign deities were simply taken into the classical pantheon as minor relations or children of the primary gods and goddesses. Prophetic religions arose, based on the teachings of evolved souls such as Buddha, Krishna, Lao Tse, Confucius, Mani and Jesus Christ. As Greece was absorbed by the Roman Empire, the Roman Empire became the host for Christianity. The combination of eastern mysticism with the humanitarian ethic and sense of time and history of the west undermined decadent Roman polytheism until it created a schism between two vast halves of the empire which allowed powerful barbarian hordes to wedge them apart as a prelude to total destruction. A similar process happened in the east as China was decimated by the Huns and Mongols from central Asia after millennia of high culture dominated by religion. The selective process central to the classical civilizations denied the primeval darkness of the psyche and crystalline culture was shattered with the Fall of Rome when Alaric sacked the greatest city in history into oblivion. The primitive had to be integrated rather than eliminated.

The earlier fertility religions of the near east were absorbed into Christianity, but certain cults resisted the bureaucratic structure of the early Church, and accepted instead the Gnostic ideal – gnosis is knowing by direct revelation. The gnostics worshipped the feminine ideal Sophia as and symbol of wisdom and the carrier of the holy spirit. By the early third century AD the books of the New Testament were chosen and translated to support the beliefs of the Christians who formed the political organization of the Church, and books which were threatening were excluded or destroyed. Similarly the direct knowing of the prophets was interpreted by their followers, often by later generations who had no direct contact with the original events and teachings. The naive accepted the surface teachings, while the initiates were forced to hide (occult) their rituals and esoteric teachings.

For Wilber this is the *Late-Ego Self* [156] of creativity, identification and mastering the various personalities while suppressing the shadow elements, i.e. all the unintegrated remnants of earlier phases.

The Virgo time in Life★Time Astrology is from 13 until 23 years, when puberty brings physical reality back to the fore. The puberty-inflicted youth, having learned the structures and rules of society, must begin to make choices, to distil and define the relationship between mind and body, refining attitudes, habits, diet, clothing and importantly, ideas. A youth detaches from family protection and recognizes that work is necessary to life. Piaget calls this the stage of Formal Operations when increased collaboration and reasoning within and with others leads to simultaneous relationships of differentiation and reciprocity which characterize the co-ordination of individual viewpoints. The use of hypothesis and testing is a recognition that the rules and laws of elders are not absolute. The earlier myths and fantasies of childhood are often eradicated or suppressed at this time, being pushed back into the unconscious. Most concrete expressions and experiences are translated into verbal and symbolic modes of expression, and rhythmic functions manifest in music, early sexuality and work activities. The choices during Virgo are usually binding and the emphasis is upon specialization and isolation.

Libra   *(AD 400 until AD 1100)*

Libra represents balance, sublimation, partnership, the search for equilibrium, law and adjustment, and falls at the midpoint of the astrological-historical time scale where unconscious influences become conscious for the first time, and where the outward arc returns to completion on the inward arc.[157] The synthesis of classical civilization began with a breakdown into opposites and ended with an east-west fragmentation which led to cross-fertilization. The forced establishment of a unified Christian Church led quickly to the political Rome-Constantinople opposition further metamorphosed into the age of monasticism exemplified by St Benedict. Fragments distilled by the Greeks and Romans were isolated into feudal enclaves and developed without much overall unity or mutual communication. The branching off of previously unified academic, musical and religious studies led to the specialization characteristic of the Dark Ages. The Athenian Schools closed in

AD 529 and knowledge of humanity almost became the exclusive property of Church theology, a situation which is still largely true.

The feudal Kings imposed order through religion and vied with the monasteries and early Popes for power. Charlemagne, King Arthur, Alfred the Great and Pepin shared power with the Popes and monastic authorities through a balance of economic leverage. Expanded feudal fiefs eventually became the states of Europe – Germany, France, England, Spain, Holland and Italy – and they related to each other under duress and only because of trade. Trading was the channel of communication and many religious, cultural and scientific innovations spread, specifically the rediscovery of classicism by the Arabic philosophers transplanted in Spain, and the revival of Buddhism in Tibet after its decline in India and China. Seeds crossed from Europe to Asia and backwards, and Erikson's voyages to the New World extended the horizon.

In China a similar division in the Eastern and Western Han Empires led eventually into warring fragments conquered by the Hsiung-nu (Huns), as were the Oxus basin, India, Iran and Europe. In composition the Huns were Tungus or Mongols, similar in shamanistic beliefs to the earliest shamans of the opposite Aries time in the scale. They had a disruptive influence on the whole civilized world – where they did not create havoc themselves, the Teutonic Goths, Visigoths and Vandals and Iranian rebels fleeing from them did so – and managed to interbreed and become assimilated into European, Persian, Indian and Chinese cultures. The spiritual vacuum of China paralleled that of the European world, and zealous Mahayana Buddhist missionaries entered China from India and Tibet and supplanted the previously dominant Taoism.

Most symbolic of Libran religion is Islam, received through the Prophet Muhammed's epiphanies from the Archangel Gabriel. The Koran, begun in 610, states that there is only one true God (Allah) and that Muhammed is the most recent and definitive prophet among Jesus, Moses, Elijah and other previous avatars. Islam absorbed its competition and instituted monotheism through its stern Law. Within a hundred years Islam spread by conquest to the East Roman Empire, Syria, Mesopotamia, Palestine, Egypt, the Persian Empire of Iraq and Iran, the Sasanian Persian Empire, Armenia and Georgia, north-west Africa, Spain, south-western Gaul, the Sind and Punjab, Uzbekistan and Turkey, and was only deterred at Poitiers in 732 from conquering France. The Koran states clearly that all those who live by the word of God must be tolerated and protected, so Christians, Jews, Zoroastrians and Hindus were integrated, but within Islam itself the struggle for succession to Muhammed created a split-off of the Shiite sect, started by Muhammed's brother Ali, which is not healed to this day.

Eastern Christendom was revitalized by Byzantine civilization as the western Christian world was by the Carolingians, culminating in the crowning of Charlemagne as Holy Roman Emperor by Pope Leo III in 800. The order was temporary, as violence erupted with the Vikings, Franks and Norse rovers overrunning Europe while Erickson reached across the ocean as far as Greenland and the New World. Even in Meso-America, barbarians sacked Teotihuacan (600) and Cholula (800), and the powerful Mayan civilization was abandoned by the ninth century. All over the world the military might (Aries) opposed the institution of the law (Libra).

The most important structure to emerge was chivalry and romantic love, exemplified by the Arthurian legends of fifth century Britain. The taming of violence by religion, and a reverence of the sublime reached its peak as Christian and prior Great Goddess cults combined through the symbolism of the Grail Legend and the magical exploits of King Arthur and the Knights of the Round Table.

According to Wilber this is the beginning of the ascent of consciousness of the *Mature Ego Self* [158] which integrates all possible personalities, dis-identifies from the ego altogether and begins to transform to higher level unity. All lower levels must be synthesized and stabilized in an autonomous, self-actualizing and intentional being.

Libra the Scales or Balance traditionally governs partnership, communal relations, the public, obligations, sublimation, justice, the law, business relationships, sociability and enemies from 23 until 42 years old. At 23 we are opposite the birth moment and have experienced the entire lower, subjective and unconscious half of the horoscope. The opposition is symbolic of the fact that in order to emerge from the unconscious, internal conflict must be fought symbolically as in the Grail legend. Marriage is the primary process through which opposing qualities may be confronted, married and integrated into a whole, and the marriage of King and Queen symbolized this as well as actually occurring. (Fig. 50) The conjunction of opposites is central to alchemy, which was a predecessor of the psychology of the unconscious. Partnership is initially a sublimation of each individual in favour of the whole relationship, but rapidly attains a higher significance as a model for balancing the psyche and transcending the personal – higher relationship is transformative and aligns with collective values in addition to satisfying personal hungers and ideals.

Scorpio   *(AD 1100 until AD 1500)*

Scorpio is the ruthless struggle for survival, passion, death and regeneration, and the transmission of life through the seed. As the opposite Taurus time was sensible contact with the physical world and cults worshipping the Earth Mother, Scorpio time is the reappearance of dark passion in the Crusades and the Inquisition, where bloodshed and warfare were justified by the winner-take-all struggle between Church and State after their uneasy alliances in Libra. Crusaders were fighting fraternities under Church rule abroad, and the inquisition eliminated heretical (read differing) practices at home; in both cases the aim was the eradication of impurity and evil. Scorpio is associated with the underworld, the incorruptible, discipline and physical and spiritual regeneration, coming as the final dissolution of the classical civilization.

The combination of high culture with historical roots, the tendency for early magical traditions to go underground in an enlightened growth of magic, and the increase in secular power and intolerance of the Church and their henchmen, the Crusaders and Inquisitors, made for a dynamic time. The primary focus of the Inquisition was the extinction of remaining fertility cults and nature worship, signalling a new materialism. The Crusades were initially great successes of strategy and financial reward by Christian expeditionary forces sent to conquer Moslem Jerusalem, but eventually turned sour as the Christians were repelled by the Moslems.

The Norman conquest of England in 1066 proved French superiority in Europe and started a great rise in Western civilization comparable to the rise of Hellenic civilization in the eighth century BC (a sextile from early Scorpio back to early Virgo). The Roman legal system was aligned with the Church and implemented by force with the age of chivalry and the ascendancy of the knights. The breakdown of the Roman governmental system into republican city-states or monarchical kingdom-states, however, utilized the rediscovery of Greek language and philosophy.

The founding of religious orders such as the Benedictines and

Cistercians, the imposed celibacy of the secular clergy and reforms in the Papacy, including its permanent move to Rome, all consolidated the power of the Church. For the first time the Curia of Cardinals elected the pope rather than powerful kings. A parallel shift in power occurred in the Islamic world as orders of chivalry, including the futuwwah, and the dervish sects were created. The Buddhists revived Buddhism in Tibet in about 1100, and the Mahayana sect was disseminated widely in Japan and northern China, and the Zen Buddhist militaristic discipline which appealed to soldiers was introduced in Japan in 1191. In China the Sung dynasty was powerful in its neo-Confucian doctrines (again, a sextile back to Confucius in early Virgo). The vast and powerful Islamic empires of the Ottomans, Mamluks and Safavis successfully repelled or integrated the Mongol influences and created highly cultured religious societies.

The fanatically religious cultures of the time found expression in the cathedrals of France and England, which were symbols of the domination of the Church and a contrast to the struggles for survival of the populace. Almost extinct mythologies were revived by schools of master masons and displayed in the rose windows[159], in the naturalistic art of Giotto, and the architecture of Brunelleschi and Bramante under the patronage of the Medicis and the Popes. Dynastic city-states created contexts for enlightened culture under the Italian Medicis, the Khans of China and the Mongols in India. There were many reactions to the disorder created by the Crusades such as the romantic literature of Dante, Chaucer and Cretien de Troyes, all of whom documented the breakdown of the previous order and prepared the stage for the transference of power to the sacred individual. To Wilber this is the stage of the *Bisocial Band Self*[160], the upper limit of membership-cognitive and physical orientation, and a stepping-stone to the higher magical through trans-verbal and trans-conceptual reality. It symbolizes going beyond conventional social barriers as the first stage of transcendence, the essential function of Scorpio time in life and history.

Scorpio the Scorpion is associated with the process of life, death and regeneration, karma, occultism and magic, survival, fanaticism, shared resources and perversity, and occupies the time from 42 years old until death in old age. During the opposite childhood Taurus time one accepts the object-like world of the body and the senses, and here the body must be relinquished at the end of life. Outer objectives have been accomplished and the inner life is rediscovered. The symbolic descent and ascent of the soul in Dante's Divine Comedy is a classic description of the Scorpio time and its lessons. Scorpio rules the various means to liberation and the inherent dangers of the failure to liberate oneself from the physical world. The power of Tibetan Buddhism, Zen, Mystic Christianity and Islam all reflect such spiritual principles. The karmic accummulation of life actions which have not been paid for come back in Scorpio, as they might have been hidden during life, a process symbolized in alchemy by the transmutation of lead into gold, paralleling the transmutation of humanity from the realm of the individual into the next Sagittarius phase of the realized being.

The Octave of Individuality (Sagittarius-AD 1500 to Pisces-AD 1950)

The Black Death plague which swept Western Europe during the 14th century was symbolic of the dissolution of classical civilization and prepared the way for the humanist age of the Renaissance, which saw humanity's great leap in knowledge and art. Enquiring minds transcended the bounds of the physical world and extended perception into outer space with the telescope and inner space with microscope, an extension to the ends of the known earth. For the first time in history, humanity could map the entire world and place it within the cosmos, perspective was discovered as a phenomenon of human perception, the entire range of musical tones was understood and heard, and the whole spectrum of colour was exploited in art. In short, humanity reached its limits and attempted to step beyond them.

1910 AD   Sagittarius to Pisces

1910 AD
Pisces
the Fishes

The Great Wars
Disintegration
Germany, USSR and USA
Matriarchal
Karmic Isolationism
Illusion
Abstraction
Nihilism
War Devices

1840 AD
Aquarius
the Waterbearer

Nationalism
Humanitarianism
Romantic Utopian Societies
Idealism
Bureaucracies and Unions
Victorian Age
Collectivization
Socialism-Communism
Modern Governmental Structure

1720 AD
Capricorn
the Goat-Fish

Industrial Revolution
Physical Perfection
England
Matriarchal
Revolutionary Materialism
Nationalism
The Reformation
Capitalist Machine Age
Ascendancy over Nature

1500 AD
Sagittarius
the Centaur

The Renaissance
Self-Realization
The Americas
Patriarchal
New Colonial Worlds
Reconstitution
Philosophical Humanism
Wholistic World View
Rebirth to Higher Mind

1950 AD

Historical Events	Religion & Mysticism	Works of Humanity

	Historical Events	Religion & Mysticism	Works of Humanity
1950	1949 NATO & Mao's China	1950 Assumption of the Virgin	1948 Antibiotics synthesized
	1947 Indian Independence	1949 Ouspensky Search Miraculous	1942 ENIAC computer
1944	1946 **United Nations**	1944 Crowley Book of Thoth	137 Whittle jet engine
	1945 **Hiroshima Atom Bomb**	1944 Jung Psychology & Religion	1935 Air transport
1939	1939 **World War II**		1932 Radio astronomy
	1933 New Deal		1930 Pluto discovered
1933	1930 Spanish Civil War		1928 Fleming penicillin
	1929 **The Great Depression**		1926 Baird television
1926	1927 Lindbergh flies Atlantic	1922 Tutankhamen discovered	1925 Radio & Mein Kampf
	1923 Munich putsch	1921 Gurdjieff Institute of Man	1920
1919	1920 League of Nations	1920 Jung Psychological Types	1915 Cinema
	1917 **Russian Revolution**	1917 Jung The Unconscious	1914 Russell Principia
1910	1914 **World War I**	1911 Frazer Golden Bough	1913 Bohr Quantum Theory

	Historical Events	Religion & Mysticism	Works of Humanity
1910	1903 Bolshevik party	1908 1st Psychoanalytic Conf	1904 Einstein Relativity
	1900 Boxer Rebellion	1907 Crowley Book of the Law	1903 Wrights' airplane
1902	1899 Boer War/Africa partitioned		1900 Freud Dreams
	1894 China-Japan War	1893 Blavatsky Secret Doctrine	1877 Gramophone
1892	1878 Treaty of Berlin	1888 Blavatsky Isis Unveiled	1876 Bell Telephone
	1871 Russo-Turkish War	1882 Soc Psychic Research	1876 Bayreuth Opera House
1881	1875 Schliemann finds Troy	1876 Muller Sacred Books	1872 Mendelkev Periodic Table
	1867 **1st Trade Union**/Serfs freed	1875 Theosophical Society	1867 Dynamite
1869	1861 **American Civil War**		1859 Darwin Origin of Species
	1857 Indian Mutiny	1865 Society Rosicruciana	1857 1st Oil Well
1856	1854 Crimean War		1851 Crystal Palace
	1849 California Gold Rush		1848 Marx Communist Manifesto
1840	1845 Neptune discovered	1841 Livingstone African mission	1840 Photography

	Historical Events	Religion & Mysticism	Works of Humanity
1840	1839 Brit-Chinese Opium Wars		1835 Marconi Telegraph
	1832 British Reform Bill	1831 Second Day Adventists	1825 Stephenson railroad
1825	1823 Monroe Doctrine	1830 Smith Book of Mormon	1807 Gas lighting
	1819 Owen Factory Act		1805 1st Museums & Galleries
1810	1815 Battle of Waterloo	1808 Inquisition abolished	1799 Beethoven First Symphony
	1812 War of 1812	1807 Hegel Phenomenon of Spirit	1787 Gibbon Decline and Fall
1790	1805 Battle of Trafalgar		1780 Uranus discovered
	1795 The Directory	1789 Wesley Sermons	1776 Smith Wealth of Nations
1770	1789 **French Revolution**	1780 Order of Asiatic Brethren	1776 Paine Common Sense
	1787 American Constitution	1760 Swedenborgian Rites	1774 Oxygen discovered
1745	1776 **American Revolution**		1769 Steam engine
	1763 Peace of Paris		1751 Encyclopedia
1720	1756 Seven Years War	1740 Secret Golden Flower	1733 Electricity discovered

	Historical Events	Religion & Mysticism	Works of Humanity
1720	1700 Great Northern War		1716 Hydrogen discovered
	1688 British Revolution		1675 Roemer speed of light
1690	1666 Great Fire of London		1666 Newton Calculus
	1642 Australia discovered		1661 Leuwenhoek microscope
1660	1638 Japan closed (until 1865)		1661 Milton Paradise Lost
	1625 Moghul Empire in India	1606 Rosicrucians founded	1623 Shakespeare Folio
1625	1620 Mayflower/Jamestown colony	1577 1st Dalai Lama	1609 Galileo telescope
	1619 Cortez conquers Mexico	1545 Council of Trent	1603 Gilbert magnetism
1590	1618 Thirty Years War	1542 Francis Xavier in Japan	1599 Globe Theatre
	1583 Raleigh Virginia Colony	1539 Society of Jesus (Jesuits)	1574 Fludd Utriusque Cosmi
1545	1519 **Magellan circumnavigates**	1533 Agrippa De occulta	
	1516 South American Inquisition	1521 Luther Diet of Worms	1520 Machiavelli The Prince
1500	1513 Balboa through Panama	1512 Lateran Council on Soul	1516 More Utopia

Sagittarius   (AD 1100 until AD 1500)

Sagittarius represents realization of the self, higher mind, philosophy, religion, wisdom, foreign influences, long journeys. After the destruction and fragmentation of Scorpio, classical principles were rediscovered as a context for the emergence of higher consciousness in the Renaissance, an age characterized by individuals who gathered, synthesized, combined and manifested many diverse strands of human knowledge and understanding and unified them in great works. The horizon was expanded in every conceivable direction; geographically, intellectually, scientifically, politically and theologically.

Voyages of discovery led to colonial empires for England, Spain, France, Portugal, India and Russia which allowed cultural trade on a world-wide scale. The colonized countries were raped, subjugated and assimilated as missionaries, adventurers and dissidents were dispatched. A time of physical plenty ensued, with great prosperity in Europe. The influx of previously unknown or rare raw materials and labouring slaves created European treasure-houses of wealth. The worldwide expansion also promoted the greatest mental and spiritual revolution since the founding of Rome, a change determined initially by a questioning and then regeneration of Graeco-Roman civilization which led finally to the emergence of independent thought.

Witches were prosecuted and executed by the Inquisition well into the Eighteenth Century, but profound men found ways to follow the mystical quest without harassment. Others paid the ultimate price for their beliefs, including Giordano Bruno (1548-1600), who proposed a system of celestial magic and Galileo. Magicians and alchemists necessarily camouflaged their true ideals and philosophies in allegory and metaphor, amidst the arts, literature and theology. The integrated celestial sciences of astrology, geometry and mathematics were understood as divine techniques for communicating with the soul of the world. Robert Fludd showed the human as a mathematical and mystical cipher of the microcosm within which the entire macrocosm lay reflected, and demonstrated that the proportions of the human body were manifest in planetary relationships and intervals of the musical scale, all of which had an integrated relationship with cosmic understanding in geomancy, the art of memory, geometry, astrology, surveying, navigation and others.

John Dee went further with his Mathematicall Preface to Euclide of 1570, which presented mathematics as a divine language for describing and attaining power over the natural world. Before this time mathematics was considered a magical art, and was not in the curriculum of either Oxford or Cambridge. Dee demonstrated the dual use of mathematics as symbolic in a Pythagorean sense and as a measurement of quantities, the second being stressed in later materialist mechanistic science. Dee was a Hermetic and Platonic philosopher and distinguished between the heliocentric theory of Copernicus, which he understood and accepted as a physical scientist, and the prevailing geocentric (earth-centred) theory of the classical world, which still applied to astrology. He was one of the few men able to grasp the concept of higher worlds of ideas governing the physical plane. Dee was advisor to the profound Elizabethan court and possessed a more complete library than any of the universities. He was a link in the transition from the Scorpionic magicians of the medieval world to the Renaissance.

The Copernican rediscovery of heliocentricity took thirty years to prove mathematically, but led to a revolution in the skies, while Galileo (1564-1642) was persecuted for inventing the telescope. Tycho Brahe (1546-1601), Kepler (1571-1630) and Newton (1642-1747) were practising astrologers, and were forced to align themselves with the fledgling science and its compromise with the Church. There was an unwritten agreement that science could investigate and describe the universe mathematically, taking over the Church's prerogative, but in exchange science was forced to suppress all speculation about the role of man in the scheme of things – an ominous devil's bargain which still seems to be in operation today. Astrologer-astronomers revolutionized scientific attitudes and formulated the mechanics of universal movements, mathematics, astronomy, physics and cosmology, but the magical component was considered heretical and was eliminated from the scientific world view. Now Newton is seen as a pure scientist, but was actually an alchemist investigating the true origin of the mysteries.

As the exterior world was explored and probed, so was the interior world of the psyche. Leonardo da Vinci (1452-1519) and Michaelangelo (1465-1560) combined architecture, painting, drawing, writing, anatomy, sculpture, mechanics, the technology of warfare and fortification. Francis Bacon (1561-1626) and Shakespeare (1564-1616) created a sublime synthesis of classical drama, poetry and lyrics with sociological, cultural, historical magical and religious material to enthrall discerning audiences at the apex of the humanist age. Bacon translated the King James' English version of the Bible and introduced a mystical context and structure which contained a magical, cryptic significance.

The Protestant reformation initiated by Luther (1483-1546), Calvin (1509-1564) and Loyola (1491-1556) created a schism within the Roman Catholic church, which then splintered into myriad reformed sects. An individual and personal approach to God mirrored the importance of logic, as intellectual attitudes became religions. Humanism supplanted organized religion as christianity could not control exclusive rights over rational explanations of the world where observation, objectivity and the scientific method were the primary ways of understanding reality. The religious wars among England, France, Spain and Germany were political power struggles masked by religion.

The striation between science and religion was exemplified by the internalization of the external world by Descartes (1596-1650), the description of a metaphysical basis of reality by Spinoza, and the assertions of Liebniz, Hume and Locke of the mathematical structure of all perception of the world as the domain of pure logic. Medicine advanced due to remembered fear of the Black Death, Boyle's formulation of chemistry, Huygens' discovery of the glass lens, and dissection, which allowed exploration of the connection between the theoretical and mystical beliefs about the human body. The body was seen as a physical object instead of the seat of the divine soul. The social contract of Hobbes (1588-1679) formalized the materialization of reality.

For Wilber a *Centauric Self* [161] emerged which reached beyond language, membership, culture, egoic logic and will to a higher level of mental reflection. This level is a transcultural but not transpersonal beginning of mystical insight.

Sagittarius is a double sign, composed of a materialist centaur body and higher healing, humanist archer. It governs the first seven weeks of gestation, when the brain structure is formed as the mother comes to the realization of her inner creative, and the first stage of initiation when the soul within is discovered.

Capricorn   *(AD 1720 until AD 1840)*

Capricorn is the centre of the field of consciousness, the ego, and represents ego-consciousness, spiritual awareness, life objectives and goals, pragmatism, materialism, reality, perfected matter, fermentation, the rigidity of old age. The ideology of Sagittarius was translated into material form, and humanistic principles were applied to whole societies, and for the first time humanity believed its position as the apex of development and more powerful than nature.

The basic building block of the physical world, the element hydrogen, was isolated in 1716 at the beginning of Capricorn. The discovery of oxygen in 1771 led to chemical formulae and the great diversity of dyes, drugs, explosives and many of the new materials of modern life. Lamarck developed systems for categorizing the natural order of the world, and Franklin, Lavoisier, Halley, Cavendish and Hershel made discoveries of a structural nature which created the mechanist-materialist science which exists today. The discovery of electricity in 1733 plunged humanity into the Industrial Revolution, which irreversibly changed the structure of the world. Electricity allowed the invention of machines which drastically affected the nature and speed of production, travel and communication, which directly altered the relationship of man to the environment, culminating in the first steam train of 1825. With the apparent direct control and participation in the world, humanity evinced a superiority over the forces of nature for the first time, as well as a sense of being a secondary operator of machines which did the work. In a sense the world contracted and the increased density generated pressure which compelled humanity to solve the remaining mysteries of the physical world – the major breakthroughs had already been made.

Technology was applied to the art of war, influencing the great revolutions. India was subjugated by the British in the 1760's and the primitive Australia was colonized by 1790. As colonial nations expanded, their appetite for imported material increased beyond bounds, and the desire to subjugate and utilize adjacent territory became obsessive. The previous dominance of Church and monarchy declined rapidly after the new Americans cast off the yoke of European colonization, creating an eqalitarian democracy, and the French Revolution established a leadership of the military, a pattern followed by revolutionary movements in South America. As a result of being forced out of the Americas, the War of 1812 brought separate national European powers directly into conflict over the territorial imperative. The practice of politics had been transformed by Machiavelli and the techniques of power infiltrated western life, showing the dominance of human mind and will over disorder, as manifest in the structure of the American Declaration of Independence (1776) and Constitution (1787), the founding of the Encyclopedia Britannica in 1771, the total control of warfare and tactics exhibited by Napoleon. The ascendency of technique over feeling and individuality transformed the spirit of humanity into exploitation of it, and led to totalitarian ethics which reduced humans to components instead of prime motivating forces.

In the intellectual sphere humanity peaked as Kant developed a formal language of cognition through mathematical language. The great German poet and novelist Goethe was also a scientist and politician, a total man who presented parallels between biological and psychological processes which were later to inspire many other philosophers and natural scientists, including Schopenhauer, who revived Eastern ideas and collaged them into his philosophical systems, reintegrating East and West.

The perfection of the music of Bach (1685-1750), Beethoven (1770-1827) and Mozart (1750-1791) was a highpoint in western culture, as were the novels of Balzac, Hugo, Scott and Coleridge and the poetry of Shelley and Keats. Romanticism surrounded the tragic lives of Schubert, Byron and Chopin, a reaction against the prevailing mechanist world view.

To Wilber this is the emergence of the *Low-Subtle Self* [162] in the causal realm where the third eye-pineal gland operates to compose the astral and psychic planes of consciousness. In yoga this is the stage beyond mastery of the physical body which operates on the world.

Capricorn is the time when the mother realizes her pregnancy and organizes the physical world to prepare for the new child as the physical structure of the body is formed and organized within. The transcendent Capricorn is higher objectives coming into manifestation in the world.

Aquarius   (AD 1840 until AD 1910)

Aquarius represents idealism, utopianism, humanitarianism, abstraction, organizations and planning. The established dominance of the material world in Capricorn quickly required more sophisticated planning, order and an idealization of world mechanisms, especially concerning the public. Basic life hypotheses were radically changed, as the independence and ascendency of the individual was finally relinquished in favour of collective social systems, coordinated and working towards similar goals.

The freeing of the underprivileged classes was a primary priority, accomplished partially through freeing of the slaves in the American Civil War, even though recently economic reasons have been advanced as the primary reasons for the war between industrial North and agricultural South. Czar Alexander liberated the serfs, and the political commentary and theory of class struggle was advanced by Marx and Engels in *"Das Kapital"* (1848), leading rapidly to the socialist movement and the formation of the first labour unions. Marx saw history as a process of class struggle towards a future "golden age" of redemption, a view which excluded a transcendental significance from history and was a rejection of the idea that a golden age exists at the beginning as well as at the end. The Marxist defense against the horrors of history is paradoxical – the attempt to achieve equality and salvation for the masses ends up putting total power in the hands of an increasingly smaller number of men, who are deified with their power.[163] Although Marxism was a reaction against capitalism, it is particularly strange as the capitalist ideals were very similar in many respects.

Unintentional support for political idealism came through Darwin's *"Origin of Species"*, which outlined a linear evolutionary view of world history as an extension of biology, implying that time is a one-way street leading into an infinite future and that the existing world order was superior to anything which had happened already. These ideal attitudes penetrated the world very quickly after weak initial resistance from those still supporting cyclical world views, and it underscored the revolution against monarchy (originated in the opposite Leo time in history) and colonialism, such as the Indian Mutiny of 1857, the Boer War of 1899, the Boxer Rebellion of 1900. Most of the few remaining monarchies were overthrown by 1910.

The resistance to the modern industrial world with its dank cities of workers was illustrated by Romantic artists, some of whom attempted to structure society by recapturing the past and integrating it into the present. Foremost of these were the socialist William Morris and the Pre-Raphaelite Brotherhood of Victorian England, who brought old handcrafts back into style and accounted the loss of such basic crafts as an undermining of all culture. Spurred on by Schopenhauer, ideas and beliefs from the East flooded into the West through channels as diverse as the Sacred Books of the East Series edited by Max-Muller, the

Theosophical Society of Madam Blavatsky, the aristocrats of Victorian society and the operas of Wagner. Many exaggerated the chaos, such as Nietzsche, Wilde, Shaw and the Impressionist painters of the turn of the Twentieth Century. Freud's "Interpretation of Dreams" of 1900 opened the door for psychological explanations for the inability of people to adapt to the new world, and his concept of a suppressed unconscious under the facade of civilization described this time very well.

For Wilber this is the realm of the *High-Subtle Self*[164] of transcendence, differentiation and integration through religious intuition, inspiration and symbolic visions. They are reflections of the highest archetypal forms of being as the summit of consciousness before dissolution into the deity.

Aquarius the Waterbearer is the middle stage of gestation when the mother's concern is humanitarian, selfless and detached from the world, concentrated within on potential new life and without on ideals transmitted to friends and groups. On the transcendent level Aquarius is the ability to create and transmit higher reality to the society beyond the range of physical contact through media, books and information.

Pisces   (AD 1910 until AD 1950)

Pisces represents karma, the end of life, seclusion and isolation, institutions, dependence upon external conditions, drugs and illusion, the psychic faculty as well as everything hidden. As the last stage of the historical process, it is the final effects of the stream of history and the collision of the many contradictory directions of humanity upon the stark reality of life.

Pisces was heralded by the founding of Psychoanalysis, the investigation of the unconscious substrata of life, conceived by Freud and Jung, and the Theory of Relativity of Einstein, which drastically altered the perception of the universe by invalidating the mechanics of Newton and forcing a total re-evaluation of the laws of the physical world. Thus the psychic and physical were relativized at the same time. The dilemma of the individual isolated by collective society was a metaphor for both fledgling sciences, and was a response to the impending collision of increasingly institutionalized powerful world states with immovable ideologies.

The competition between capitalism and socialism escalated from the Russian, Mexican and Chinese Revolutions of the early twentieth century to the full-blown conflict of the First World War. Interim attempts at reconciliation by forming a

League of Nations were ineffective. The shift of the industrialized nations to war economy led to great, although artificial, prosperity which forced the Great Depression of 1929. The new power of media allowed Hitler in Germany, Mussolini in Italy and Stalin in Russia to proclaim nationalistic beliefs. With the technological advances of mobility, flight, chemical and explosives allied to the warlike stance, the Second World War crippled the entire planet by the detonation of the atom bombs in Japan.

The collapse of every facet of civilization occurred during Pisces: in music Stravinsky, Mahler and Schoenberg left classical sounds for atonal and arhythmic composition; in art the cubists and constructivists shattered the classical sense of form; in philosophy Bertrand Russell, Alfred North Whitehead and de Chardin attempted to confront the collapse of society; in literature James Joyce, Eliot and the existentialists Sartre and Camus exploded the classical conception of language; in entertainment the celluloid fantasy world of Hollywood movies created an illusory world beyond reality; in science Einstein, Bohr, Pauli and Heisenberg upset the predictable Newtonian physics and created the technological access to diabolical instruments of destruction.

For relief from the tension and negativism of the world state many people plunged into excessive indulgence in alcohol, the products of the burgeoning pharmaceutical industries, the distortion of reality of surrealism, the worship of artificially created movie stars and a dream of stockpiling huge fortunes like the reclusive millionaires. The rush for instant profit despite the insecurity of a wartime world forced an abandonment of traditional values, added unpredictable drugs to most foods, produced a destructive military-industrial complex and created a lowest class in western societies who were, amidst plenty, undernourished and poverty-stricken. The shift to dependency upon external values created counter-movements by Steiner, Crowley, Jung, Hesse and Suzuki in a spiritual and magical direction.

For Wilber this is the *High-Causal Self* [165] which leads to Atman, the perfect knowing of formlessness, pure radiance which is trans-temporal, eternal and transcendent. It is the container of all previous stages in the evolution of consciousness and the final transformation. The self dissolves into and becomes co-extensive to the archetypal deity, contacts to a single point, and vanishes into the void.

With the end of Pisces the world cycle drew to a close in a

mood of universal dissolution and annihilation of all positive values. The symbol of Pisces is two fishes swimming in opposite directions, but tied together by the tail, representing unconscious forces pulling both down into deeper unconsciousness and up to consciousness. Pisces is the last stage of pregnancy when the mother gains weight, becomes sensitive to influences from the world, and must sacrifice herself for the welfare of the child within. On the transcendent level Pisces is the final dissolution into the boundless.

The End of the World Age

> That ye which have followed me in the regeneration, when the son of man shall sit in the throne of his glory, ye also shall sit upon twelve thrones, judging the twelve tribes of Israel. And every one that hath forsaken houses, or brethren, or sisters, or father, or mother, or wife, or children, or lands, for my name's sake, shall receive an hundred-fold, and shall inherit everlasting life. But many that are first shall be last, and the last shall be first.[166]

The parable of Jesus means that to accept the death and resurrection of the individual and the world age, one must experience the twelve thrones (the twelve zodiacal houses) and judge (live through and identify with) the twelve tribes or stages in the process of the world age. By abandoning identification and thoughts of stabilization in any one stage, everlasting life shall be inherited. Those that are first (most powerful or materialistic) will be last, and the last (powerless or humble) shall be first. Access to spirit is beyond worldly existence. The disciples were initially shocked by this, but as John observed of Jesus, "He was in the world, and the world was made by him, and the world knew him not".[167] Being beyond the purely physical or historical world places one in the spiritual world.

The end of Pisces in 1950, after the detonation of the Hiroshima atom bomb, is the end of the World Age. With the twelve phases of the time scale, humanity has accelerated from the emergence of consciousness to the self-destruction of civilization. The cycle returns to its final point, which coincides with its beginning. Humanity programs itself to believe that the present world is the height of civilization, yet clearly the powers of destruction are at a peak. What seems like the achievement of the goals of evolution is attended by a stripping bare of the meaning of life, leaving spiritual vacuum and nihilism. Collective humanity is cut off from its roots, initiating a breakdown into component parts.

At the moment of death the life process passes before the mind's eye in an instant. During gestation all history is recapitulated from the creation of life to the moment of birth. In death visions, called by Steiner "the great panorama" or "life-tableau" and more recently "panoramic memory", the images of the entire life repeat very quickly. The etheric body is the receptacle of memory and as it exists for a period of time after the death and dissolution of the physical body, the etheric body is the medium of the death memory.

In the history of humanity the same process is experienced collectively. The entire cycle of history is compressed into one-thousandth of the time — the fifty year unit of the Time Scale. As the individual reexperiences his individual life at death, the world age experiences its history at the end of a world age. The repetition of all history occurs with every individual returning to experience the whole. Similarly, the burst of energy at conception is identical to the similar shattering of consciousness at death. The last judgement, when the dying civilization experiences the memory loss of the River Lethe, synchronizes with the seed creation of the next world age. Death is required for redemption, two counter-trends create a simultaneous split and synthesis at the cataclysm point. It is quite obvious in the world at the present time that such a striation is happening. The collective death moment is the rising of the dead of all ages, the "second death" mentioned in Revelations. The first death is the death-blow delivered to the world age by the explosion, resultant pollution and genetic damage of atomic energy, and the second death is the culmination of the last judgement in the time approaching the year 2000.

The transition from octave to octave in the time scale is like the "shock points" in life at conception, birth, the end of childhood and death. In the World Age every individual soul is present during the time of the last judgement, all potentially able to experience the trials which determine the difference between reincarnation into the next world age or transcendence to the right hand of God. It is important to understand the nature of the great confrontation in order to understand the transcendence of history and the way to liberation.

History and all women and men who have ever lived repeat the entire historical cycle. To the extent that one creates a clearly defined historical identity, one is obliged to return in each recurrent World Age to perform the particular role in the same manner, amidst the same conditions. The closer the historical individual comes to personal integration, the greater the freedom in choice for following lifetimes.

Paradoxically, the more public one's identity, the less freedom is available to the soul animating the identity. Politicians, movie stars, great thinkers and the famed remark about the apparent inevitability of their lives; they cannot do other than they must in life. While it seems to the mass of humanity that such lives are more desirable and freer, that notable people have the world as their oyster, the reality as experienced by such people is very different. There is a strange fatedness which fame brings which is more of a burden than a liberation. It is very interesting that the most famous individuals in history, those who have had the most profound influence upon the course of history, seem to be outside of or beyond historical reality. Individuals of whom this is true are Buddha, Lao Tze, Jesus Christ and, closer to our time, Shakespeare. They all "lived" in recorded historical times which should have located them, but there are controversies about their actual lives. The first three are all avatars, while the life and works of Shakespeare are definitely godlike. A linking factor to all three is a crystal clear understanding of beingness, a doctrine that there is life after death, and that eternal return is inevitable unless one transmits and identifies with the whole.

The Tibetan Buddhist Book of the Dead, the Bardo Thodol, is a guide for the forty-nine days after death, when the soul experiences states from the Clear Light to rebirth in the next womb of the next incarnation. The initial state of enlightenment should be recognized, but the soul typically passes through the state rapidly. Therefore, the first instruction to the soul is: "Thine own intellect, which is now voidness, yet not to be regarded as of the voidness of nothingness, but as being the intellect itself, unobstructed, shining, thrilling and blissful, is the very consciousness."[168] The void of the pure light is beyond individual and historic time. The soul loses its confining body and becomes one with the radiant godhead, as every human does upon physical death, and as the entire population at the moment of the end of history, as in the universal superorganism envisioned by Peter Russell, the Supermind of Sri Aurobindo or the Omega of Teilhard de Chardin. The recitation from the Bardo Thodol during the post-death state is an attempt to guide the soul to transcendence, resisting the temptation to be attracted to another womb, and its analogy, a particular historical time which compels the soul to exist again and take up a body. In order to transcend time and history, one must relinquish the craving to return to time and history.

The fifty years approaching the target year AD 2000 is a highly compacted version of the entire Time Scale in one-thousandth of the time, according to the same diminishing spiral. The World Age reached back 50,000 years, 5000 years, 500 years and 50 years, and divisions within the 50 year period are fifty years, five years, 0.5 years or six months, and 0.05 years or eighteen days. The two processes when shown adjacent to each other are as follows:

Table 6   The Last Judgement

AD 1950	(−50yrs)	0 Aries	Dec 1999	(−0.05yrs)
		REALIZATION		
AD 1500	(−500yrs)	0 Sagittarius	Jul 1999	(−0.5yrs)
		INDIVIDUALITY		
3000 BC	(−5000yrs)	0 Leo	Jan 1995	(−5yrs)
		MYTHOLOGY		
48000 BC	(−50000yrs)	0 Aries	Jan 1950	(−50yrs)

The events and developments which occur during the original manifestation of the World Age, together with the individuals who participate in them, recur with the object being to not be trapped in the historical process (maya), mistaking it for reality. The soul can easily mistakenly believe that its home is in the historical age rather than in the limitless realm of the spirit. Similarly, in the passage through the Bardo states the soul is tempted into various existences which at first appear attractive, but quickly lose their lustre, become gray and lifeless. The soul then descends into lower levels, or "hells" of existence. The collective mass of society does not understand the illusory nature of reality, is unaware of the concept of maya and is psychically overloaded merely existing. The Darwinian illusion of a linear continuation of preceding ages of history creates a temporal vortex into which a majority of souls are mechanically attracted. The attraction to past forms and patterns is very seductive, and the wandering soul tries to attach itself to a familiar past with which to reattach and reidentify. The same principle is active in ghosts, disembodied spirits which return to the scenes of their earth-life as phantoms. The tremendous renewal, after AD 1950, of Hinduism, Buddhism, fundamentalist Christianity, Islam, the worshipping of gurus and religious teachers support this view, and the obsession with the past in fashion, cinema, literature and every other field reflects the eternal return.

The overemphasis upon media is frighteningly similar to the lurid Bardo states. In a 1985 statistic, American children watch an average of 29 hours of TV weekly, including 250 acts of violence, not to mention the prevalence of "video nasties". By definition, media represent either (a) events which have already happened, (b) events happening somewhere else at the same time, or (c) cinematic fantasies which never have and never will happen. Participation is one-way because the time spent watching television, video-recorder or movie is passive, with no participation other than changing the channel or turning it off. Time spent on such activities is lost forever. The viewer is a captive of the media. The selection of objects and times is totally programmed. Illusion interpenetrates reality until it is impossible to discriminate between the two. Is the President of the US really an actor playing a role? The observer is bound into a time framework beyond individual control. Programs are chosen with the majority in mind, if you can call it mind.

A primary manifestation of the power of the past is the world of fashion, the structure of which is to identify with previous times by dressing suitably. Fashion has existed throughout history, but during the recapitulation time of fifty years, the cycles of fashion intensify, until they pass very rapidly and govern masses of people. Certain eras are represented by tastemakers as significant and great effort is made to copy every detail of appearance and affectation. Entire subcultures recreate a particular agreed-upon era, like the fifties, and every garment and gesture is copied faithfully, like a live period drama. The possibility of style reflecting continuing evolution is undermined and the orientation towards the past is total. Each fashion has its own compartment, and when outmoded in weeks or months disappears as rapidly as it appeared. Every transition must be totally embraced or one becomes unfashionable. The ability to consciously or unconsciously determine the next style allows tastemakers to dictate commercial directions to the public. Since 1950, nostalgia craze has swept the entire western world.

Involvement in the past overwhelms individualistic impulses. Previous times and places seem to be more vital, more real and easier to imitate, duplicate and document, as well as to understand. The ability to be present is lost and the automaton is born. Mass psychological reality has supplanted individual trends, and the follower and comformist are envied. People buy advertising on clothes, perfumes, cars and in many other products as a way of identifying their tastes. Consciousness ceases due to the great pressure to process the increasing flood of information and the senses are overloaded with input. The room becomes psychically stagnant and the mannikins stand around performing, all according to pattern and plan. The world is asleep.

Last Judgement of History

The time from 1950 until 2000 is a microcosm of the entire cycle of humanity and every person has an opportunity to experience harmonics of the periods of time in history when they were active, to relive collective development in individual life. (Table 6) It is a time of potential synthesis unavailable in the rest of history. Developmental phases are greatly compressed and history is repeated in a higher, denser harmonic. Developments evolved over immensely long eras are compacted into very short periods. Everything is compressed, including population, into one thousandth of the time. Developments happen ever more quickly, and more and more information is generated and transmitted. It is estimated that in the 1980's the average western person is exposed to as much information each day as an educated person was in a lifetime only one hundred years ago: quite a staggering statistic.

The higher octave of *Aries* from 1950 to 1972 evokes our primitive beginnings. Mass-transportation allowed many people to travel, echoing nomadic stages. Traditional values were abandoned, the increasing power of science and technology dehumanized life and led to Arian reactions epitomized by the "beat generation" which went on the road to leave the nihilism of civilization behind. The popularity of television encouraged the mindlessness and vicarious experience characteristic of modern life. The activities most prized by the post-war generation were shamanistic and primitive, such as the ecstasy of rock'n'roll, the rejection of bourgeois materialistic values, fragmented nonverbal communication and eventually, dropping out. The poetry was reactive, an emphatic free verse as spontaneous and emotional as shamanistic trance ravings.[168] Hippies grew long hair like Cro-magnon ancestors, returned to nature, moved in groups, cross-bred and were addicted to rhythmic, primitive drumming. The reaction against traditional religion was a return to celestial worship, and the practice of astrology was reborn. Young millions were converted instantly to revitalized ancient religions and cults revering Eastern gurus. The I Ching became a bible and born again Christians and Islamic fundamentalists emerged from American slums and the wilds of Africa. The increasing adherence to vegetarianism reflected early nomadic gatherers. At one level society degenerated and fell into the destructive Cold War split between the USA and Russia, while the undercurrent provided the roots for a regeneration.

The primal Aries time led in the more stable, settled and matriarchal *Taurus* time from 26,000 BC until 14,000 BC, announced by Venus figurines and Earth Mother cults. In the higher Taurus time from 1972 to 1984 the rebellious generation became more domesticated with the shift to health foods and the industries associated with organic revitalization, such as naturally grown grains, herbal medicines and drugs, a search for roots and a return to nature. The counter-trend in the outside world was the mechanization of farming, the scientific programming of livestock and plants, battery breeding and a large-scale shift of country populations into the cities and small towns. As farming machines eliminated the human element from agriculture, people all over the world were deprogrammed from knowing how it was done in the first place. The use of chemical fertilizers and hybrid plants and animals replaced human contact with huge agro-technological combines cultivating millions of acres and raising thousands of animals in mechanical conditions. The creation and rise of the Women's Movement emphasized the shift from left-brain linear logic to right-brain holistic thinking, natural childbirth and a return to organic ways of carrying and birthing children.

The *Gemini* time from 14,000 BC until 7000 BC parallels its higher octave from 1984 to 1991, and focuses on communication, language and a change in instincts. Communication is the primary focus of civilization after 1984, with computers and the media being central. Paradoxically, the literacy rate worldwide plummets down as population increases and "improved teaching methods" like phonetic spelling and New Math contribute to the loss of the basis of language and mathematics. Existing language degenerates through slang and misuse, amusingly called "Haigspeak" in honour of the US Secretary of State in the 80's who butchered language, evoking memories of the Tower of Babel. Computer technology not only puts millions of industrial labourers out of work, but the primary occupation in the world becomes information and its transmission. The countercurrent to the disinformation produced by computer logic and the decline of education is in the creation of a new language based upon Pythagorean mathematics, the new physics and cosmology, and the decoding of prehistoric monuments. A transformational and transcendent communication network as a countercurrent is a force for transforming the traditional world and knowledge. The Gemini time is tribal and diversifies into New Age business, government, ecology, information technology, politics, education, publishing, media and many others.

The higher *Cancer* time is from 1991 until 1994, during which time all beings are involved with the emotional reality. The breakdown of cellular family for the masses coincides with the reestablishment of a higher level of heart contact among those who remain awake. The change may occur through a transformation in psychotherapy, higher spiritual impulses or through the shock generated by the decline in order in the world.

The second octave, from *Leo* (January 1995) *to Scorpio* (July 1999), evokes the time from 3000 BC until AD 1500, and is highly compacted into less than five years, during which time the civilizations created in the World Age dissolve into a vague echo of feudal times, complete with world-threatening plagues which sweep humanity.

The third octave of completion, from *Sagittarius* (July 1999) *to Pisces* (12 December 1999), is the final breakdown of the World Age into its constituent parts, like the 500 years from the Renaissance compacted into six months.

The options confronting every individual soul approaching the end of the Twentieth Century derive from the historical process. The media explosion and the increased influence of cinema creates pictures of previous ages which have highly formative influences on the world. The first octave of development in history was instinctive and unconscious, and the higher octave judgement will see a majority of humanity returning to levels of consciousness similar to the dawn of history, through identification with primitive levels of consciousness. The mechanization of the masses was predicted by George Orwell in "1984" as a monolithic transcontinental government run by the media in total control. The actor-President of the US is an uncomfortable echo of Big Brother, especially in his media orientation and the revival of blind patriotism as a primary virtue. There was much discussion in 1984 about how the modern world is unlike that predicted by

Orwell, but the similarities are much more subtle and insidious. The burning of books and disinformation Orwell depicted is going on now through the dominance of computers and video, and the only way to transcend the downward trend is to understand the higher octave cultural and historical messages.

The world will not disappear, but existing structures must die before a renewed world can emerge. The dissolution of the outer forms of civilization and their re-integration from the beginning reflects the disintegration of all bodies and beings in both the micro- and macro-worlds.

Aware individuals attracted to particular historical trends, cultural ideas or religious belief systems must retain the integrity of soul in higher transpersonal or transcendent realms rather than identification with physical, emotional or mental constructs. The eastern concept of nonattachment to the result of one's actions is a natural law. The barrage of information in the fifty years of the last judgement tempts every soul to form attachments to an individual life, life in general or history itself – all represent the desire to reincarnate. All information must be decoded, processed, assimilated and passed through, but not allowed to capture the soul. Attachment to a particular time creates mechanicality, unconsciousness and the impossibility of liberation. In the blunt terms of Gurdjieff, sleep must be fought every step of the way. Awareness of the historical process and disidentification is the sole way to transcend it.

Everyone contains a spiritual and genetic memory of the entire process of the world age, which is perpetually reactivated during the astrological cycles to which all living organisms are exposed. One's primary historical roots are described in the birth horoscope, which is circuited every day by the rotation of the earth on its axis, every month by the moon, every year by the sun, and in the larger and longer cycles of the other planets. The positions of planets in the birth horoscope define predispositions toward particular times in history, genetic characteristics and cosmic karmic actions which create the individuality of each being. During the fifty-year compacted death moment, the soul experiences the whole World Age and will be attracted and attached to those time periods of most powerful identification. The mechanism is easy to identify: affinities with artifacts, books, poetry, knowledge, religion, ideas and physical locations are all indicators of formative influences. The California follower of the Krishna cults in the 1960's has a Hindu root in the Cancer time in history, while the

Tibetan Buddhist is locked into the late Libra or early Scorpio time in history. The wanderer, the farmer, the religious fanatic, the media freak, the warrior, the magician and the auto mechanic all unconsciously reverberate to their times of origin, recreate such times in their lives, and signal others by assuming the trappings of their past lives, in order to relive the previous times when they were "home". Everyone is affected by a succession of influences and attractions, sometimes becoming bonded to a particular time and place and its attendant influences, while others carry a hodge-podge of historical influences which vie for attention.

Ken Wilber represents the historical process in an abstract form as the Complete Life Cycle in Fig. 32. The outward arc of

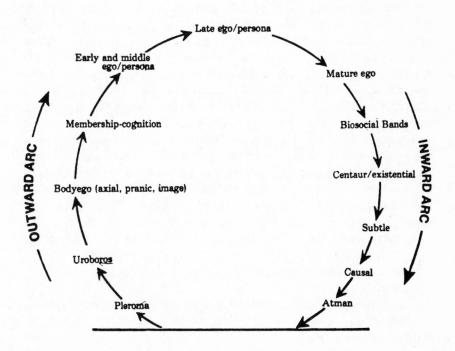

Fig. 32: The Complete Life Cycle
Ken Wilber divides the complete life into an Outward Arc from subconsciousness to self-consciousness and an Inward Arc of the return from self-consciousness to superconsciousness. These halves correspond to the stages of the Time Scale from Aries to Libra and Libra back to Aries. *(Wilber, The Atman Project)*

the first six stages is the battle to break free from subconsciousness by the hero, leading to self-consciousness and individuality. The inward arc is a return from self-consciousness to superconsciousness, the path of eternity beyond the path of time. The cycle of history is the developmental cycle of consciousness.

Zen Buddhism is based on the principle of regaining the purity of the Self through not letting the senses or feelings obscure the primal state. If the Self is understood as a crystal ball, the process of wiping the surface clean is superficial, compared to procedures which induce the original clean state of the crystal. The true state in astrology is the centre of the horoscope, the centre of the Self, which includes the entire periphery as well. The periphery is the residence of the personality, ego, senses, environment and other qualities, in short, the place wherefrom beingness manifests. Beingness arises at conception and grows and changes and increases in force until the periphery dominates the centre. Individual nature accepts these qualities as the boundary of the Self, rather than the Self itself. The periphery is the samsara round of birth, sickness and death. Living through and experiencing life, when understood in the context of the Self, leads to the realization that the world and its qualities are the way the world is, but are not the world. Once one dies to the world of illusion, if even for a second, the higher Self awakens forever, and brings a recognition that the illusory nature of the universe and life leads to eternal repetition of identification and involvement. Every life is merely a variant of the Buddhic Self. The collective and individual unconsciousness is the source of all human and natural qualities, but every being interprets them from an individual viewpoint. True individuality through individuation is seeing the flow of reality rather than being absorbed in one or the other part of the process. Freedom is absorption in the Self, the centre.

The techniques for determining your previous incarnations in the world age are given in detail in the following chapter on reincarnation.

★ Chapter Six ★
★ The Universal Time Scale ★

Lifetimes proportional to complexity. The fifty million year Age of Mammals. Aries through Pisces. The appearance of Neanderthal and Cromagnon. The fifty billion year Era of Creation. Our gyroscopic context. The past and future of the Milky Way. Into the microcosm. The Cellular World. The Molecular World. The Atomic World. The Subatomic World. History and the Eightfold Path. The spiral of time and universal process. Schopenhauer and the whole world. True relativity. The end and the beginning of time. Spirit and black holes. The Faustian anti-universe.

The Time Scale of humanity has two phases of development: the *World Age* of 50,000 years and the *Last Judgement* of 50 years, the panoramic memory of the historical world age. The ratio of 50,000:50 is the same as the ratio between the human lifetime of 1000 lunar months (77 years) and the one lunar month of the ovum. These are only two octaves out of the total of eight which grade the universe from the subatomic world to the duration of the universe. The logarithmic mathematics governs throughout.

$$\frac{\text{Ovum lifetime}}{\text{Human lifetime}} = \frac{\text{Last Judgement}}{\text{World Age}} = \frac{1}{1000}$$

Darwinians understand humanity as the apex of evolution, but The Divine Plot restores humanity to the centre of the scale of lifetimes in the universe. The short duration of human history is like the narrow spectrum of visible light in the electromagnetic scale. Carl Sagan used the image that if all creation were compacted into one year, the existence of humanity would begin at 22:30 pm on the 31st of December.[169] The true position of humanity is defined relative to scales shorter and longer than the World Age. The whole range of scales within which humanity exists is the Universal Time Scale.

The ratio of octave to octave of 1:10 and the compaction throughout a three-octave world age of 1:1000 are the ratios which govern the Universal Time Scale. The human life represents the enfoldment of the universe in space and time, as a metaphor and mathematically. The same ratios hold true at every level from the shortest unit of time, the lifetime of a subatomic particle, to the longest unit of time, the lifetime of the universe, and there is resonance from level to level. The range of the scale defines the universe within which humanity is embedded and which it in turn reflects.

Every cosmos has natural access to three levels of awareness or temporal dimensions above and below it in the cosmic scheme, and the possibility of extending perception beyond, as in Collin's table of cosmoses in Chapter Three. Each being has basic consciousness of its own life, a superconscious level above it (a shorter temporal dimension) and an unconscious level below it (a longer temporal dimension). Jung perceptively stated, ''Whereas we think in terms of years, the unconscious thinks and behaves in terms of thousands of years''.[170] Our unconscious may be equated to the World Age, as our spiritual dimension may be equated to the molecular world.

Table 7 shows *The Universal Time Scale* complete with its eight octaves. The fifty thousand-year World Age of humanity is shown adjacent to the fifty-year Last Judgement. The *Age of Mammals* is one thousand times longer than a World Age, a duration of fifty million years, graded by the same twelve astrological-developmental stages, in the same proportions.

Table 7   The Universal Time Scale

The Universal Time Scale shows all eight scales from the longest, the Big Bang, to the shortest, the Subatomic world — four in the macrocosm and four in the microcosm. Each scale is one thousand times longer than the scale to its left and one-thousandth the scale to its right.

The Macrocosm

Sign	Octave IV — Last Judgement	Octave III — The World Age	Octave II — Age of Mammals	Octave I — Era of Creation	Sign
Pis	Dec 1999 Trial by Fire	1950 Atomic Bomb	50,000 Multiple pigmentation; 75 Primate Stock	50,000,000 Saurian Extinction; 70 Primate Stock	Pis
Aqu	Nov 1999	1910 The Great Wars; Relativity	90,000 90 Protomodern Humans; 120 Neanderthalers	90,000,000 90 Winged Reptiles; 120 Flowering Planets	Aqu
Cap	Nov 1999	1840 Age of Nationalism; Telegraph	160,000 160 Toolmakers; 200 Brain increase	160,000,000 170 Birds; 235 Dinosaurs	Cap
Sag	Sep 1999	1720 Industrial Revolution; Electricity; Renaissance	280,000 250 Archaic Homo Sapiens; 450 Pithecanthropus	280,000,000 280 Insects; 400 Land Vertebrates	Sag
Sco	Jul 1999 Trial by Pestilence	1500 The Black Death; The Middle Ages	500,000 Hominid Transition; 900 Peking Man	500,000,000 Swimming Vertebrates; 600 Mollusks	Sco
Lib	Feb 1999	1100 Cathedrals; The Dark Ages	900,000 1.5 Homo Habilis extinct; 1.6 Homo Erectus	900,000,000 1 Sexual Repro; 1.3 Supercontinents	Lib
Vir	Jun 1998	AD400 Fall of Rome; Classical Age	1,600,000 2.5 Stone tools; 3.0 Ice Ages begin	1,600,000,000 1.6 Protoanimals; 3.1 Bacteria/Algae	Vir
Leo	Mar 1997	800BC Greece and Rome; Kingly Civilization	2,800,000 3.7 Homo Habilis	2,800,000,000 3.5 Genetic Code; 4.55 Earth	Leo
Can	Jan 1995 Trial by Water	3000 The Great Flood; Neolithic Age	5,000,000 Manlike Apes; 6 Australopithecus	5,000,000,000 The Solar System; Tidal Universe	Can
Gem	Feb 1991	7000 Cities; Tribal Societies	9,000,000 10 Ramapithecus; 14 Hominids	9,000,000,000 Symmetry-Duality	Gem
Tau	Mar 1984 Computer Language; Return to Nature	14000 Writing; Earth Mother Cults	16,000,000 16 Volcanic activity; 20 Proconsul	16,000,000,000 Form-matter	Tau
Ari	Nov 1971 Womens Liberation; Alternative Culture; Jan 1950 Hydrogen Bomb	26000 Painting and Sculpture; Celestial Shamans; 48000 Consciousness	28,000,000 25 Mountain chains; Mammal upsurge; 50,000,000 Mammals	28,000,000,000 Existence; 50,000,000,000 The Big Bang	Ari
	50 years	50,000 years	50 million years	50 billion years	

The Microcosm

	Octave V Cellular World	Octave VI Molecular World	Octave VII Atomic World	Octave VIII Subatomic World	
Pis	.00005y = 26.25m Bacterium Fission	1.575s One Breath	1.6×10^{-4}s One Millisecond	1.6×10^{-7}s One Billisecond Low Frequency Radiation	Pis
	.0005y = 4h32m	15.7s Day of Blood Cell 18s Life of Molecule	1.6×10^{-3}s Electron Life	1.6×10^{-6}s Hadronic Era	
	.005y = 1.82d Small Cells Blood Cell One Week	2.625m	1.6×10^{-2}s One Perception 1s Pulsar Lepton Era	1.6×10^{-5}s Light Photons	
Ari	0.5y = 18.2d	26.25m	1.6×10^{-1}s	1.6×10^{-4}s	Ari
	18.2 days	26 minutes	1.6 seconds	1.6×10^{-4} seconds	

The Age of Mammals

About the time when the last dinosaurs became extinct, the Age of Mammals who were to replace them as the primary species began in the Eocene Era. While the geological and cosmological reasons for the extinction of the dinosaurs is still under dispute, it is usually recognized that a radical change in the earth's climate about 50my (million years) ago is the primary cause, either through a shift in the earth's axis, collisions with comets or asteroids, or the effects of Nemesis. Astronomers are currently studying the "Nemesis" theory which postulates a twin star to the sun which has eradicated most life on earth on a regular cycle of 25 million years.[171] The modern land masses had just been formed, and the great mountain chains had not yet been pushed up through the damp marshy swamps of the saurian era. The splitting of the continental plates cooled the temperature and lowered sea level. The climate became drier, great plains were created and mammals and birds became dominant, replacing the saurians. The vegetation was tropical and luxurious, and smaller plants had just begun to evolve into trees, providing a habitat for the first protoprimates.

The Age of Mammals is divided into three developmental octaves like the World Age, and the growth of mammals parallels the developmental levels of humanity during a World Age, correlating with the sequence of twelve signs.

In *Aries* (−50 to −28my) mammals, birds and the protoprimates came into dominance parallel with the attainment of consciousness for humanity. Marsupials and archaic carnivores from the previous era evolved into modern predators. Hoofed mammals became dominant, including sheep, the totem animal of Aries, as large as rhinos. In addition, whales, rodents and hoofed animals, including dog-sized horses, proliferated. The continental plates then separated into continents, threw up the Alps and Rockies, and changed the movement of the sea which progressively lowered the temperature.

In *Taurus* (−28 to −16my) climatic changes killed the older mammals which were replaced by giant hoofed animals, dogs and rhinos, as well as pigs and bears. The Aegyptopithecus (−28my), still both monkey and ape, transformed into the more mobile Proconsul and Dryopithecus (−20my). Softer vegetation, flowers and plains grasses fed an inundation of grazing mammals, the bovoid ancestors of modern sheep and cattle (Taurus the Bull?).

Throughout *Gemini* (−16my to −9my) the earth suffered a succession of volcanoes and earthquakes, leading to radical oscillations in temperature. Ramapithecus, apes with man-like teeth, were forerunners of orang-utans and the proliferation of grazing animals, birds and other smaller creatures continued.

In *Cancer* (−9my to −5my) the forests receded, the plains were criss-crossed by the great rivers and the milk-producing mammals were generated. The anthropologist Richard Leakey identified a "fossil gap" between −8 and −4my, which is resonant to the Great Flood in the World Age. At both times extraneous species were made extinct by climatic changes and the surviving species contained vestigal qualities of those they superseded, as in the myth of Noah's Ark. In Hebrew Kaballa the Ark, understood as the body of Noah, was the vessel which contained pairs (chromosomes?) of all known species.

In *Leo* (−5my to 2.8my) great man-like apes such as Australopithecus Africanus were disinherited from their three kingdoms by the recession of the huge forest areas which covered central Africa and Asia, creating great plains. Environmentally-caused individuation created three branches − gorillas, apemen and chimpanzees. These early primates differentiated themselves by attempting to break the bondage of tree-life and gorillas lived in dense forest, the monkeys in mor eopen forest and the manlike apes at the forest edge near the plains. The higher primates walked upright, became carnivorous and learned to use tools to protect themselves as the forest gradually began to vanish before them. Early horses and cats (Leo the Lion?) were beginning to appear, as did very quick and dangerous giant cheetahs. By about −3my a land bridge was created between North and South America, leading to the destruction of many of the species entrenched in South America.

In *Virgo* (−2.8my to −1.6my) ice ages generated noticeable cold and the first small stone tools were made by Australopithecus Robustus, and the decrease in rainfall allowed the development of the first true human, Homo Habilis the tool-maker. They had large brains and as their diet consisted of a range of scavenged meat and collected plants, their tools were primarily for cutting and cleaning flesh. Homo Habilis was the first species to form family groups, exchange food and specialise to increase survival possibilities. They gathered plants and hunted small animals, but had to be very careful of the dangerous cats which prowled the savannah.

In *Libra* (−1.6my to −900,000 years) a more sophisticated and stronger alternative species appeared. Homo Erectus were more hunters than hunter-gatherers at the start of the Pleistocene Era, and a time of rapid proliferation ensued. The two brain halves began to affect the handedness of early humans, and the polarities of hunter-gatherer and of male-female. A quantum jump was made by the more intelligent, faster and more mobile Homo Erectus. They were nomadic, used fire and moved in groups for a million years.

In *Scorpio* (900,000 to 500,000 years ago) were many catastrophes, possibly caused by a shift of the earth's axis. Human traces show cannibalism and increased proficiency at killing the many creatures available. Many of the animals which are common features of Chinese astrology, such as the rat, the wolf and the domestic dog, came into being.

In *Sagittarius* (−500,000 years to −280,000 years) a change corresponding to the self-realization of AD 1500 was the drastic shift from the manlike ape Homo Erectus to the more developed Pithecanthropus or Peking Man of 500,000 years ago. This earliest version of Homo Sapiens is characterised by the matriarchal transmission of heredity and starts an extensive period of little outward change. They travelled in bands, used a variety of weapons and harnessed the power of fire, stolen from forest fires or places struck by lightning and carried while wandering as hot coals, but they were unable to start the miraculous fire themselves. Fire was particularly useful in the Ice Ages where warmth and dominion in the caves inhabited by cave lions and bears was necessary for survival. The final mammalian cycle was the development of the homo sapiens who were forced to contend with the inclement Ice Ages.

In *Capricorn* 280,000 years ago the shift to technical archaic homo sapiens was accomplished. The final creation of modern man in an elongated "gestation" coincided with the introduction of ego-consciousness at zero degrees Capricorn in the World Age. Human bone structure became more subtle and human, and although still beetle-browed and very clumsy, the brain capacity increased rapidly to modern size. The animals we know today were domesticated, including the goat, the totem animal of Capricorn.

The primary shift in the *Aquarius* time beginning 160,000 years ago was the development of more sophisticated flint weapons to attack and eat the woolly mammoths on the plains of Europe and Asia as they migrated yearly to avoid the glacial movements. The Neanderthals inhabited Europe and Asia, had even larger brains than modern humans and developed their own culture. The primary leap in evolution was internal – the development of higher awareness of life which was absent before.

In *Pisces* from 90,000 to 50,000 years ago, development led to Tanzanian man with a form similar to modern humanity, who had no apparent evolutionary prototype but just appeared. They were much less efficient or civilised than even the Neanderthalers, who remained the most numerous species. The Neanderthalers used herbal medicines, painted their bodies and buried their totem animals and their dead, advancing almost to the fringe of civilization. They worshipped the cave bears and lions with whom they were forced to compete for caves, survived the harsh climate and created a culture of sorts.

At the end of the Age of Mammals the Neanderthalers had to adapt or perish after the appearance of Cro-magnon Man, just as the individuals at the end of the world age must transcend consciousness or be imprisoned in the repetition of another world age cycle. Beings of superior consciousness appear at the end of a world age as miraculously as the Cro-magnons appeared about 50,000 years ago. Cro-magnons were taller, had a larger brain capacity, were highly intelligent and very well organised. Over a period of about 15,000 years, they completely wiped out the Neanderthaler. Their great weapon was speech, and the rise of our World Age ensued. At the borderline of the Age of Mammals and the beginning of the World Age of humanity, the apes which did not make the transition gradually regressed until they formed the genera of apes which we know today, or hid as the Yeti or Abominable Snowman in Himalayan reaches.

During one cycle of mammals, humanity could go through one thousand cycles of creation, development and extinction. The World Age of humanity is a death memory for the Age of Mammals which passes by in an instant and carries a dreamlike quality. Human beings have a discrete lifetime and an individuality, but in the animal kingdom species reflect each other from generation to generation. The cows or sheep in the fields are virtually the same creatures which existed in vast numbers before humanity.

It is particularly interesting that the succession of totem animals and images of the twelve astrological signs are very accurately represented in the Age of Mammals, encoded in our memory and genetic code.

The Age of Creation

The *Age of Creation*, one thousand times longer than the Age of Mammals and one million times longer than the World Age, is fifty billion years in duration, (Last Judgement 50 years, World Age 50,000 years, Mammals 50,000,000 years and Creation 50,000,000,000 years) which extends back to the origin of the universe. (Table 7) the Big Bang is reciprocal to the creation of mammals after a temperature rise made the dinosaurs extinct, the creation of humanity after the explosion of the first Atomic Bombs and the greenhouse effect of fossil fuels. All creations involve increases in temperature and are related to the fire sign Aries. Each octave begins as a result of the end of the previous octave, and fits in with the idea that the Big Bang which created our universe was the death of a previous imploded universe.

It is fascinating that the earliest stages in the creation of the universe after the Big Bang closely parallel the first four zodiac signs.

Aries (−50 to −28by) is pure existence and the dissipation of enormous energy spewing outwards at close to the speed of light, which occurs in an instant but is followed by billions of years of steady state.

In *Taurus* (−28 to −16by) the world of form is created from the pure energy and the particulate nature of the universe is determined.

In *Gemini* (−16 to −9by) the universe is symmetrical, galaxies are formed and the intrinsic dualistic nature of the world comes into being.

In *Cancer* (−9 to −5by) the universe is tidal as galaxy formation creates a home for what later became planetary systems.

In *Leo* (−5 to −2.8by) the creation of the Sun and Solar System in the Age of Creation coincides with the individuation of manlike apes one octave higher and human individuality and self-consciousness two octaves higher in 3000 BC. Beginning with the formation of earth 4.55 billion years ago, and throughout the Leo time of 2.2 billion years, the earth was molten and then liquid, covered by seas. Genetic code was created signalling the beginning of life about 3.5 billion years ago and the earliest microfossils of primary life forms date back to this time.

In *Virgo* (−2.8 to −1.6by) the primary life form diversified to produce ocean-breeding blue-green algae (−3.1by), filament algae −2.7by, nuclear cells in −1.7by and then fungi in the

Hypozoic era.

In *Libra* (– 1.6by to 900my) a supercontinent was formed by – 1.3by and one billion years ago the Proterozoic Era began, leading to the first multi-celled beings recorded as fossils.

In *Scorpio* (– 900 to – 500my) an acceleration in the diversity of the primitive life forms was the advent of sexed life and sexual reproduction, a primary separation and division from the previously unified and undifferentiated life. This was paralleled by the breaking apart of the continental plates in the beginning of the Cambrian Era about 600 million years ago, also the time of the first mollusks.

The last octave of the Creation Era began 500 million years ago in *Sagittarius* (– 500 to – 280my) with a rapid proliferation of life all over earth, coinciding with the settling of the continents, and a shift of life forms from the sea onto dry land. Shellfish (– 50my), fish (– 450my) and corals (– 450my) populated the seas and led to the vascular land plants – 400my ago. Very quickly the land was filled with insects (– 395my), seed producing plants created the forests (– 380my) and amphibious creatures (– 350mh) bridged water and land.

The undisputed kings of *Capricorn* (– 280 to – 160my) were the reptiles which developed from shelled sea creatures and proceeded to dominate the land, ruling the primeval swamp by their number and size. Previously dominant life forms declined in their favour, and a positive outgrowth of the rapid changes was the first primitive mammals, which were very small, herbivorous creatures in about – 22my. The supercontinent Pangea broke apart, providing separate areas for development all over the earth. It is particularly interesting that the primary coal deposits were made at this time, exactly two octaves before the industrial revolution in the later Capricornian time in the World Age when they were first used on a massive scale.

In the Mesozoic era of *Aquarius* (– 160 to – 90my) birds became the bearers of the great evolutionary leap and nature proliferated in the shadow of the dinosaurs, beautifying the landscape with flowering plants (– 140 to – 120my).

In the final *Pisces* age (– 90my to – 50my) was the destruction of the dinosaurs, probably brought about by the decrease in temperature of the earth, caused by collision with asteroids or comets, or the passage of Nemesis, the twin star to earth. The decline of the dinosaurs took place from – 65 to – 50my, coinciding with the separation off from the mammals proper the first hint of primate stock in about – 70my. Then, about 55 million years ago the cold began and wiped the dinosaurs off of the face of the earth, leaving their inheritance in the reptilian creatures and closely related birds, still alive today.

In the context of the Universal Time Scale, each life form developed according to a natural and essential pattern, following one another in evolution to complete the overall earth-organism, just as atoms from which inner electrons have been blasted away first jump inwardly to complete the structure, creating intermediary elements along the way. Life is the organism continously changing, but always containing the essential unity, whatever the outer form.

Timing the Time Scale

Not only is it impossible for things to be other than they are, it is even impossible that the initial situation of the universe could have been other than what it was. No matter what we are doing at a given moment, it is the only thing that was ever possible for us to be doing at that moment.[172]

Zukav, The Dancing Wu Li Masters

Dating developmental stages of a Universal Time Scale is very contentious. The same logarithmic ratios govern in the World Age, the life of the individual human being and in the Age of Mammals and Creation. Among scientists there is great deviation in the dates attributed to early events in the age of the universe, although the age of the solar system and the earth are quite universally accepted to be between 4.55 and 5 billion years. The creation dates of the various life forms which populate earth are in great question, particularly by specialists. In the twelve years that the author has researched The Divine Plot the accepted age of the universe has increased from seven to almost fifteen billion years, an increase of more than 200%. The important factor is therefore not the exact times at which developments occurred, but the ratios inherent in the process. The overall view is more important and illuminating than the details from which the overview is created.

Parallels exist across the horizontal file of the Universal Time Scale. Movement from bottom to top in each file is linear development, like Darwinian evolution, punctuated by the shock points from octave to octave and the great leaps at the beginning of each three-octave scale. But there are other more powerful, if less obvious, organisational mechanisms at work in the creation and maintenance of life in the universe. Resonance along the horizontal file is the way in which information is transmitted throughout the development of life on earth.

Scientists, with the exception of Sheldrake, ignore inter-scale resonance in favour of linear evolution, but it is a very important organising principle of existence. Similarities of sign manifestations in higher or lower octaves are in the form of the life, in the same way that the many people with the sun-sign Leo have striking inner similarities but appear different. Vertical movement in the Universal Time Scale diagram is physical lineage, while horizontal movement is morpho-genetic, governed by other than physical transmission.

The complete picture describes all life forms as integral parts of octaves and ages, yet each part is a whole. A being composed of billions of separate molecules is still an individual. Each era in the historical development of the universe is whole in itself, but is populated by beings of a much shorter lifespans, and leads to eras of much longer duration. Each life form performs an essential role in the whole as a stage in the development of consciousness and spiritual impulse.

The earliest stages of creation remain in the continuous formation and annihilation of galaxies in deep space. Galaxies created at the same time as the Milky Way move away from each other at close to the speed of light. All energy and matter in the universe is expanding at an unimaginable speed, yet since all parts are expanding at similar rates, the relative position of everything remains close to being the same as it must have been just after creation. Distances away from earth are measured by the length of the spectrum of light reaching us. The greater the red shift, the further away and the older the galaxy. It is clear that galaxies are differentiated primarly by their apparent size and angle of rotation, which could be the only difference between the microcosmic and macrocosmic worlds.

Rodney Collin investigated the nature of galactic perception in *"The Theory of Celestial Influence"*. (Fig. 33) The zodiac belt of constellations lies in the plane of the ecliptic, at an angle of 23½ degrees to the plane of the equator, and is used as a reference circle to measure the cycles of earth. The Milky Way galaxy of which the solar system is a part is tilted at an angle of 55 degrees to the plane of the zodiacal ecliptic. The sun orbits around its sun, the star Sirius, the planet the Egyptians worshipped as the supreme deity and around which they oriented their yearly calendar. Sirius orbits around the galactic centre, presently at 26 degrees of Sagittarius. The earth therefore orbits around the sun, which orbits around Sirius, which orbits around the galactic centre in a period of 250,000,000 years. There is a

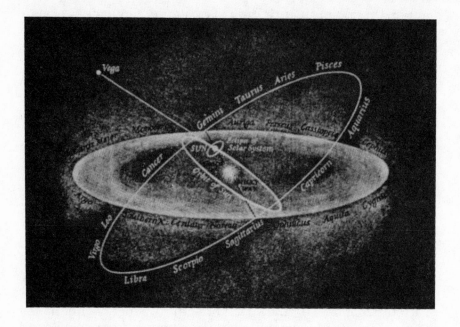

Fig. 33: Solar System in Context
The earth orbits around the sun, which orbits round the centre of the
Milky Way Galaxy in an estimated 250 million years. The zodiacal
constellations are in the ecliptic plane of the Solar System, which is
inclined to the plane of the galaxy. The entire mechanism is every
much like a gyroscope. *(Collin, Theory of Celestial Influence)*

 yroscopic interaction between all these systems of which earth
is a part, just like the multitude of orientations which exist
among the various atoms, molecules and cells of which we are
made. The zodiacal belt is the present of earth, but to look above
the ecliptic, towards the north pole star, is looking into the
future where earth is going, while looking towards the south
pole is looking towards the past where earth has already gone.
    The plane of the ecliptic intersects the plane of the Milky Way
in the signs Gemini and Sagittarius, which to Collin is the
"cross-section of the ship intersecting the surface of the sea".[172]
(Fig. 34) Looking towards Sagittarius is looking towards the
centre of the galaxy, and looking towards Gemini is looking
away from the galactic centre. The nearer Gemini edge is 10,000

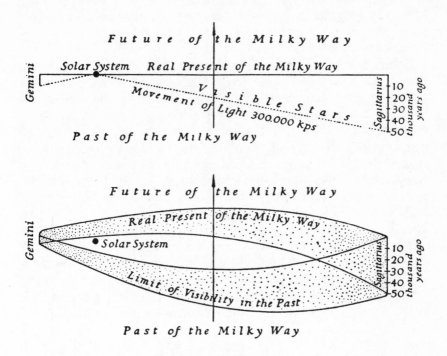

Fig. 34: Milky Way Cross-section
The present of the Milky Way is the plane of its long axis as the galaxy hurtles through space and time. Light received from the direction of Sagittarius takes 50,000 years to reach earth, therefore looking towards Sagittarius is looking into the past. (*Collin, Theory of Celestial Influence*)

light years away and the farther Sagittarius edge is 50,000 light years away. The distance away of these stars is reflected in the vast period of time it takes light to reach earth from their positions. It takes light 60,000 years to cross the Milky Way. The stars in Gemini are in the positions they occupied 10,000 years ago, while the stars in Sagittarius are where they were 50,000 years ago, at the time when humanity became conscious. Looking into space we see the past and future of the Milky Way. Perception of the universe is limited by the speed of light, and Collin suggested that there must be an energy, with which humanity has not yet become acquainted, which is far faster than light.[173]

As the sun is the source of energy for earth, to face Sagittarius is to align with the centre and source of creative energy of the Milky Way galaxy. In this perspective, the zodiacal signs measure our position relative to the galactic centre at various times of the year.

Collin investigated and catalogued the relations between many cosmoses at levels from that of the Electron to the Absolute, and determined that the relationship between each level of consciousness or development in the universe is exponential, as in the Universal Time Scale. The fact the duration of each age is the cube of its next lower age, as is the case in the UTS, implies the "introduction of plan, purpose and possibility."[174] All levels of organisation — cell, human body, nature, earth, solar system and milky way — are complete in themselves, yet part of the whole. (See Table 1 in Chapter Three) All systems contain the pattern and possibilities of the whole. God created humanity in his own image, a divine image of the universe. The Divine Plot of the Universal Time Scale is an image of humanity and its universe, all related mathematically. Humanity occupies a relative position in the middle of the scale of existences in the universe.

The Microcosm

Four successively longer phases of the universe in the macrocosm have been described:

IV	The 50-year cycle of	The Last Judgement
III	The 50,000-year cycle of	The World Age of Humanity
II	The 50,000,000-year cycle of	The Age of Mammals
I	The 50,000,000,000-year cycle of	The Era of Creation

The mathematical organization of each cycle reflects that of the others, and each cycle is one-thousandth of the previous cycle and one thousand times longer than the following cycle. The ratio 1:1000 describes the Last Judgement or panoramic memory of every cycle in the time scale. The World Age of Humanity is merely an instant within the Age of Mammals, and mammals observe quietly the coming and going of a thousand historical world ages in each developmental stage. Likewise, relative to the Era of Creation, the Age of Mammals represents a recapitulation of the earliest cycle encapsulated within the mammals. It is as though the cells of the body were conscious of the whole.

Each successive cycle is shorter by a factor of one thousand, and the density increases as the number of life-forms is constant. Cycles become shorter and the apparent fullness of life is greater, but the overall reality of each octave is constant. The number of souls remains the same.

The macrocosm is the world of the cosmos, but there are realms of the microcosm still to be mapped. The fifty-year cycle of the Last Judgement approximates an average human lifetime throughout an entire world age, and smaller cycles represent realms which may be encompassed within a life. The macrocosm and the microcosm reflect each other, both possessing four development cycles. (Table 7) Microcosmic cycles contain as many events as longer cycles, but happen rapidly in what is the realm of particle physics.

Cycle V, *The Cellular World*, extends from 18.26 days (0.05 year) to 26.2975 minutes (0.00005 year). In the first octave is one week, the approximate life time of a human blood cell, and three days, the life time of small cells in the human body. Towards the end of the cycle is the reproductive cycle of bacterium fission.

Cycle VI, *The Molecular World*, extends from 26.2975 minutes to 1.58 seconds (five ten thousandths of a year), which is one breath. In the midst of the cycle is one minute and molecular cycle of 18 seconds.

Cycle VII, *The Atomic World*, extends from 1.58 seconds to 1.58 x 10^{-4} seconds, or one milli-second. In the beginning of the cycle is one second, the cycle of the pulsation of a pulsar, and entrance into the realm of subatomic particles. Movement into the infinitely small echoes the infinitely large as the structure of the atomic level of organization reflects the macroscale of solar systems. At the equivalent of the Leo time of the cycle is the duration of one perception of about 1/4th of a second, and at 1/1500th of a second is the duration of a quantum of an electron, at the equivalent of the Sagittarius time.

Cycle VIII, *The Subatomic World*, extends from 1.58 x 10^{-4} seconds to 1.58 x 10^{-7} seconds (one millionth of a second), which is the fastest perceptual scale, where everything breaks down into pure energy. The visible universe is created, and lifetimes shorter than those in the cycle are in the realm of transitory subatomic particles and high frequency sound, areas in the electro-magnetic spectrum which are beyond human comprehension. In the Hadronic Era, 10^{-7} seconds after the Big Bang, the universe is a seething mass of particles and antiparticles formed from photons, within which proton-antiproton pairs annihilate each other. The dissolution into pure energy is reflected at microcosmic and macrocosmic levels.

After Cycle VIII are the processes of creation which overlap into the macrocosmic world.

The Universal Time Scale has eight stages of development from the lifetime of the universe to the lifetime of atoms, the longest and shortest wavelengths which bind the world. Once again, each cycle is one thousandth of its predecessor and one thousand times longer than its successor.

The eight stages of the Universal Time Scale inescapably parallel the Eightfold Path of Buddhism. The intention of Buddhism is to attain *"nirvana"* or Buddhahood, which is awakening, but also the disappearance of being from the eternal round of incarnations, an escape into the immeasurable and infinite. There actually is no attainment because it cannot be desired and nothing is acquired. Nirvana can only arise spontaneously when the impossibility of grasping has been perceived. Buddha is neither above nor below the round, but has transcended all such distinctions. The Eightfold Path describes Buddhic "dharma" − the method by which futility is ended. The first four are thoughts and the second four are actions. The process is the key to liberation from the universe described in the Universal Time Scale.

The Spiral of Time

The Universal Time Scale can be represented in two ways, each clarifying a different mechanism. One is as a spiral cylinder through time and the other is as a series of spirals seen end-on.

The UTS can be shown as a cylinder with the Big Bang at the bottom and the lifetime of the atom at the top. (Fig. 35) Within each stage is movement along the cylinder and around the circle, as the whole UTS recurs eternally. Once it manifests, it can only repeat its development in time in infinite permutations, as there is no other way for it to manifest. Each stage repeats and the entire process also repeats.

The UTS describes repetitive creation and the manifestation of form in the world of action and the microworld where only

Fig. 35: Universal Time Scale Cylinder
The UTS represented as a cylinder, with creation at the bottom and the micro-world at the top. Order decreases and information increases as the spiral ascends. The unit of one day is at the exact centre between macrocosm and microcosm, and past and future.

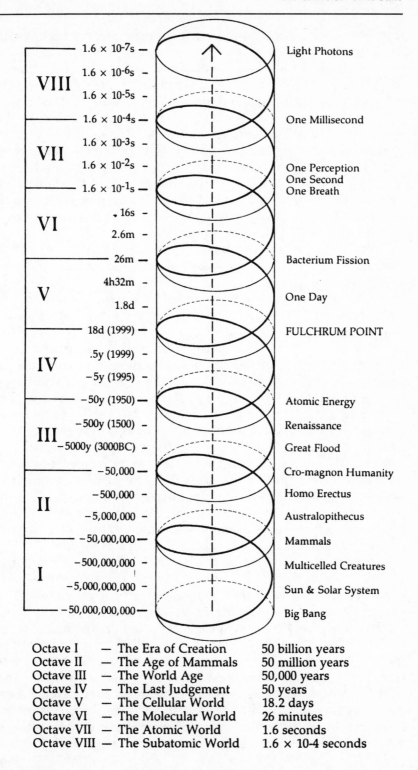

	$1.6 \times 10^{-7}s$	Light Photons
VIII	$1.6 \times 10^{-6}s$	
	$1.6 \times 10^{-5}s$	
	$1.6 \times 10^{-4}s$	One Millisecond
VII	$1.6 \times 10^{-3}s$	
	$1.6 \times 10^{-2}s$	One Perception
	$1.6 \times 10^{-1}s$	One Second / One Breath
VI	$.16s$	
	$2.6m$	
	$26m$	Bacterium Fission
V	$4h32m$	
	$1.8d$	One Day
	$18d$ (1999)	FULCHRUM POINT
IV	$.5y$ (1999)	
	$-5y$ (1995)	
	$-50y$ (1950)	Atomic Energy
III	$-500y$ (1500)	Renaissance
	$-5000y$ (3000BC)	Great Flood
	$-50,000$	Cro-magnon Humanity
II	$-500,000$	Homo Erectus
	$-5,000,000$	Australopithecus
	$-50,000,000$	Mammals
I	$-500,000,000$	Multicelled Creatures
	$-5,000,000,000$	Sun & Solar System
	$-50,000,000,000$	Big Bang

Octave I	— The Era of Creation	50 billion years
Octave II	— The Age of Mammals	50 million years
Octave III	— The World Age	50,000 years
Octave IV	— The Last Judgement	50 years
Octave V	— The Cellular World	18.2 days
Octave VI	— The Molecular World	26 minutes
Octave VII	— The Atomic World	1.6 seconds
Octave VIII	— The Subatomic World	1.6×10^{-4} seconds

thoughts exist – each contains four stages. The organization of the whole is repeated within each component cycle, reflected in the workings of the natural world at every level of perception. Movement from the macrocosmic Era of Creation in the past towards the microcosmic Subatomic World is accompanied by a decrease in order. Information is stored and recorded in the temporal process by "entropy", the translation of information into events. The universe continuously exchanges energy, in the form of information, for existence, accompanied by a decrease in order, which is why subatomic events exhibit what appear to be less order and more randomness. Entropic exchange is a universal process which can be perceived from an infinity of possible viewpoints within.

Every being carries every level of the universal process within simultaneously, as well as recapitulating the process through life. Previous stages back to the Big Bang have "already become" and the cycles of the subatomic world are always in the process of "becoming," therefore there is always a balance within between being and becoming. The rapid cycles of the subatomic world resonate with those in the macrocosm, and every breath is a recapitulation of the entire universe in time. In recurrence, every level is whole in itself, yet is a summation of the larger whole of which it is a part. Each cycle is itself, yet also a spiralling back into the previous cycle and a progression forward into the next cycle. Each world is a judgement of its next longer world, and the seed of the next shorter world.

In the UTS spiral the centre point is somewhere between a year and a day: the *"eternal present"*. The present moment is always here, and always contains the rest of time -- the centre of the universal process from the macrocosm to the microcosm. Humanity is not the ultimate development in the universe, but the central perception from which its is experienced.

The natural way to view the spiral is with the Past at the bottom, which makes the upper half the microcosmic world, the Future. The arrow of time points from bottom to top. The slower cycles of the past and faster cycles of the future reflect our perception of time. Any phenomenon, event or being, from the particles of the microcosm to the galaxies and suns of the macrocosm, has a primary perception within a particular cycle from I-VIII, its past in the next lower cycle and its future in the next highest. The cycle lengths determine how often shock points occur, at which transition to finer and more spiritual cycles becomes possible. For example, it takes hundreds of millions of years for objects in the mineral world to pass through their lifetime, and only at the end of the cycle might they be broken down in death and synthesized in a mammalian body. The human body contains traces of all minerals and elements, which date back to the origin of Earth, which in turn is composed of matter split-off from the Sun. Yet the minerals and elements presently exist in the finest combined form of which they are capable. In the accompanying Fig. 36, the Universal Time Scale and the Periodic Table of the elements are represented as spirals – the similarity of both to atomic structure is powerful. Larger cycles and entities exist towards Cycle I, while smaller cycles exist towards Cycle VIII, but each being perceives the passage of its lifetime as being the whole of history.

Schopenhauer defined "maya" as a dream of the whole knowledge of the world. Humans have two realities – one is the *subject*, the knower and the known, the supporter of the world and all that exists in the world, in short, it is the world, but the body is an *object* among other objects and is conditioned by the laws of objects. The subject is present, entire and undivided in every being. Schopenhauer states that, "any one percipient being, with the object, constitutes the whole world as idea just as fully as the existing millions do; but if this one were to disappear, then the whole world as will and idea would cease to be".[175] In death we experience the end of the world and believe it is contingent upon us. As death coincides with the end of the world (as will and idea), so conception coincides with creation. *Every being is the entire universe.*

The new physics corroborates Schopenhauer. Phenomena only exist relative to an observer. There is no preferential objective frame of reference from which to experience the world, we have to be in it. Every being is the centre of its universe, and the present moment is the eternal present, the fulcrum of the Universal Time Scale. The space-time continuum, which correlates every moment of time with every other moment, is the "web of maya" from which the soul wishes to escape. Once we come into the universe, we become entire universe. The object becomes the subject, and the knower the known. The dilemma of existence is the artificial separation of these two principles, where we feel split off from the whole.

Relativity theory is derived from religious ideology. In relativity the universe is curved and time is circular. The universe begins with a Big Bang, manifests in curving time, and then ends when all order is gone and randomness prevails, and

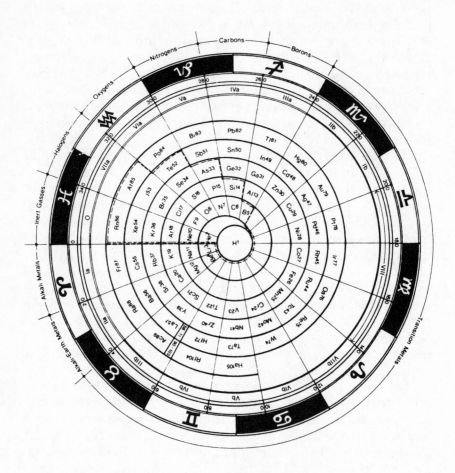

Fig. 36: Spiral Periodic Table
The Periodic Table of the Elements may be represented as spiralling
out from hydrogen. Each layer of the table is defined by the number
of electron rings filled out from the centre of hydrogen. An inert gas
forms the basis for each layer.

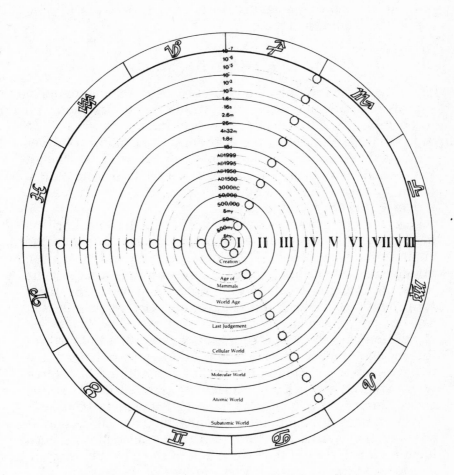

Fig.36 Spiral Universal Time Scale
The UTS as a series of circles with creation at the centre, showing unity, and the eight octaves in concentric rings – the diagram looks both like the atomic model and the diagrams of Fludd.

compaction of all matter in the universe in a singularity, followed by another Big Bang. The end state creates a new beginning. Understanding the universe is to return to discover how it was created. The word "religio" means "to link back" and the function of religion also is to regain access to pure Spirit, the Unity, the One.

The End is the Beginning

The process of the universe is circular as is each component system of the universe. The wholes interlock and are inseparable. And the end is the beginning, just as it is in individual life. In Life★Time Astrology, conception coincides with death. At conception life is all potential, while at death it is all actual. Any stage in life is a phase of the transformation of potential into actual reality. Life transforms reality as the universe transforms information.

Like the ouroboros snake biting its tail, the end and the beginning of the Universal Time Scale join. Fig. 37 shows the eight spiral cycles of the UTS joined end to end, making a doughnut shape called a torus. Arrows on the surface of the torus indicate the local flow of time. In physics the torus furnishes what is called "different connectivity", where the self can be simultaneously separate and connected with the rest of the universe.[176] Arthur Young discovered that the formula for the volume of the Einstein–Eddington universe, the hypersphere, was $2\pi^2R^3$, the same as the volume of a torus with an infinitely small hole. The flow over the surface of a torus is also similar to the pattern of the earth's magnetic field.

When end and beginning are connected, the interaction at their junction is crucial. Subatomic particles called mesons have lifetimes much shorter than Cycle VIII of the UTS, but they are considered "transitory" particles. Suddenly, below Cycle VIII, subatomic particles have lifetimes that are infinite. Subatomic particles bridge the gap between the macrocosm and the microcosm. At microscale, cause and effect lessen and linear time vanishes. Entropy reaches a maximum and randomness is the result, producing a vortex, like the infinity symbol, at the crossover between the micro- and macro-worlds.

The physicist E. H. Walker speculates that photons are conscious because they exhibit organic qualities and seem to "know" how and where to move, process information and act on it. Photons exhibit qualities which belong to both macrocosmic and microcosmic realms. Taking it one step

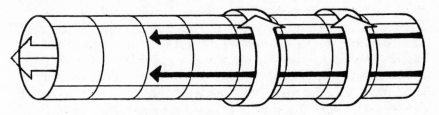

The Arrow of Time

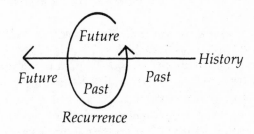

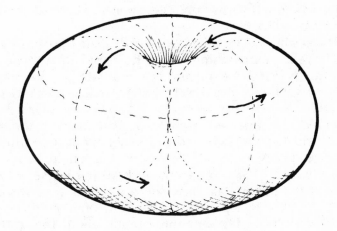

Fig. 37: UTS Torus

When the rectilinear table is bent into a cylinder, the beginning and end of each octave meet, creating an image of circular history within each octave, shown by the large encircling arrows. The length-wise arrows show the process of evolution and history, from Creation at the right to the Subatomic realm at the left. When the cylinder is wrapped around to form a torus shape, the intersections of each octave at conception and death all coincide, and the point when each octave begins and ends is always the same point. The simultaneous spiral and circular movements are also those of electrons encircling the nucleus. The torus shape shows all these interactions.

farther, subatomic particles such as the photon are not particles at all, but rather "sets of relationships".[177] Elementary particles are creations of the physicists' theories, mathematics and observational devices. Photons do not exist by themselves as discrete entities – they do not exist apart from the whole. Photons are pure energy which become manifest as bound electrons enriching the atomic nucleus. Since photons move at the speed of light, their time is infinite according to relativity. They live in the microworld, but live forever. They only have time when bound in matter. Spirit is subject to time when attached to a body, and liberation is a release of energy and freedom from time.

Another explanation of the linkage between end and beginning concerns black holes. Physicists accept that stars are born, live and die just like man.[178] When a star reaches the end of its lifetime, its gravitational field becomes so strong that it recloses upon itself and compacts not only its mass but the space in its vicinity, forming a funnel towards the point of disappearance. Within is a spherical egg like a mini-universe, a separate whole which has only one point of contact with the universe: the black hole.

Black holes have their own laws which seem to defy physics. A time traveller approaching a black hole appears from outside to slow down, but due to an anomaly in relativity takes an infinite time to get there. The time traveller would experience great speed and enter an alien world "crossing the Schwartzchild". "Our explorer's time will come back to its start in the same space . . . the traveller is here the prisoner of a cyclical universe where periodically, with each turn of the black hole, he will live the same event."[179] Black hole time unfolds in reverse order. In our universe phenomena decrease in order as they develop, while in a black hole negentropy rules and phenomena increase their order as they develop. Information about the universe decreases, but in a black hole it increases. Charon speculates that black hole space-time is a "space of thought" or "space of memory". He ascribes similar qualities to the constitution of the electron, making it a micro black hole, a "bearer of the spirit". An electron has a quasi-eternal lifetime, constitutes a universe on its own and can exchange information at a distance with other electrons.[180] The electron contains a space-time of the spirit, and as a micro-universe with cyclical time it reactivates past states of its own space, increasing entropy (information) in the process.

Charon's attribution of psychic qualities to particles resonates with the Unus Mundus, the unity of all things of the alchemists. The electron is basic to everything in the universe, and through black holes is able to create the transition from matter to spirit and back again. The electron is the shock point crossover between cycles and octaves in the time scale. The electronic realm is an eternal universe within which there is no death, only changes of state.

The Faustian Universe

Table 8 shows the structure of the early universe.[181] The lefthand column is Cosmic Time dated from 0 to 20 billion years from top to bottom, while the righthand column is Years Ago dated from 20 billion years to 10 thousand years from top to bottom. The two scales run in opposite directions, yet both are accurate. The events which happen in the macrocosm after creation billions of years ago are the same events which happen in the microcosm in daily life. The "arrow of time" is considered by scientists to be one-directional and irreversible but it is clearly bi-directional. Nobel Laureate Ilya Prigogine considers the problem of the reversibility of time the primary and most controversial topic in the physical sciences, "Think of Einstein, Proust, Freud, Teilhard, Pierce or Whitehead."[182]

In the spiral scheme of the eight worlds, time in the universe runs from creation at the bottom to the electronic realm at the top, but there is another time which acts concurrently with the time of the universe. For every particle in the universe, there is an anti-particle in the anti-universe, the *"Faustian universe"* of the physicist Stannard. Like the space-time of the black hole, in the Faustian universe the arrow of time runs backwards. The present moment is an intersection between universe and anti-universe where the future of the universe is the past of the Faustian universe, and the past of the universe is the future of the Faustian universe – they are parallel but mirror-image universes. As the universe moves towards the electronic realm where there is maximum disorder and minimum information, the Faustian universe has maximum order and maximum information – a total antithesis. The two mirror universes run in opposite directions in time, and when the universe ends, the Faustian universe is being created, and vice versa, thus ensuring a continuum and implying a repetitive, eternal world plan. Access to the workings of the universes is through spirit, available to anyone at any time in history.

The Faustian universe is "outside of time" and is the realm

explored by mystics, yogis, spiritual teachers and everyone who has experienced spiritual or peak experiences, pre-cognitive dreams, deja vu, or near-death experiences, as well as the realm in which mantic arts such as tarot, I Ching, geomancy and others operate. It may also be co-existent to the "unconscious" which contains all information about the future of our universe in its past. The Platonic world of ideas is also correlative to the Faustian universe. It is accessible to anyone at any time, and contains all information potential to our system. Jean Charon has proposed a "theory of complex relativity" in which the anti-universe has inverse laws which seem more mental than physical.

Frank Barr has suggested that a universal pigment in all living organisms, the organic superconductor *melanin*, has properties similar to a black hole and may be the major organizing molecule for living systems.[183] He believes it is a regulating mechanism and the "key to understanding evolution, embryological development, tissue repair and regeneration, consciousness and altered states of consciousness, and the trigger-like biasing of mental states". Others think that melanin may be the matrix for the construction of DNA, RNA and proteins. It also seems to be self-organizing and self-synthesizing, a key in the quest for the answer of the mysteries of life, mind and biological organization.

The correlation of the subatomic realm with higher consciousness does not consider the realms beyond the physical universe. The highest states are unmanifest, unknowable and exist beyond the universe. In Hebrew mysticism such a realm is called Ain Soph, the eternal state of being which results when all qualities are removed – the unconditioned state of all things. The highest state is both the centre of the circle and its territory, the periphery of the universe and its contents; in short, God.

Table 8   Cosmic Time

The left-hand scale shows Cosmic Time from the singularity of the Big Bang to the creation of Homo Sapiens, while the right-hand scale shows time in Years Ago. The developments of the clustering of the galaxies which create astrological reality and the microscopic life forms of primitive DNA are created in the corresponding central zone of both scales.

COSMIC TIME	EPOCH	RED SHIFT	EVENT	YEARS AGO
0	SINGULARITY	INFINITE	BIG BANG	20×10^9
10^{-43} SECOND	PLANCK TIME	10^{32}	PARTICLE CREATION	20×10^9
10^{-6} SECOND	HADRONIC ERA	10^{13}	ANNIHILATION OF PROTON-ANTIPROTON PAIRS	20×10^9
1 SECOND	LEPTONIC ERA	10^{10}	ANNIHILATION OF ELECTRON-POSITRON PAIRS	20×10^9
1 MINUTE	RADIATION ERA	10^9	NUCLEOSYNTHESIS OF HELIUM AND DEUTERIUM	20×10^9
1 WEEK		10^7	RADIATION THERMALIZES PRIOR TO THIS EPOCH	20×10^9
10,000 YEARS	MATTER ERA	10^4	UNIVERSE BECOMES MATTER-DOMINATED	20×10^9
300,000 YEARS	DECOUPLING ERA	10^3	UNIVERSE BECOMES TRANSPARENT	19.9997×10^9
$1-2 \times 10^9$ YEARS		10-30	GALAXIES BEGIN TO FORM	$18-19 \times 10^9$
3×10^9 YEARS		5	GALAXIES BEGIN TO CLUSTER	17×10^9
4×10^9 YEARS			OUR PROTOGALAXY COLLAPSES	16×10^9
4.1×10^9 YEARS			FIRST STARS FORM	15.9×10^9
5×10^9 YEARS		3	QUASARS ARE BORN; POPULATION II STARS FORM	15×10^9
10×10^9 YEARS		1	POPULATION I STARS FORM	10×10^9
15.2×10^9			OUR PARENT INTERSTELLAR CLOUD FORMS	15×10^9
15.3×10^9 YEARS			COLLAPSE OF PROTOSOLAR NEBULA	4.7×10^9
15.4×10^9 YEARS			PLANETS FORM; ROCK SOLIDIFIES	4.6×10^9
16.1×10^9 YEARS	ARCHEOZOIC ERA		OLDEST TERRESTRIAL ROCKS FORM	3.9×10^9
17×10^9 YEARS			MICROSCOPIC LIFE FORMS	3×10^9
18×10^9 YEARS	PROTEROZOIC ERA		OXYGEN-RICH ATMOSPHERE DEVELOPS	2×10^9
19×10^9 YEARS			MACROSCOPIC LIFE FORMS	1×10^9
19.4×10^9 YEARS	PALEOZOIC ERA		EARLIEST FOSSIL RECORD	600×10^6
19.55×10^9 YEARS			FIRST FISHES	450×10^6
19.6×10^9 YEARS			EARLY LAND PLANTS	400×10^6
19.7×10^9 YEARS			FERNS, CONIFERS	300×10^6
19.8×10^9 YEARS	MESOZOIC ERA		FIRST MAMMALS	200×10^6
19.85×10^9 YEARS			FIRST BIRDS	150×10^6
19.94×10^9 YEARS	CENOZOIC ERA		FIRST PRIMATES	60×10^6
19.95×10^9 YEARS			MAMMALS INCREASE	50×10^6
20×10^9 YEARS			HOMO SAPIENS	1×10^5

★Chapter Seven★
★Reincarnation★

Transmigration. Law of Karma. Reincarnation beliefs. The Four Bodies: physical, emotional, mental and spiritual. Higher bodies: atmic, monadic and logoic. Planetary reincarnation. Astrologarithmic Reincarnation Time Scale. Dating reincarnation. Planets and reincarnation personifications. Reincarnation case histories: Napoleon, Nostradamus, Hitler, Thomas Mann. Famous supporters of reincarnation. Varieties of reincarnation. Plato and recurrence.

> Gautama Buddha speaks: With this heart thus serene, made pure, translucent, cultured, devoid of evil, supple, ready to act, firm and imperturbable, the saint directs and bends down his mind to the knowledge of the memory of his previous temporary states. He recalls to his mind. . . one birth, or two or three. . . or a thousand or a hundred thousand births, through many an aeon of dissolution, many an aeon of both dissolution and evolution.[184]

Reincarnation was an essential part of Vedic India, Egypt, Buddhism, Taoism, Zoroastrianism, Sikhism, Judaism, Christianity, Gnosticism, Islam, shamanism and many other religions. In its simplest form it is the periodical reappearance on earth of the same soul. In the Krishna cult, only heroes, leaders and teachers reincarnate — for the masses the process is more vague.

The *transmigration of souls* is reincarnation through all life forms and introduces an element of morality through reward and punishment. The soul passes through a sequence of increasingly complex animal bodies until a human body is attained.

The *law of karma* is the universal action of cause and effect governing reincarnation and transmigration. Present life is a product of the qualities of past lives and determines the quality of future lives. Psychic traces of previous lives are passed on through the soul without a connecting ego. Every action, thought, emotion and idea affects karma, which places responsibility upon every being, although the soul itself remains pure. While for most people reincarnation is a matter of faith, yogins and some others do recall past lives in meditation or regression.

The cycle of birth, death and rebirth is symbolized by the *wheel of samsara*, liberation from which is enlightenment. Possessing a body impels ceaseless wandering in material existence, while liberation is freedom from compulsion into eternal bliss. Some souls choose to incarnate voluntarily, as do the thousand living Buddhas who renounce nirvana to help others attain enlightenment.

Two fundamental concepts of Buddhism are the concept of Brahman, a metaphysical absolute out of which all things come and to which all things return, and the concept of atman, the soul or universal self, which is identical to Brahman. Atman experiences successive lives, becoming identified with the body and immersed in the world throughout a succession of incarnations. When the identity of the two is re-established, the quest for salvation is complete. Ken Wilber calls this quest for ultimate unity-consciousness The *Atman-Project*.[185] (Fig. 38)

The Eastern approach to reincarnation was brought to the West by the Rosicrucians and the Theosophical Society in the 19th century. In the East the circular mechanism of time is something from which to escape, while the time-dominated Westerners are immersed in linear time and wish to live forever. The concept of linear time was formulated by St Augustine (at the mid-way point in the Time Scale at AD 400). Previously there was little conception of time in either East or West. Time is contingent upon consciousness and objectivity, and Libra signals an increased awareness of humanity. The first, lower half of the Time Scale is subjective and unconscious, and transition to the objective and conscious upper half happens at AD 400. Individual life contains a subjective childhood, when impressions and behaviour patterns from the family system are received, and an objective adulthood, when one acts upon the received principles. Repetitive history is a development of consciousness which brings both subjective and objective attitudes into play. The development of time concepts in history parallels the similar development in individual life. Aries and Taurus periods are timeless, Gemini is

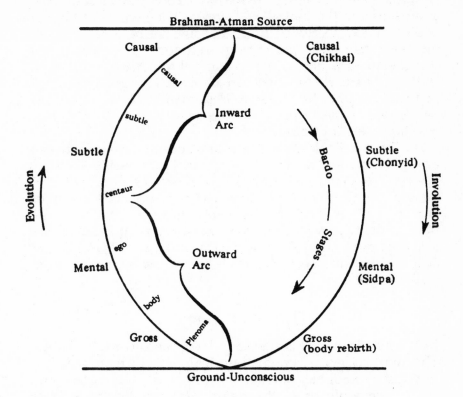

Fig. 38: The Bardo Passage
The stages of evolution and involution are recapitulated in our lives, and in compacted form in the 49 days between lives in what the Buddhists call the Bardo Passage. Every sentient being experiences the entire process, and then seeks the appropriate Karmic level.
(Wilber, The Atman Project)

an immediacy of present time, Cancer is an extended present, Leo is a primal grasp of temporal sequences, and Virgo is an extended linear time. The passage of time is not understood until about the twenty-third year, or its equivalent historical time of AD 400. Modern concepts of time are very recent, as mechanical clockworks date back only five hundred years, to the same time that visual perspective was understood. A world-wide time standard only came into being in 1833.

The soul is subjected to temporal laws when incarnate, but is capable of transcending the space-time continuum and its laws. A soul may have its next incarnation thousands of years ago, and its last incarnation hundreds of years in the future. In eternity, there is no time. The soul is conceived in the boundless and returns to the boundless, tarrying for periods of time in bodies in the world of time, but always returning to the timeless, like the pure-energy photon. The stream of consciousness is like a river passing through many different lands and natural conditions. In all mystical philosophies, the godhead emerges from the timeless void, and only after this emergence is time created. The return to unity with god is beyond time but through time.

The Tibetan Book of the Dead describes the events between physical death and rebirth into a new womb as the Bardo states. The soul seeks transcendence in the clear light, vouchsafed all sentient beings, but most are attracted to previous reality or illusory states which are mere substitutes or shades of the transcendent purity. The soul passes through the entire universal process between each birth, and also in the birth and death of each moment. All levels are eternally present, from God to reptile.

The Four Bodies

Reincarnation happens on many levels and to many bodies. The four bodies of graduating subtlety which incarnate – physical, emotional, mental and spiritual – are analogous to the elements of earth, water, air and fire. Each body metamorphoses in its own way, and indicates emphasis on specific personal and collective developmental stages.

The *Physical Body* is created in gestation and reincarnates in two ways. First, it constantly interchanges and modifies its material substance and force with the physical world by chemical changes, physical effects and renewal and exchanges with other organisms, and second, it reproduces. The body exchanges its substance with the earth continuously through life, in a series of bodily incarnations linked by the same individuality which wear out, pass off, and then are replaced by a new body. Death occurs when the processes of renewal are not as strong as the processes of destruction, what Wilber calls the struggle between Eros and Thanatos.[186] Eros is the drive to perpetuate one's own existence and Thanatos is everything which carries or threatens dissolution. These two counter-forces are analogous to the Hindu gods Vishnu and Shiva, or God as Father and Holy Ghost. Reproduction creates an unbroken line through protoplasmic substance from generation to generation within the same family. Geneology traces such

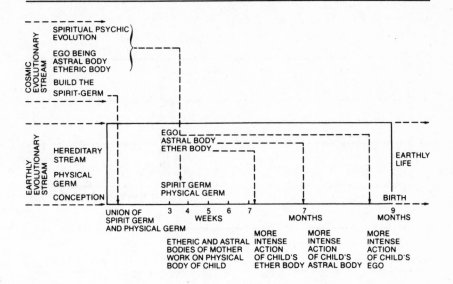

Fig. 39: Embryonic Phases
The spirit germ activates the physical germ at conception, after seven weeks (49 days) the etheric body is formed. The astral body enters at about seven months after conception, and the ego, having entered with the astral, becomes stronger just before birth. *(Wachsmuth, Reincarnation)*

physical connections back into history. The succession of physical bodies is the most basic form of reincarnation.

The physical body is composed of three components which enter in sequence during gestation. (Fig. 39) First, at conception, the *spiritual germ* unites with the *hereditary stream* in the physical act of conception. Four weeks after conception, the cellular body begins formation when the fertilized ovum attaches itself to the wall of the uterus, and the *etheric body* links with the spiritual-physical germ. The etheric body is the architect of physical processes, which derives its instructions from the formative forces in the surrounding world and the cosmos. The etheric body is a name for genetic codes which govern and control the formal evolution of the physical body. In Scientology it is called the Genetic Entity (GE), which jumps from physical line to physical line. (Fig. 40) The energetic pattern or morphogenetic field which creates genetic code is the same for all life forms, but utilizes varying combinations of individual components of the code. During gestation we recapitulate the developmental stages of all life from a one-

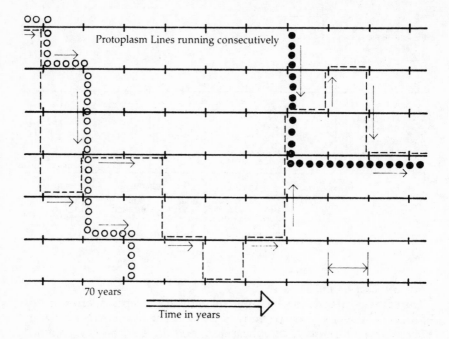

Fig. 40: Scientology Reincarnation
The parallel unbroken lines of protoplasm through time form family
generations, father, son, grandson, etc. The dashed line of the
Genetic Entity chooses different protoplasm lines from generation to
generation, random in choice. The circles of the Theta Being skip
from generation to generation without regard to either protoplasm or
GE lines. Homo sapiens requires a combination of protoplasm, GE
and Theta Being lines, which accounts for the variety of beings even
within the same family. *(After Hubbard, The Ages of Man)*

celled ovum to modern humanity. The process is similar
for everyone as a transmission of collective unconscious
development. As individual as we feel, we have a common
developmental process which is never separate from all other
beings. The pure life-force of the etheric body carries instinctual
urges for survival, sustenance, organ-formation, reproduction
and our inner dynamics.[187] Just before birth the astral body,
derived from planetary and stellar realms, enters the physical
matrix and provides a counterpoint to the biological vital
processes of the etheric influence. The astral limits development, makes it concrete and formal, and signals the beginning

of consciousness, which is itself a limiting mechanism to pure growth.

The *Emotional Body* is created during childhood from birth to about seven years old within the context of the home and family system, and contains instinctive and learned responses to the world, behaviour patterns, value systems, emotional expression and the identification of an individual identity. As the focus in gestation is upon the physical and tangible, in childhood the focus is upon the relative emotional values to which we are exposed. Personality is the sum total of the various ways in which we see, understand or mask ourself, and includes the many sub-personalities which we contain. In astrology the emotional body includes planets in the first four houses and sub-personalities symbolized by planets on or in aspect to the Ascendant. The emotional body surrounds and penetrates the physical body, and being more subtle, senses and perceives a wider range of influences coming from within and the outside world as an instrument of perception, but is in turn still highly influenced by the atmosphere and nature of the family system.

The *Mental Body* is created during maturity and surrounds and penetrates the physical and emotional bodies, making a trinity of levels of being in the mature human. In the first logarithmic half of its development, from seven to twenty-three years old, the mental body is created as an intellectual perspective formed by family, school, religion and society. Later it is the ability to create a position in the world and a family, both of which are generators of further karma, and the formation of a "world view" which will determine future incarnations.

The *Intuitive* or *Spirit Body* transcends the triad of personal bodies and is the transition beyond physical, emotional and mental planes to a realm which activates the others and is in direct connection with the godhead. In Life★Time Astrology the spirit body is the higher octave of gestation, including impulses and energies transformed beyond the "real" life into transpersonal or transcendent life, utilized through creativity and higher purpose. The spirit body is symbolized by and identified with Christ- consciousness or Buddha-nature.

The distribution of planets in the horoscope by octave and element shows the proportional emphasis upon each of the bodies. Gestation (9th, 10th, 11th and 12th house) planets function both on the physical and transcendent levels. Horoscopes with a majority of planets in childhood (1st, 2nd,

3rd and 4th houses) focus in the emotional body and in maturity (5th, 6th, 7th and 8th houses) in the mental body. The element earth is physical, water is emotional, air is mental and fire is intuitional or spiritual. Everyone is a combination of both systems and contains most if not all four elements and all three octaves. The overall aspect pattern connecting planets and octaves shows the degree of possible integration between components of the self and historical ages. Aspects which contact the centre of the horoscope also provide "windows to the soul", and access to higher levels of consciousness.

Higher Levels of Being

The scheme of the four bodies is a basic model of the development of consciousness, but there are more elaborate models which utilize seven levels or planes of consciousness through which the soul progresses to reunite itself with the Divinity. A typical model of seven planes is described by Alice Bailey in "*A Treatise on Cosmic Fire*," related to the progress of the soul, the chakras (centres in the energetic body) and the states of enlightenment of Buddhism. (Fig. 41) Each of the seven planes of existence has seven sub-planes within, making a total of forty-nine levels of awareness. The first three planes are personal, and entrance onto the Intuitional plane through initiation is symbolized by the thousand petalled lotus, evoking the mathematical scheme of The Divine Plot. The first four planes correspond to the four bodies of Plato.

The *Atmic-Nirvanic Plane* is the fifth plane, the first spiritual plane of the Permanent Atom, and the apex of a spiritual triad of energies. The planes and their chakra energy centres are likened to lotuses floating on the surface of eternity with varying numbers of petals. The first five lotuses contain a total of fifty petals, again reflecting the mathematics of The Divine Plot.

The *Monadic Plane* is a higher level of unity and the Logos, the word, where the three qualities of Will, Wisdom and Active Intelligence originate.

The primary *Logoic Plane* is the realm of pure spirit before manifestation.

Sevenfold planes of existence are refered to in Christianity, Theosophy, Buddhism, Hinduism, Yoga, Judaism, Rosicrucianism, Sufism, in ancient Greece and Egypt, Zoroastrian religion and the spiritual beliefs of the Polynesians, and such a structure is essential to the understanding of any

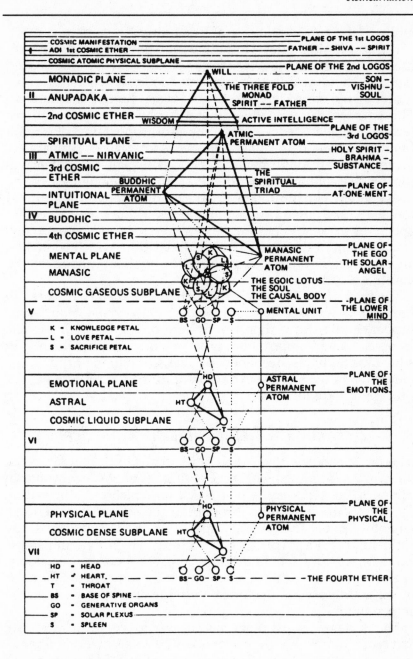

Fig. 41: Bailey Bodies
The lower half of the diagram contains the physical, emotional and lower mental planes. The higher mental plane is a synthesis of these and a stepping-stone to the higher intuitional, atmic-nirvanic, monadic and logoic planes of manifestation. *(Bailey, Treatise on Cosmic Fire)*

study of the subtle anatomy of humanity.[188]

The sevenfold model is naturally transposed onto a planetary model of the seven planets of the ancient world (although called planets, they include the Sun and Moon as well as the five innermost planets Mercury, Venus, Mars, Jupiter and Saturn). The passage through the planetary spheres is central in the Jewish Kaballah, and also in the Anthroposophy of Rudolf Steiner, where it is called *"Etheric Astronomy"*. Humanity's ascent passes through stages related to the planetary spheres in the process of uniting with the cosmos. Steiner locates the passage between life and death as a living through the world of the stars, and identifies earlier phases of humanity in earlier epochs as a transition through the spheres. Mundane astrology is a remnant of the ancient primeval wisdom which contained an exact methodology describing the metamorphosis of the spiritual-psychic being of humanity.

The pattern of evolution through the planetary spheres in Steiner follows the pattern: Moon, Venus, Mercury, Sun, Mars, Jupiter, and Saturn, then the Sphere of the Fixed Stars. The complex and important process of enlightenment in Anthroposophy is described by transformation through the planetary spheres of the evolution of humanity reflected in the process of individual life.

Astrological Reincarnation Time Scale

The Divine Plot is applied to individual reincarnation on the *Astrological Reincarnation Time Scale (ARTS)* on the facing page in Fig. 9 . The ARTS is the matrix within which the information shown on the page tops throughout the sequence of signs in Chapter Five, The World Age. The ARTS describes the influences of The World Age in a form which determines the times in history when primary and secondary incarnations register, the historical events to which they are related, and the gods, goddesses and historical individuals who symbolize the incarnations.

The scheme is astrologically based to conform with the structure of the horoscope process of twelve zodiacal signs divided into seven planetary categories. The ARTS is used with the Scale of Dates from 48,000 BC until AD 1950 in Table 10.

The Scale of Dates tabulates the time in history for each degree of each zodiacal sign. For example, 19 Taurus is equivalent to 17,527 BC, 27 Libra is AD 1058 and 4 Aquarius is August 1853. The scale compacts logarithmically so that one degree in early Aries is on the order of 1000 years, in early Leo about 100 years, while a degree in the end of Pisces is one year. It takes one thousand times longer for humanity to experience or perceive developments at the beginning of the time scale than at the end. Time passed one thousand times slower, and the world was one thousand times less dense than now. Degrees in the first four signs, from Aries through Cancer, are longer than a lifetime, and therefore describe many generations or lineages of people, like the biblical records of Genesis. From Leo through Scorpio each degree is a lifetime or less, while from Sagittarius through Pisces a degree is a quite short period of time, until they represent singular events rather than lives.

Dates before the historical era of 3000 BC encompass long periods of time when no tangible historical events may be dated, but reading across each line shows the harmonics of the original primordial event, bringing it into the recent past.

Table 9   Astrological Reincarnation Time Scale

The ARTS shows the gods and individuals which animate the historical World Age from 50,000 years ago to AD 1950. To find your previous planetary incarnations, locate the exact date of each planet in your horoscope in the Table of ARTS Dates following and then locate the nearest historical prototypes in the appropriate planets's column in the ARTS tables in this section. As the Ascendant and MC are not specifically related to a particular column, read across the entire width of the appropriate sign at the correct date.

Personal Inner Planets

Sun
Creators, fathers, sun gods, heroes, kings, patriarchs, popes, emperors, presidents, lords and the masculine, conscious and objective archetypes.

Moon
Creatrix, earth mothers, chthonic goddesses; Queens, empresses, heroines, significant women, matriarchs, unconscious and subjective archetypes

Mercury
Titans, twin gods, dioscuri; Intellectuals, orators, authors, critics, mystics, alchemists, magicians, mental and communicative archetypes

Venus
Fertility and grain goddesses, deities of rhythm, harmony and integration, artists, musicians, architects, poets, play-wrights, dramatists, aesthetic and creative archetypes

Mars
Heroic, deities of war, energy and destruction; heroes, conquerors, generals, politicians, explorers, tyrants, martyrs, athletes, masculine aggressive archetypes

Jupiter
Wise, procreative, expansive deities; Prophets, religious leaders, philosophers, psychologists, sages, saints, expansive and wise old man archetypes

Saturn
Paternal, orderly, material deities; Scientists, doctors, mathematicians, inventors, bankers, and the repressive father archetypes

Collective Outer Planets

Uranus   Magicians, inventors, eccentrics, intuitive scientists

Neptune   Psychics, mediums, sensitives, drug addicts, dreamers

Pluto
Warriors, statesmen, politicians, transformers, revolutionaries

Personal Points

Ascendant   Personality, personal characteristics, environmental qualities, ways of acting, physical appearance, milieu

Midheaven   Spiritual awareness, ego-consciousness, objectives, sense of purpose

48000 BC   Aries to Cancer

		Sun		Moon		Mercury

7000 BC
Cancer the Crab

		Sun		Moon		Mercury
City Religion		Sun		Moon		Mercury
Feeling and Emotional		Apollo		Artemis		Hermes
Matriarchal		Dionysius		Diana		Mercury
Tigress-Euphrates		Bacchus		Hera		Iris
Nuclear Family Homes		Hercules		Hestia		Keryx
Integration		Talos		Demeter		
Neolithic Societies		Mithras		Kore		
Cities and Nations				Sati		
Mythological Religions	N	Vil	N	Idunn		
Buildings						
	E	Horus/Osiris	E	Isis	E	Thoth
	H	Manu				

14000 BC
Gemini the Twins

		Sun		Moon		Mercury
Tribal Language		Sun		Moon		Mercury
Verbal		Helios		Selene		Metis
Patriarchal		Eos		Skylla		Mnenosyne
Mediterranean		Hyperion		Io¹		Coeus
Instinctive Movement				Cybelle		Kaius
Communication						Charybdis
Diversification						Muses
Music and Dance						Sirens
Multi-god Cults						
						Kabiri
	B	Tammuz	B	Sin	B	Bel
	E	Amun/Amon	E	Nut		
	H	Prajapati	H	Soma		

26000 BC
Taurus the Bull

		Sun		Moon		Mercury
Earth Mother Fertility Cults		Sun		Moon		Mercury
Physicality		Ouranos		Gaia/Earth/Da		Sky
Matriarchal		Nature		Chthon		Psyche
European		Pan		Io		Monos
Fertility				Fates		Idyia
Domestication of Animals				Moirae		Telesta
Possessions				Nemesis		Tyche
Bull and Skull Cults						
Tools	B	Anu	B	Ishtar/Ea		
	E	Ra/Aten	E	Hathoor	E	Nut
	H	Varuna/Aditya				

48000 BC
Aries the Ram

		Sun		Moon		Mercury
Celestial Nomads		Sun		Moon		Mercury
Self Consciousness		Heaven		Earth		Aither (Air)
Patriarchal		Wind		Eurynome		Boreas
African		Sky		Tethys		Aeolus
Primitive		Ophion		Nya (Night)		
Self-Assertion				Auka		
Hunting Bands				Neith		
Celestial Cults						
Weapons			N	Ymir	N	Odin/Wotan
	B	Apsu	B	Tiamat		
	E	Nun	E	Maat	E	Ptah
	J	Jehovah/Adonai				
	H	Brahma/Vishun	H	Maya/Kali	H	Vayu

N = Norse, E = Egyptian, H = Hindu, J = Jewish, B = Babylonian

3000 BC

	Venus		Mars		Jupiter		Saturn
	Venus		Mars		Jupiter		Saturn
	Venus		Mars		Jupiter		Saturn
	Europa		Ares		Zeus		Athena
	Daedalus		Adonis		Philos		Proserpina
	Phaethon		Atlas		Balleus		Asklepios
			Priapus		Ktesius		Pan
			Pluto		Prometheus		Minerva
N	Bragi	N	Tur				
E	Nepthys					E	Set
H	Parvati	H	Shiva				

	Venus		Mars		Jupiter		Saturn
	Venus		Mars		Jupiter		Saturn
	Nemesis		Hades		Themis		Kronos/Rhea
	Narkissos		Crius/Krios		Eurymedon		Nepthys
	The Graces		The Gorgons				Hydra
	Lamia		3 Eryines				Echnida
			3 Graiae				Sabazius
B	Beltis	B	Nergal	B	Marduk	B	Ninurta
		E	Typhon			E	Geb

	Venus		Mars		Jupiter		Saturn
	Venus		Mars		Jupiter		Saturn
	Sea		Cyclopes		Poseidon		Mala/Era
	Leda		Neith		Achelos		Persephone/Styx
	Ceres		Adonis		Dike		Cybelle
	Aphrodite		Priapus		Python		Delphyne
			Haephestos				Moros
B	Astarte	B	Baal				
				H	Brahaspati	H	Bhuta

	Venus		Mars		Jupiter			Saturn
	Venus		Mars		Jupiter			Saturn
	Phanes				Okeanos	G		Chronos
	Protogonos				Metis	G		Erebos
	Iao/Iahu				Eileithya	G		Tartaros
	Hemera					G		Ais
N	Frigga	N	Baldr	N	Thor			
H	Kama	H	Agni	H	Indra	H		Yama

3000 BC   Leo to Scorpio

	Sun	Moon	Mercury

1100 AD
Scorpio the Scorpion

The Middle Ages	Sun	Moon	Mercury
The Black Death Plagues	1491-1527 Henry VIII	1488-1561 Ma Shipton	1486-1535 Agrippa
Medieval Societies	1466-1520 Montezuma	1485-1536 Cath Aragon	1463-1494 Mirandola
Matriarchal	1452-1485 Richard III	1480-1519 L Borgia	1433-1499 Ficino
Medieval Europe	1449-1497 Lorenzo Great	1451-1504 Isabella	1378- Rosencreutz
Inquisition and Crusades	1389-1464 Cosimo Medici	1474-1539 Isabelle Este	1330-1410 Flamel
Separation	1348-1413 Henry IV	1412-1431 Jeanne d'Arc	1265-1321 Dante
Feudal and Monastic	1350-1405 Timurlane	1363-1429 De Pisan	1260-1327 Eckhardt
The Cathedrals	1284-1327 Edward III	1347-1380 Cath Sienna	1235-1316 Lully
	1274-1329 Robert Bruce	1303-1380 St Birgitta	1206-1280 Albert Magnus
	1216-1294 Kubla Khan	1271-1309 Jean Navarre	1160- Chretien
	1212-1250 Frederick II	-1290 Matilda	1145-1202 Joachim Floris
	1137-1193 Saladin	1256-1301 Gertrude	1126-1198 Maimonides
	1162-1227 Genghiz Khan	1122-1204 Eleanor Acq	1126-1198 Averroes

400 AD
Libra the Scales

The Dark Ages	Sun	Moon	Mercury
East-West Balance	1167-1216 John I	1098-1179 Hildegard	1039-1105 Rashi
Patriarchal	1157-1199 Richard I	c -1097 Trotula	1020- Psellus
China and Islam	1068-1135 Henry I	978-1015 Lady Murasaki	1000-1070 Avicebron
Sublimation	1027-1087 William I	935-1002 Hrosvitha	980-1037 Avicenna
Law and Justice	848-900 Alfred Great	901-964 Theodora	772-846 Po Chu-I
State-Religion Schism	790-823 Mamun Great	752-803 Empress Irene	750- Cybewulf
Zen	742-814 Charlemagne	-855 Pope Joan	735-804 Albinus
Troubadours	720-768 Pepin	664- Empress Wu	721-775 Geber
	688-741 Chas Martel	612- Bertha	610-650 Hsuan-Tsung
	c590-628 Li Yuan	c520- Iseult	c490- Procopius
	c500-550 King Arthur	c510- Guinevere	c480- Merlin
	400-453 Attila	508-548 Theodora	c450- Pseudo Dyonysios
	400-461 Leo I	420-500 St Genevieve	450-540 Eudo

800 BC
Virgo the Virgin

Classical Civilizations	Sun	Moon	Mercury
Discrimination	331-363 Julian	325-410 Marcella	340-420 Jerome
Matriarchal	272-337 Constantine	370-415 Hypatia	293-373 Athanasius
Greek and Roman	245-313 Diocletian	307-367 Catherine	185-254 Origen
Distillation	121-180 Aurelius	-230 St Cecilia	150-220 Clement Alex
Classical Learning	76-138 Hadrian	210-254 St Agnes	100- Vitruvius
Culture	37-68 Nero	170-230 Julia Domina	c75- Apollonius
Christianity and Buddhism	63-14 Augustus	130-212 Irenaeus	23-79 Pliny
Classical Architecture	102-44 Julius Caesar	BC20-50AD Mary	106- Metrodorus
Rationalism	300-230 Asoka	69-31 Cleopatra	372-29 Mencius
	356-323 Alexander	470-410 Aspasia	500-428 Anaxagoras
	597-562 Nebuchanezar	Deodema	582-507 Pythagoras
	668-626 Assurbanipal	612- Sappho	551-479 Confucius
	c820- Romulus & Remus	6th- Judith	606-563 Ezekiel

3000 BC
Leo the Lion

First Great Civilizations	Sun	Moon	Mercury
Self-Consciousness	970- Solomon	850- Jezebel	
Patriarchal	1090- King Wen	1194- Helen of Troy	
Babylonian and Egyptian	1150- David	1200- Medea	1122- Duke Chou
Individuality	1300- Moses	1320- Miriam	
Organizations	1360-1340 Tutankhamen	1360- Meritaton	
Civilizations	1375-1350 Amenhotep	1370- Ankhsenamon	
Monotheism	1377- Rameses	1400- Nefertiti	1760- Joseph
Temple Monuments	1900- Abraham	1503-1480 Hatshepsut	
Divine Kings	2181-2123 Hammurabi	1580-1536 Bathsheba	
	2300- Sargon	1750- Amat-Namu	
	2400- Gilgamesh	2489-2460 Neter	
	2750- Zozer	2500- Shub Ad	
	2852- Tai Ho	2600- Hetep	

1500 AD

Venus	Mars	Jupiter	Saturn	
Venus	Mars	Jupiter	Saturn	
1497-1543 Holbein	1485-1546 Cortez	1491-1556 Loyola	1490-1541 **Paracelsus**	1500
1483-1570 **Raphael**	1485-1557 S Cabot	1483-1546 **Luther**	1473-1543 **Copernicus**	
1465-1560 **Michaelangelo**	1480-1521 **Magellan**	1478-1538 Thomas More	1466-1536 **Erasmus**	1450
1471-1528 Durer	1460-1524 Da Gama	1469-1539 Guru Nanak	1436-1476 Regiomontanus	
1452-1519 **Leonardo Vinci**	1469-1527 **Machiaveli**	1486-1538 Chaitanya	1401-1464 Nicholas Cusa	1395
1444-1514 Bramante	1451-1506 **Columbus**	1452-1498 Savonarola	1397-1468 Gutenberg	
1404-1472 Alberti	1454-1512 Vespucci	1370-1415 Huss	1340-1400 Cresca	1335
1386-1466 Donatello	1450-1498 John Cabot	1304-1374 Petrarch	-1297 Campanus	
1377-1446 Brunelleschi	1250-1300 Marco Polo	1265-1308 Duns Scotus	-1288 de Voraigne	1265
1340-1400 **Chaucer**	1232- Marburg	1225-1275 **St Th Aquinas**	1257-1327 Cecco	
1313-1375 BOccaccio	1220-1263 Nevsky	1214-1249 Roger Bacon	1202- Fibonacci	1190
1267-1337 **Giotto**	1122-1190 Barbarossa	1212-1273 Rumi	1114-1202 Lille	
1165-1240 Ibn Arabi	1117-1170 Becket	1081-1170 St Francis	1100-1150 Thierry	1100

Venus	Mars	Jupiter	Saturn	
Venus	Mars	Jupiter	Saturn	
1120-1200 Chu Hsi	1070- De St Omer	1090-1153 Gampopa	1033-1109 St Amselm	1100
c -1123 Khayyam	1070- De Payens	1057-1135 Milarepa	973-1040 Al-Biruni	
995-1050 D'Arezzo	1042-1099 Urban II	1011-1100 Naropa	965- Alhazen	1020
940-1020 Firdusi	1040-1099 El Cid	968-1069 Tilopa	865-925 Rhazes	
c900- Beiruni	994-1035 Eriksson	c-747 **Padmasambhava**	786-886 Albumasar	925
768-824 Han Yin	994-1035 Canute	c -800 Shankarcharya	740-814 Alcuin	
c -762 Li Po	956-1015 Vladimir	638-713 Hui Neng	680-741 Leo III	815
670- Caedmon	764-809 al-Rachid	c502- Isadorus	673-735 Bede	
500- Anthemius	541-604 Sui Wen Ti	570-632 **Mohammed**	c 687 Ibn Nafis	695
c550- Taliesin	c510- **Parzifal**	c534- St Columba	c598- Brahmagupta	
540-604 Gregory	c500- Launcelot	433-468 St Patrick	560-630 Isidore	565
400-480 Kalidasa	454-526 Theodoric	410-485 Proclus	483-565 Justinian	
c450- Musaeus	440-500 Clovis	480-544 St Benedict	c450- Capella	400

Venus	Mars	Jupiter	Saturn	
Venus	Mars	Jupiter	Saturn	
c350- Macrobius	370-410 Alaric	354-430 St Augustine	233-303 Porphyry	400 AD
c250- Ossian	330-380 Sallustus	216-277 Mani	280-330 Iamblicus	
204-270 **Plotinus**	160-205 Chang Chou	c200- Patanjali	129-182 Ho Hsiu	260
123-170 Apuleius	53-117 Trajan	4-64 St Paul	129-199 Galen	
46-120 Plutarch	9-79 Vespatian	0-33 **Jesus Christ**	100-178 **Ptolemy**	84 AD
99-55 Lucretius	74-4 Herod	300- Chuang Tsu	287-212 Archimedes	
100-29 **Virgil**	247-183 Hannibal	284-322 **Aristotle**	c300- Euclid	108 BC
106-45 **Cicero**	490-449 **Pericles**	429-347 **Plato**	469-379 Hippocrates	
496-406 Sophocles	514-449 Themistocles	484-424 Herodatus	c500- Empedocles	321
495-406 Euripides	521-486 Darius	479-399 **Socrates**	c540- **Democritus**	
c500-432 Phidias	c500- Nehemiah	563-483 **Buddha**	c520- Hesiod	554
525-463 Aesculus	c570- Solon	c600- **Lao Tse**	640-546 Thales	
620-560 Aesop	590-529 Cyrus	620-551 Zoroaster	c600- Miletus	800

Venus	Mars	Jupiter	Saturn	
Venus	Mars	Jupiter	Saturn	800 BC
850- Homer	1190- Menelaeus			
Demodocus				1095
	1170- **Ulysses**	1000- Zoroaster	1376- **Asklepius**	1405
1350- **Orpheus**	**Aeneas**			
	1250- Jason	1500- Seheb		1750
	1300- Cadmus			
		2000- Melchizedek		2130
2600- Imhotep	2716- **Theseus**		Ur-engur	2545
	Perseus			
	Odysseus	Fu Hsi		3000

1500 AD   Sagittarius to Pisces

| | Sun | | Moon | | Mercury |

1910 AD
Pisces the Fishes
The Great Wars

	Sun			Moon			Mercury
Disintegration			1941-	Baez	1943-	Fisher
Germany, USSR and USA	1948-	Prince Charles	1934-	Loren	1935-	Sagan
Matriarchal	1944-	R Gandhi	1932-	Taylor	1929-	Osborne
Karmic Isolationism	1937-	Aga Khan IV	1929-	J Onassis	1927-	Grass
Illusion	1935-	Hussein	1929-1983	Kelly-Rainier	1923-	Mailer
Abstraction	1927-	Castro	1926-1962	Monroe	1918-	Solzhenitsyn
Nihilism	1921-	Edinburgh	1926-	Elizabeth II	1915-1985	Welles
War Devices	1918-1981	Sadat	1921-	Friedan	1913-1960	Camus
	1918-1963	J F Kennedy	1919-	Fonteyn	1913-	Briten
1950 AD	1916-	Wilson	1918-19	Bailey	1912-	Williams
	1913-	Nixon	1917-1984	Gandhi	1912-1968	Ionesco
	1911-1974	Pompidou	1911-1937	Harlow	1911-1982	McLuhan
	1911-	Reagan				

1840 AD
Aquarius the Waterbearer
Nationalism

	Sun			Moon			Mercury
Humanitarianism	1897-1978	Paul VI	1901-1978	Mead	1901-	Ebertin
The United States	1893-1976	Mao Tse-Tung	1898-1937	Earhardt	1901-1978	Disney
Patriarchal	1890-1970	De Gaulle	1895-	Langer	1899-1982	Hitchcock
Romantic Utopian Societies	1889-1945	**Hitler**	1890-1960	Th Neumann	1891-1946	Fortune
Idealism	1884-1962	Truman	1884-1962	E Roosevelt	1887-1950	Carter
Bureaucracies and Unions	1883-1945	Mussolini	1882-1941	Woolf	1890-1943	Zimmer
Victorian Age	1882-1945	F Roosevelt	1878-1927	Duncan	1878-1965	Evans-Wentz
Collectivization	1879-1953	**Stalin**	1874-1946	Stein	1875-1947	Crowley
Socialism-Communism	1876-1958	Pius XII	1861-1937	Salome	1861-1925	Steiner
Modern Government	1868-1918	Nicholas II	1859-1924	Duse	1860-	Waite
	1858-1914	T Roosevelt	1858-1950	Lagerloff	1859-1930	Doyle
	1859-1941	Wilhelm II	1844-1879	Bernadette	1854-1918	Mathers
	1845-1886	Ludwig	1844-1923	Bernhardt	1842-1933	Besant

1720 AD
Capricorn the Goat-Fish
Industrial Revolution

	Sun			Moon			Mercury
Physical Perfection	1835-1867	Maximillian	1821-1910	Eddy	1831-1891	Blavatsky
England	1830-1916	Franz Joseph	1820-1912	Barton	1821-1880	Dostoevsky
Matriarchal	1818-1881	Alexander II	1820-1910	Nightengal	1823-1880	Max-Muller
Revolutionary Materialism	1809-1865	Lincoln	1820-1906	Anthony	1812-1870	Dickens
Nationalism	1796-1855	Nicholas I	1819-1901	**Victoria**	1810-1875	Eliphas Levi
The Reformation	1773-1850	Lou Phillipe	1804-1876	Sand	1809-1849	Poe
Capitalist Machine Age	1769-1821	**Napoleon**	1804-1861	Browning	1802-1870	Dumas
Ascendancy over Nature	1767-1845	Jackson	1759-1797	Wollstonecraft	1802-1885	Hugo
	1757-1828	Karl August	1763-1814	Josephine	1799-1850	**Balzac**
	1754-1793	Louis XVI	1755-1793	Antoinette	1785-1859	De Quincey
	1740-1786	Fred Great	1746-1793	Du Barry	1775-1817	Austen
	1738-1820	George III	1750-1848	Herschel	1743-1795	Cagliostro
	1732-1799	**Washington**	1729-1796	**Cath Great**	1743-1803	St Martin

1500 AD
Sagittarius the Centaur
The Renaissance

	Sun			Moon			Mercury
Self-Realization	1712-1786	Fred Prussia	1717-1780	Maria Theresa	1602-1681	Lilly
The Americas	1710-1774	Louis XV	1709-1762	Eliz Russia	1586-1654	Andraeae
Patriarchal	1672-1725	**Peter Great**	1684-1727	Catherine I	1575-1624	Boehme
New Colonial Worlds	1650-1702	William III	1665-1727	Anne	1574-1637	Fludd
Reconstitution	1638-1715	**Louis XIV**	1607-1678	Schurman	1568-1639	Campanella
Philosophical Humanism	1630-1685	Charles II	1623-1701	Jane Leade	1565-1622	Meier
Wholistic World View	1600-1649	Charles I	1596-1662	Eliz Palat	1561-1626	F Bacon
Rebirth to Higher Mind	1566-1625	James I	1591-1643	Hutchinson	1554-1586	Sidney
	1556-1605	Akhbar Great	1542-1587	Mary Stuart	1548-1600	**Bruno**
	1532-1592	Wilhelm IV	1533-1603	**Elizabeth I**	1547-1616	Cervantes
	1530-1584	**Ivan Terrible**	1519-1589	Cath Medici	1534-1577	Luria
	1520-1566	Suleimann	1516-1558	Mary I	1527-1608	**Dee**
	1500-1558	Charles V	1515-1582	Theresa Avila	1503-1588	**Nostradamus**

1950 AD

Venus   Mars   Jupiter   Saturn

Venus		Mars		Jupiter		Saturn		
1941-	Dylan	1942-	Muhammed Ali	1935-	Erhard	1942-	Sheldrake	1950
1940-1980	Lennon	1931-1955	Dean	1933-	Dalai Lama XIV	1942-	Hand	
1935-1977	Presley	1929-	Moss	1931-	Rajneesh	1939-	Capra	1944
1930-	Warhol	1929-1968	M L King	1927-	Laing	1935-	Sagan	
1928-	Stockhausen	1928-1967	Guevarra	1925-	Casteneda	1934-	Gargarin	1939
1928-	Albee	1925-1968	R Kennedy	1923-1982	Karmapa XI	1930-	Armstrong	
1925-	Rauschenberg	1923-	Kissinger	1920-	Leary	1928-	Gauquelin	1933
1925-	Boulez	1919-1949	Hillary	1918-	Graham	1926-	Hefner	
1924-	Brando	1919-	Trudeau	1915-1982	Watts	1922-	Bernard	1926
1924-	Baldwin	1918-	Schmidt	1913-1969	Pike	1921-	Glenn	
1918-	Bernstein	1916-	Heath	1913-	Makarios	1914-	Salk	1919
1912-	Cage	1914-	Heyerdahl	1911-	Hubbard	1913-	Lovell	
1910-	Anouilh	1913-	Ford	1910-1955	Collin	1912-	Von Braun	1910

Venus		Mars		Jupiter		Saturn		
1882-1941	Joyce	1906-1975	Onassis	1905-1980	Sartre	1901-1976	Heisenberg	1910
1882-1971	Stavinsky	1905-1976	Hughes	1888-1974	Assagioli	1897-1957	Reich	
1881-1973	Picasso	1900-1945	Himmler	1881-1955	de Chardin	1900-1958	Pauli	1902
1875-1955	Mann	1900-1976	Mountbatten	1879-1950	Maharshi	1885-1962	Bohr	
1875-1926	Rilke	1897-1945	Goebbels	1877-1945	Gurdjieff	1880-1926	Spengler	1892
1874-1951	Schoenberg	1890-1970	Eisenhower	1875-1968	Suzuki	1879-1950	Einstein	
1871-1922	Yeats	1885-1945	Patton	1875-1965	Schweitzer	1874-1937	Marconi	1880
1866-1946	Wells	1879-1940	Trotsky	1875-1961	Jung	1867-1934	Mme Curie	
1862-1918	Debussy	1874-1965	Churchill	1872-1970	Russell	1863-1947	Ford	1870
1860-1911	Mahler	1871-1916	Rasputin	1869-1948	Gandhi	1856-1940	Thompson	
1856-1950	Shaw	1870-1924	Lenin	1856-1939	Freud	1854-1932	Eastman	1855
1854-1897	Rimbaud	1853-1902	Rhodes	1856-1918	Sai Baba	1847-1922	Bell	
1844-1896	Verlaine	1847-1934	Hindenburg	1844-1900	Nietzsche	1847-191	Edison	1840

Venus		Mars		Jupiter		Saturn		
1833-1897	Brahms	1822-1890	Schliemann	1836-1886	Ramakrishna	1837-1915	J P Morgan	1840
1820-1910	Tolstoy	1822-1885	Grant	1820-1903	Spencer	1834-1907	Mendeleev	
1813-1883	Wagner	1818-1883	Marx	1817-1862	Thoreau	1831-1879	Maxwell	1825
1810-1849	Chopin	1815-1898	Bismarck	1801-1877	Brigham Young	1822-1865	Mendel	
1801-1886	Liszt	1807-1882	Garibaldi	1796-1859	H Mann	1822-1895	Pasteur	1808
1797-1827	Schubert	1804-1881	Disraeli	1788-1860	Schopenhauer	1809-1882	Darwin	
1795-1821	Keats	1783-1830	Bolivar	1786-1856	Webster	1766-1844	Dalton	1790
1792-1824	Shelley	1769-1852	Wellington	1776-1822	Hoffman	1738-1822	Herschel	
1788-1824	Byron	1771-1858	Owen	1770-1831	Hegel	1744-1829	Lamarck	1770
1770-1827	Beethoven	1768-1818	Tecumseh	1759-1803	Schiller	1743-1794	Lavoisier	
1757-1827	Blake	1761-1806	Pitt	1749-1832	Goethe	1733-1815	Mesmer	1745
1750-1791	Mozart	1757-1834	Lafayette	1737-1787	Gibbon	1731-1810	Cavendish	
1732-1790	Haydn	1740-1794	Robespierre	1724-1804	Kant	1723-1790	Adam Smith	1720

Venus		Mars		Jupiter		Saturn		
1685-1759	Handel	1708-1796	Pitt	1717-1778	Rousseau	1706-1790	Franklin	1720
1685-1750	Bach	1700-1750	Walpole	1711-1771	Hume	1701-1783	Euler	
1632-1723	Wren	1689-1755	Montesquieu	1709-1784	Sam Jonson	1646-1716	Leibniz	1690
1632-1675	Vermeer	1643-1687	La Salle	1694-1778	Voltaire	1642-1727	Newton	
1608-1674	Milton	1604-1660	Mazarin	1688-1772	Swedenborg	1632-1723	Leuwenhoek	1660
1606-1669	Rembrandt	1600-1658	Shah Jahan	1686-1761	Law	1627-1691	Boyle	
1573-1631	Donne	1599-1658	Cromwell	1632-1704	Locke	1578-1657	Harvey	1625
1567-1633	Monteverdi	1585-1642	Richelieu	1632-1677	Spinoza	1577-1644	Van Helmont	
1564-1616	Shakespeare	1583-1634	Wallenstein	1623-1662	Pascal	1571-1630	Kepler	1590
1564-1593	Marlowe	1552-1618	Raleigh	1596-1650	Descartes	1564-1642	Galileo	
1552-1597	Spenser	1540-1596	Drake	1585-1642	Richelieu	1550-1614	Napier	1545
1508-1580	Palladio	1536-1598	Hideoyoshi	1542-1591	St John Cross	1546-1601	Brahe	
1511-1574	Vasari	1526-1630	Babar	1509-1564	Calvin	1512-1594	Mercator	1500

LOGARITHMIC TIME SCALE

Degree	Pisces	Aquarius	Capricorn	Sagittarius	Scorpio	Libra
00	Jan 1911	Nov 1841	Oct 1719	●Jan 1500	1109 AD	419 AD
01	Oct 1912	Nov 1844	Mar 1724	Jul 1509	1128	449
02	Jun 1914	Nov 1847	May 1729	Oct 1518	1143	478
03	Jan 1916	Sep 1850	Jul 1734	Dec 1527	1161	507
04	Aug 1917	Aug 1853	Aug 1739	Dec 1536	1177	536
05	Mar 1919	May 1856	Jul 1744	Sep 1545	1192	564
06	Oct 1920	Jan 1859	May 1749	●May 1554	1208	591
07	Apr 1922	Oct 1861	Mar 1754	Nov 1562	1223	618
08	Sep 1923	May 1864	Nov 1758	Feb 1571	1237	644
09	Mar 1925	Dec 1866	Jun 1763	Jan 1579	1252	670
10	Aug 1926	Jun 1869	●Dec 1767	Apr 1587	1266	695
11	Jan 1928	Dec 1871	Apr 1772	Feb 1595	1280	720
12	May 1929	May 1874	Aug 1776	Nov 1602	1294	744
13	Sep 1930	Oct 1876	Nov 1780	May 1610	1307	768
14	Jan 1932	Feb 1879	Jan 1785	Oct 1617	1320	791
15	Apr 1933	Jun 1881	Feb 1789	Jan 1625	1333	814
16	Aug 1934	Sep 1883	Feb 1793	Mar 1632	1346	837
17	Oct 1935	Nov 1885	Feb 1797	Mar 1639	1358	859
18	Jan 1937	Jan 1887	Dec 1800	Jan 1646	1371	881
19	Apr 1938	Mar 1890	Sep 1804	Oct 1652	1383	902
20	Jun 1939	●Apr 1892	Jun 1808	May 1659	1394	● 923
21	Jul 1940	Apr 1894	Jan 1812	Oct 1665	1406	943
22	Sep 1941	May 1896	Aug 1815	Mar 1672	1417	964
23	Oct 1942	Apr 1898	Feb 1819	Jul 1678	1428	984
24	Nov 1943	Mar 1900	Aug 1822	Jul 1684	1439	1002
25	Dec 1944	Feb 1902	Dec 1825	Jul 1690	1450	1021
26	Jan 1946	Dec 1903	Apr 1829	May 1969	1460	1040
27	Jan 1947	Oct 1905	Jul 1832	Mar 1702	1470	1058
28	Jan 1948	Aug 1907	Sep 1835	Oct 1707	1480	1076
29	Jan 1949	May 1909	Oct 1838	May 1713	1490	1094
30	●Jan 1950	Jan 1911	Nov 1841	Oct 1719	●1500 AD	1109 AD

N.B. 0° and 30° of the next sign are synchronous.

Table 10 ARTS Dates 48,000 BC to AD 1950 — The World Age

The table shows when in history each planetary incarnation registers. Just find the horizontal file for the correct sign, i.e. Aries or Sagittarius, then read down the column for the correct degree, i.e. 7 degrees or 26 degrees. By reading across the degree file you can find the Harmonic Incarnations before and after the Primary Incarnation.

DATES FROM 48000 BC TO 1950 AD

Virgo	Leo	Cancer	Gemini	Taurus	Aries	Degree
811 BC	●3000 BC	6891 BC	13811 BC	26117 BC	●48000 BC	00
758	2905	6722	13511	25583	47050	01
705	2818	6557	13216	25059	46118	02
654	2720	6394	12927	24544	45203	03
604	2630	6234	12643	24040	44306	04
554	2543	6078	12365	23545	43426	05
506	2456	5924	12092	23059	●42563	06
458	●2371	5774	11824	22583	41716	07
412	2288	5626	●11561	22116	40885	08
366	2206	5481	11304	21658	40070	09
●321	●2127	5339	11050	●21208	39270	10
277	2048	5200	10803	20767	38486	11
233	1971	5063	10559	20334	37716	12
191	1896	4928	10321	19910	36962	13
149	1822	4597	10087	19493	36221	14
108	●1749	4668	9857	19085	35494	15
68	1678	4501	9632	18684	34782	16
29 BC	1608	4417	9411	18291	34083	17
10 AD	1540	4295	9194	17905	33397	18
● 48	1472	4175	8981	17527	32725	19
● 84	1406	4058	● 8772	17156	32065	20
121	1341	3943	8567	16792	31417	21
157	1278	3830	8366	16435	30782	22
192	1216	3719	8170	16084	30159	23
223	●1155	3610	● 7976	15741	29548	24
●260	1095	3503	7787	15404	28948	25
293	1036	3399	7601	15073	28360	26
325	978	3296	7418	●14748	27783	27
357	921	3196	7239	14430	27217	28
388	966	3096	7064	14118	28662	29
419 AD	811 BC	●3000 BC	6891 BC	13811 BC	26117 BC	30

LOGARITHMIC TIME SCALE (SECOND OCTAVE)

Deg	Pisces	Aquarius	Capricorn	Sagittarius	Scorpio	Libra
00	28 Nov 1999	3 Nov 1999	19 Sep 1999	1 Jul 1999	9 Feb 1999	2 Jun 1998
01 02 03 04		4 Nov 1999 5 Nov 1999 6 Nov 1999 7 Nov 1999				
05	1 Dec 1999	8 Nov 1999	29 Sep 1999	18 Jul 1999	11 Mar 1999	25 Jul 1998
06 07 08 09	(11.94 hr)	9 Nov 1999 10 Nov 1999 11 Nov 1999 12 Nov 1999				
10	4 Dec 1999	13 Nov 1999	7 Oct 1999	2 Aug 1999	8 Apr 1999	11 Sep 1998
11 12 13 14	(19.28 hr)	14 Nov 1999 15 Nov 1999 16 Nov 1999 17 Nov 1999				
15	6 Dec 1999	18 Nov 1999	15 Oct 1999	16 Aug 1999	2 May 1999	24 Oct 1998
16 17 18 19	(8.43 hr)	19 Nov 1999 20 Nov 1999 20 Nov 1999 21 Nov 1999				
20	8 Dec 1999	22 Nov 1999	22 Oct 1999	29 Aug 1999	24 May 1999	2 Dec 1998
21 22 23 24	(2.97 hr)					 1 Jan 1999
25	10 Dec 1999	25 Nov 1999	28 Oct 1999	9 Sep 1999	13 Jun 1999	8 Jan 1999
26 27 28 29	(2.39 hr)					
30						
30	12 Dec 1999	28 Nov 1999	3 Nov 1999	19 Sep 1999	1 Jul 1999	9 Feb 1999

Table 11 ARTS Dates 1950 to 1999 —
The Last Judgement

The table shows the dates when the entire zodiacal sequence compacts in the last fifty years of the Twentieth Century.

FROM JANUARY 1950 TO DECEMBER 1999

Virgo	Leo	Cancer	Gemini	Taurus	Aries	Deg
10 Mar 1997	1 Jan 1995	9 Feb 1991	9 Mar 1984	18 Nov 1971	1 Jan 1950	00
30 Mar 1997	3 Feb 1995	11 Apr 1991	28 Jun 1984	1 Jun 1972	12 Dec 1950	01
17 Apr 1997	9 Mar 1995	11 Jun 1991	13 Oct 1984	10 Dec 1972	18 Nov 1951	02
6 May 1997	12 Apr 1995	9 Aug 1991	27 Jan 1985	15 Jun 1973	18 Oct 1952	03
23 May 1997	15 May 1995	6 Oct 1991	10 May 1985	17 Dec 1973	10 Sep 1953	04
11 Jun 1997	16 Jun 1995	3 Dec 1991	20 Aug 1985	15 Jun 1974	29 Jul 1954	05
29 Jun 1997	17 Jul 1995	28 Jan 1992	28 Dec 1985	9 Dec 1974	9 Jun 1955	06
1 Jul 1997	17 Aug 1995	24 Mar 1992	5 Mar 1986	1 Jun 1975	14 Apr 1956	07
3 Aug 1997	17 Sep 1995	16 May 1992	9 Jun 1986	19 Nov 1975	11 Feb 1957	08
19 Aug 1997	16 Oct 1995	8 Jul 1992	11 Sep 1986	26 Jul 1976	6 Dec 1957	09
5 Sep 1997	15 Nov 1995	29 Aug 1992	12 Dec 1986	16 Oct 1976	23 Sep 1958	10
21 Sep 1997	13 Dec 1995	19 Oct 1992	2 Jan 1987	26 Mar 1977	7 Jul 1959	11
7 Oct 1997	11 Jan 1996	8 Dec 1992	13 Mar 1987	31 Aug 1977	15 Apr 1960	12
22 Oct 1997	7 Feb 1996	26 Jan 1993	29 Aug 1987	2 Feb 1978	14 Jan 1961	13
7 Nov 1997	6 Mar 1996	15 Mar 1993	29 Nov 1987	4 Jul 1978	21 Sep 1961	14
21 Nov 1997	1 Apr 1996	1 May 1993	21 Feb 1988	30 Nov 1978	3 Jul 1962	15
6 Dec 1997	27 Apr 1996	17 Jun 1993	14 May 1988	2 Apr 1979	21 Mar 1963	16
20 Dec 1997	23 May 1996	1 Aug 1993	3 Aug 1988	15 Sep 1979	1 Dec 1963	17
4 Jan 1998	17 Jun 1996	14 Sep 1993	21 Oct 1988	4 Feb 1980	8 Aug 1964	18
17 Jan 1998	11 Jul 1996	28 Oct 1993	7 Jan 1989	22 Jun 1980	11 Apr 1965	19
31 Jan 1998	5 Aug 1996	10 Dec 1993	24 Mar 1989	4 Nov 1980	7 Dec 1965	20
13 Feb 1998	29 Aug 1996	21 Jan 1994	27 Feb 1989	17 Mar 1981	23 Jul 1966	21
26 Feb 1998	20 Sep 1996	3 Mar 1994	19 Aug 1989	25 Jul 1981	21 Mar 1967	22
11 Mar 1998	11 Oct 1996	13 Apr 1994	30 Oct 1989	30 Dec 1981	3 Nov 1967	23
24 Mar 1998	4 Nov 1996	22 May 1994	9 Jan 1990	26 Mar 1982	14 Jun 1968	24
5 Apr 1998	26 Nov 1996	20 Jun 1994	19 Mar 1990	6 Aug 1982	19 Jan 1969	25
17 Apr 1998	18 Dec 1996	7 Aug 1994	26 May 1990	4 Dec 1982	22 Aug 1969	26
29 Apr 1998	15 Jan 1997	14 Sep 1994	31 Jul 1990	2 Apr 1983	20 Mar 1970	27
10 May 1998	28 Jan 1997	21 Oct 1994	5 Oct 1990	27 Jul 1983	13 Oct 1970	28
22 May 1998	18 Feb 1997	26 Nov 1994	8 Dec 1990	18 Nov 1983	3 May 1971	29
22 May 1998	18 Feb 1997	26 Nov 1994	8 Dec 1990	18 Nov 1983	3 May 1971	30
2 Jun 1998	10 Mar 1997	1 Jan 1995	9 Feb 1991	9 Mar 1984	18 Nov 1971	30

N.B. 0° and 30° of the next sign are synchronous.

The *Sun* is the primary masculine incarnation and describes fatherly qualities, consciousness, self-awareness and sense of objectivity. The Sun in one of the first four signs creates a paternal sense which is mythical and often omnipotent, in the sign Leo kingly, in Scorpio inquisitorial, or in Aquarius victorian.

The *Moon* is the primary feminine incarnation and shows motherly feelings, emotions, the ability to nurture, protect and the valuing mechanisms. The Moon in the first four signs is the mythical divine mother in her protective form and in her devouring form as Kali, in Aries evoking the emotional reality of a cavewoman, in Virgo of an early Christian virgin, in Scorpio of a Joan of Arc, in Aquarius a Victorian matron.

Mercury is the intellect, the quality of intelligence, communicative abilities, mental set and ideas about the self and the world. Mercury in Gemini is a continual invention of language or means of communication, in Virgo is the classical scholar, while in Pisces is media and cinema oriented.

Venus is the aesthetic sense, creativity, cultural affinities, and the quality of relationships, as well as sexual mores, attractions and taste in people. Venus in Taurus is dominated by raw sensuality, in Libra by chivalric idealism, in Sagittarius Shakespearean bawdiness.

Mars is the warrior, aggressive, changing by force and exploratory, and the urge to destroy and revel. Mars in Aries is celestial assertion, in Virgo the Homeric hero, in Scorpio the Crusader and in Capricorn the robber baron.

Jupiter is the religious belief system or philosophical stance which creates a world view. Jupiter in Taurus worships the earth mother, in Cancer the home and family, in Aquarius worships the machine. Religions change from sign to sign. Jupiter in mid-Virgo would be early Christians contemporary with Jesus Christ or gnostics, in Scorpio crusaders, in Sagittarius reformation Protestants, in Pisces atheists or existentialists.

Saturn describes the incarnation which determines the attitude to reality and the degree of scientific understanding and the material attitude. Saturn in Aries accepts only what it can see and touch, in Leo accepts the divine right of the king, in Libra Roman law, and in Aquarius the rule of the capitalist factory owner.

The *Outer Planets* move slowly and in birth horoscopes describe collective influences shared by entire generations. In respect reincarnation they do not have their own column of influence, but are described by a band across all seven planets with a strong focus on the planet of which it is a higher octave. *Uranus* is the higher octave of Mercury and is an incarnation representing eccentricity, individuality, independence and inventiveness. *Neptune* is the higher octave of Venus and is an incarnation representing psychic influences, mediumship, sensitivity, weakness and contact with disease. Often Neptune registers when psychic regression is the keynote, and are times in history which contain mystical and magical connections. *Pluto* is the higher octave of Mars and indicates the incarnation which was most revolutionary, transformative and had the greatest contact and influence upon the masses.

The *Personal Points* are more general influences which describe a band across the entire ARTS. The *Ascendant* is very important as it describes the time in history of the personality, physical appearance and environmental characteristics. The *Midheaven* is ego-consciousness, spiritual realization, and objectives in life related to an incarnative time in history. The personal points are often a combination of many influences, rather than one in particular.

Constellations of more than one planet signify powerful times of influence where multiple influences are in operation. If the Sun and Venus are conjunct in 10 degrees of Sagittarius in the birth chart, indicating artistic or aesthetic aspirations and awareness, the reincarnative influence could be a man who was artistic in 1587, or a young woman who exhibited a very strong consciousness, and the influence combines the two categories. Planets such as Mercury (intellect), Jupiter (religion) and Saturn (practical influences) in the sign Virgo, the time of Classical civilization, would be appropriate for a classicist who specialized in language and religions.

Aspects in the horoscope indicate planets which are in relationship with each other, and the same logic is transposed into the reincarnation scheme. Aspects in the ARTS show connections between historical periods and their equivalent incarnations. For example, planets in opposition between the signs Leo and Aquarius are in opposing eras in history. The Leo time (3000 to 800 BC) is the age of kings when the individual was highly valued, while the Aquarius time (1840 to AD 1910) is the antagonistic Victorian era when social causes and the collective national attitudes totally dominated society and signalled the effective end of monarchy. Supportive aspects such as trines show octaval developments of a similar theme. In Leo time the individuality originated and self-consciousness developed, and in the next fire sign Sagittarius the humanistic Renaissance man was valued. The aspects are harmonics, and are shown by reading along the same horizontal file of Table 11.

Reincarnation Case Histories

The positions of the planets and personal points in the horoscope indicate twelve primary incarnations and their historical times. The mechanism may be symbolized by historical characters who influence future generations with their ideas or personalities, and may have been influenced by previous generations. Although the mathematics of The Divine Plot is quite specific, a certain leeway should be accepted, in keeping with the acceptable margin of error in astrology of one degree each way, a deviation of 00.27%.

A well-known case is that of *Napoleon Bonaparte* (Fig. 42), who believed himself to be a reincarnation of Alexander the Great (356-323 BC is 9° to 10° Virgo) and Charlemagne (AD 742-812 is 12° to 15° Libra). Napoleon has Neptune (psychic connection) at 9° Virgo, which registers in 377 BC; Mars, (warlike influence) at 12° Virgo, which registers in 233 BC; and a square from Uranus (individuality and inventiveness) at 11° Virgo retro-

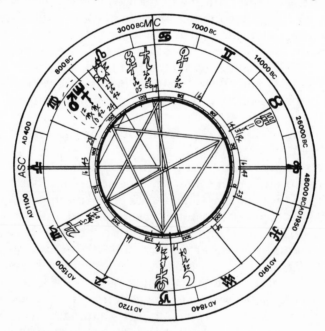

Fig. 42: The Horoscope of Napoleon
Born 15 August 1769 at Ajaccio, Corsica.

grade (moving backwards), which registers in 254 BC. The Ascendant in Napoleon's horoscope is 16° Libra, showing that his personality is within one degree of the time of Charlemagne.

The great prophet and seer *Nostradamus* (1503-1566) (Fig. 43) is one of the most mysterious and magical individuals in history, and no one has ever presented a theory to explain the uncanny accuracy of his predictions. The author gave astrological advice for the second edition of *"The Prophecies of Nostradamus"* by Erika Cheetham, and a series of remarkable facts became clear. While to look at the structure of The Divine Plot from a time after its end is intellectually satisfying, it must be remembered that the mathematical principles, the structure of astrology and the nature of the space-time memory system were intact in ancient times, and could have been constructed by such as Nostradamus, either as part of a secret tradition or intuitively. The horoscope of Nostradamus is interesting because one planet, Pluto, registers during his lifetime and a number of planets register after his lifetime in the ARTS, coincidentally at the times of his most accurate future prophecies. The implication must be that Nostradamus had experienced and remembered his future as well as past

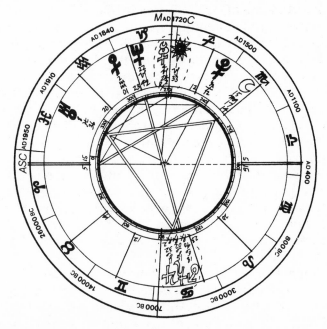

Fig. 43: The Horoscope of Nostradamus
Born 14 December 1503 at St Remy, France.

incarnations. Pluto registers at 6° Sagittarius 12°, equivalent to a date of 1556, when Nostradamus was 53 years old. The year is highly significant because of the story of Nostradamus' most famous prediction. In the first edition his Centuries in 1555, Nostradamus predicted the death of King Henri II in Century I, 35, in a duel where "He will pierce his eyes in their golden cage; two wounds in one, then he dies a cruel death".[189] As a result of the prediction, he was summoned to the French court by Queen Catherine de Medici on 14th July 1556, to explain the prophecy. The prediction was astonishingly fulfilled, because in 1559 Henri II died in a joust by accident when an opponent's spear shattered, piercing his golden helmet and also wounding him in the neck. He lived in agony for ten days before he died. Nostradamus also predicted that four of Catherine and Henri's children would be kings, which was true. The registration of Pluto (the masses and powerful people, magical influence over others) in the 8th house of death and the sign Sagittarius of sporting events, merged in the most critical time of his life.

The planets which register in the ARTS after the lifetime of Nostradamus are highly significant. Coincident with the Sun at 1° Capricorn, Nostradamus predicted the Accession of George I in 1714. In Century III,77 he predicted the exact date of a treaty between the Persians and Turks in October 1727, within a degree of his Midheaven at 2° Capricorn. The registration of Neptune in 22° Capricorn, dated in 1815 fits with his numerous and very precise predictions concerning Napoleon's 100 days, his escape from Elba and the Battle of Waterloo in 1815 in Centuries I,23, II,70, IV,75 and X,24. At the registration of Venus at 2° Aquarius in 1848, he accurately predicted the creation of the National Assembly of 1848 (IX,5), very descriptive of Venus (integration) of a group (Aquarius), the involvement of Napoleon III in French revolutionary activity, and the Marriage of the Count de Chambard. One of the more notorious quatrains, describing the Munich Putsch started by Adolf Hitler in 1923, coincides exactly with Uranus at 8° Pisces. The opposite point to his Saturn at 15° Cancer coincides with the French Revolution of 1789 to the year. The correlations are truly astonishing.

Another example is the horoscope of *Adolf Hitler* (Fig. 44), the maniac who professed strong belief in a mystical inheritance of the Aryan racial memory and was obsessed with the Grail legend. The strong and unconscious influence he had upon the German nation can be understood in six planets and the Midheaven which register in the first four signs, Aries, Taurus,

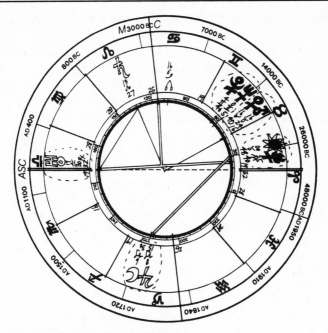

Fig. 44: The Horoscope of Adolf Hitler
Born 20 April 1889 at Branau, Austria.

Gemini and Cancer. The conjunction of Neptune and Pluto describes "the supernatural, clairvoyant visions, a magical influence over the masses, as well as manias, self-torment, peculiar states of soul experience and possession,"[190] and its location in Gemini indicates a magical power from the use of language and communication alone, a fact in Hitler's rise to power.

A most fascinating example of reincarnation theory is the great German novelist *Thomas Mann* (1875-1955) (Fig. 45) and his masterwork *"Joseph and His Brothers"*, started in 1927 and not finished until 1944. In the first of the four volumes, *"Tales of Jacob"*, Mann frequently refers to the astrological heritage of Joseph's time and specifically describes the positions of the planets and personal points in the horoscope of Joseph using Persian terminology. When translated, Joseph and Thomas Mann have the same horoscope! In both horoscopes the Gemini Sun is conjunct the Midheaven, indicating a noon birth, the sign Virgo is rising on the Ascendant, and the Moon is in Cancer:

As there is no knowledge that Thomas Mann knew any astrology, it would be natural for him to use his own horoscope as that of Joseph, but the agreement between the two lives is striking. It would seem obvious that Mann felt a sympathy and strong connection to Joseph, but the life parallels are beyond chance because the plot of the Joseph story is recorded in the Bible. What is amazing is that the life of Joseph is prophetic of Thomas Mann's life during the years when he wrote the novel. Many of the events in Mann's life happened after he had written about them in Joseph's story. The parallels are sketched below:

Joseph	Thomas Mann
– the youngest son in large family	– the youngest son in large family
– competitive with older brothers	– competitive with brother Heinrich
– mocked his brothers	– Buddenbrooks exposed the bourgeois
– given Coat of Many Colours	– awarded the Nobel Prize
– abandoned by brothers in a well and sold to traders	– rejected by Heinrich and ejected by the Nazis
– lived in exile in north Egypt	– lived in exile in Switerland
– moved again to southern Egypt	– moved again to Princeton, USA
– supported by Potiphar	– supported by publisher in New York
– rejected advances from P's wife	– rejected advances from p's wife
– moved again to acclaim	– moved to California with acclaim
– interpreted the Pharaoh's dream about the coming of a war	– convinced Roosevelt about WW2 coming
– was honored for patriotism	– honored for support
– reunited with his brothers	– sponsored Heinrich in the US

It is tempting to assume that Thomas Mann was formerly Joseph in the biblical story, as it was the very powerful novel which occupied seventeen years of his most creative time.

Another interesting aspect of Thomas Mann's horoscope is its connection to the ARTS times when his novels were set. Mann's primary concern was with language, reflecting the Sun (spiritual centre and vitality) and the Midheaven (ego-consciousness and spiritual awareness) both in Gemini, the time when language was developed. The mythical Moon in Cancer corresponds to an ancient Indian legend about the true love of a woman in *"The Transposed Heads"*. Uranus in Leo registers at the time of the patriarch Abraham, very much contemporary to the Joseph story, and very near the time of the short story *"The Tables of the Law"*. Jupiter in AD 964 falls near the time of Pope Gregory, the central character in *"The Holy Sinner"*. Mars in Capricorn occurs at about the time of his short novel *"Royal Highness"*. The most significant correlation, however, is the registration of Saturn (hereditary influences) at the time when his first great novel *"Buddenbrooks"*, about a

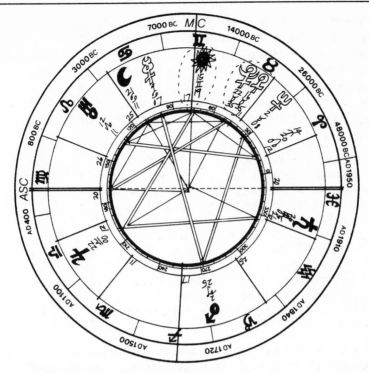

Fig. 45: The Horoscope of Thomas Mann
Born 6 June 1875 at Lubeck, Germany.

family dynasty based upon his own family, took place. The principle that creative people work out reincarnation influences that derive from the times in history when their planets register is a very helpful and intriguing way to use the mechanism of the ARTS.

Varieties of Reincarnation

The history of reincarnation ideas is very wide and vague. Two wonderful books describe people and groups in history who have supported some form of reincarnation. *"Reincarnation: An East-West Anthology"* by Head and Cranston includes quotations from over 400 western thinkers, including those already mentioned, as well as Thomas Huxley, Albert Schweitzer, Thomas Edison, Walt Whitman, Emerson, Thoreau, Tom Paine, William James, Carl Jung, Hesse, J. B. Rhine, Darwin, Einstein, Planck, Schrodinger, Fromm, Henri Bergson, Flaubert, Kierkegaard, Ibsen and many others. A sequel, *"Reincarnation: The Phoenix Fire Mystery"*, is a comprehensive look at reincarnation with a focus on scientists and various national cultural contexts. Terms used include palingenesis, preexistence, transmigration and rebirth, as the word "reincarnation" did not come into vogue until the French introduced the term in the middle of the last century.

While the actual mechanism of reincarnation is unknowable except on a psychic level, the most thorough understanding of it is Eastern:

> The ancient Indian thinkers believed that the happenings in an individual's present life are to be understood against the background of the previous life, which itself is to be looked upon as the nearest link in a beginningless series of rebirths. 'Avidya' itself is something that does not have a beginning in time: it is beginningless. Thus it is supposed that the mind of a newborn infant is, at birth, full of traces (samskaras) of those actions that were made over countless past lives, for the embryo in the mother's womb is itself supposed to be equipped with these samskaras, for they form a part of the subtle body luga sharira, which leaves one gross body at the time of death, entering into an embryo as guided by the samskaras.[191]

The discovery of genetic code has allowed the concept of reincarnation to be seen in a different light. Reincarnation is a collective phenomenon because all life is the cumulative effect of many former lives, parallel to the action of genetics. Every being carries, via genetics, a history back to the first life, and before that to the creation of the world. The qualities which differentiate one individual from another are the result of the dominance of certain genetic impulses over others, in turn formed by the karma of the incarnating soul. Everyone has the same fund of possibilities, but the drive to manifestation varies in strength and qualities. That certain qualities are derived from father or mother, or grandparents is verifiable, but to go further back is impossible due to the lack of information, i.e. photographs, birth records, biographical information, etc. When one's genetic line is taken back one hundred years, the qualities inherited from any one ancestor is 1:4000, while back one thousand years, a brief time in the total span of history, all family lines converge, and 15,000 years ago even racial differences disappear. The similarities between all present humans is more than 95% of the total pattern. Reincarnation is the forerunner of genetics, and is a superior knowledge because it is concerned with more than only the protoplasmic line, and addresses the differential requirements of the other, higher bodies in the process of cosmic manifestation. The Divine Plot is the integration of traditional reincarnation technology and modern genetics, and an attempt to quantify and qualify the individual inheritance.

Individuals *"remember"* past lives when they feel the resonance of historically-based genetic and spiritual impulses activated by contact with artifacts, places, other individuals or information. Instead of valuing only those inherited qualities which are quantifiable, like hair and eye colour, facial structure, weight and height, the qualities derived from historical ways of behaving, holding a world view or instinctively acting can be correlated with astrological qualities which may be checked against a birth horoscope. Although in the early stages, a new science of reincarnation is beginning.

The concept of planetary bodies implies multiple ways of reincarnation. The physical incarnation process is tangible and follows the protoplasmic family trees without the freedom to deviate, and is carried strictly through the protoplasmic line. The physical line carries all impulses derived from the family descent, but focuses on those which are activated by the Ascendant position in the horoscope. The emotional incarnation is a finer process, not limited by the direct substance of which the body is composed but changes, jumping from family to family within a general racial and hereditary pattern, and is activated by the Moon in the horoscope. The Moon characteristics may lie dormant for generations, and may activate qualities which originate from outside of the direct protoplasmic line. The Moon is equivalent to the Genetic Entity. Each planetary body reincarnates at certain times in history, has an effect upon the individual life, and passes on to other lives.

The relative importance of the historical periods or incarnations represented by the planets is determined by planetary positions in the birth horoscope. Planets near the Ascendant are highlighted because they are sub-personalities. Planets near the MC, at the apex of the horoscope, are the most conscious. Planets in the 7th house would affect the nature of partners and relationships.

The integration of a birth chart is symbolized by a group of space-time beings in various historical manifestations attempting to discover a higher purpose. Afflicted planets are difficult individuals in their time or indicative of imperfect understanding of a particular life time. Each planet tries to dominate the whole by recreating its natural time and mode of consciousness and behaviour, as sub-personalities can dominate an individual. Present-time reality is a collage of historical beings and their times joining, conflicting or integrating. Everyone is a multi- temporal being, eternally shifting from one identity to another. The only ordering possible is to encompass all time and determine how to express all natural instincts and modes of consciousness. Each individual component is unique and potentially dominant, but the whole is served by integration which experiences all components. The parts must be identified with before we can be liberated from them.

According to the *pattern* of the birth chart, there is either a representative selection of times (splay shape), a concentrated focus (bundle shape), an awareness of half of reality (a bowl shape) or a see- saw from one constellation of attitudes to others opposite (sling shape). Closer groupings weight the whole towards one particular attitude and its time, and show an attempt to revive the spirit of the time irrespective of the other times. The process works two ways. Each person has certain interests and a world view derived from the times in history which struck a familiar chord, and seeks confirmation of those approaches to life. Some people are carried away by their love of historical games or attitudes, at the expense of the whole.

The aware individual has primary consciousness only of the stage in which they live in the present time, with partial access to the octave immediately before or after. In gestation previous lives are simultaneously lived, and in childhood, the gestation octave of previous lives is still sensed, although in most societies such memories are suppressed. There have been many cases of young children remembering past lives so vividly that objects, words and ideas totally alien to their new life are recognized instantly. Such a process is in action in the selection of Tibetan Buddhist lamaic incarnations. The accompanying horoscope is a western young man who was recognized as the incarnation of a very high Tibetan Buddhist lama at the age of seven years old in Kathmandu (Fig. 46). Usually, once the fifth house cusp has been passed at about seven years old and the octave of maturity entered, the memories of previous incarnative influences begins to fade, if not disappear totally.

Taste, fashion, faddism, revivalism, romanticism, historicism and pragmatism are all snares to entrap the unwary in history. One can be reabsorbed into the past, drawn into attitudes which mirror illusory parts and take away from the whole, just as in life the trap of family or individual psychological patterns are often total and binding. The mechanism of former realities

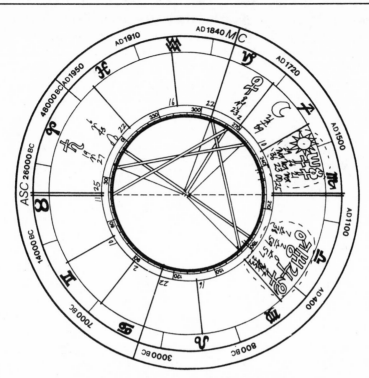

Fig. 46: A western Tibetan Buddhist Lama incarnation
Born 21 November 1968, at Great Barrington, Mass., USA.

can dominate, cycle after cycle. It is necessary to disidentify from such historical patterns in order to transcend their bondage. Attraction influences future incarnations, as similar periods of time are returned to, time after time. Multiple personalites result when the identities have no knowledge of each other and create inner collisions. The creative process of collating spatio- temporal existences is part of the individuation and transpersonal processes in psychology. The necessary connection is the perception of various identities as related to each other, no matter how unlikely, and to combine them to generate a true whole.

Plato believed that most people are so bound in their lives that when given the opportunity at death to transcend their limitations, to move to a higher state, will choose to live their previous life again, regardless of the pain or entrapment implied by that life. The fear of the unknown is stronger than the desire for liberation. This principle permeates not only the individual in the incarnation process, but also our world age. In order to transform our world, everyone must be willing to give up their past patterns of which they are enamoured. The nature of life and the world must be known before liberation can free the life and the world.

★Chapter Eight★
★Up the Golden Path★

The end of the World Age. The nature of The Divine Plot. The Four Worlds. World in crisis. Contemporary theories of universal history. The Reflexive Universe. The Invisible Landscape. Up From Eden. Earth Ascending. Exo-psychology. UFO's and Space Fertilization. Jung's saucers. Astral travellers. Chariots of the Gods. Pyramid mysteries. Prodigies. The End of Time.

The world itself is the judgement of the world.[192]
Schopenhauer

The end of a World Age of humanity is a terrifying prospect, one many would think a very negative speculation. Not only is it a possible projection of the immediate future, but it is also a story which forms the nucleus of all mythical representations of the nature of the world. Myths are the essence of religious, political and social systems. Investigating the mechanism of the End of the World allows speculation on the elusive key to what is happening in the world now, where the evolution of consciousness is leading, and presents a way to come to terms with The Divine Plot.

There are many ways to interpret The Divine Plot; as history, as a metaphysical mechanism, as a programme for the biocomputer, as a religious stance, or as a description of the physical world. The scientist might criticize the free use of science, where some principles are accepted and used as evidence, while others are openly negated, but that is common scientific practice. The search for physical laws is fruitless because laws must be changed as understanding increases. The psychiatrist might resist combining behavioural principles with the workings of the mundane world. The astrologer might resent the sacred science dragged down into physical manifestation. The transpersonal psychologist might feel that a circular view of time is too fated and closed, and would not allow freedom for self-expression. The historian might find the history described inaccurate and incomplete, dealing as it does with both inner and outer history. The optimist might resist what seems like a negative picture of the world – after all, the Aquarian Age is just around the corner. It is difficult to satisfy everyone, but everyone is a part of time and history.

In the west the focus is upon extending the duration of life, thereby conquering time, while the traditional eastern goal is liberation from the wheel of time and karma, an end to the series of incarnations. In this sense history is a programming from which we must escape. Rodney Collin's "Four Worlds" are shown in Fig. 47. The two horizontal circles are the 1000 lunar month lifetime of the cellular body, and the one lunar month lifetime of the ovum. They intersect like the symbol for infinity at the point of conception and death. An individual experiences an entire lifetime in essence during the lunar month of the ovum, and the cellular life then unfolds in its own time. By using the familiar factor of 1000 Collin states that the next longer phase of 80,000 years would be equivalent to life in the mineral realm where change is excruciatingly slow, pressure is great and heat intense, like what we call hell. At the moment of death, at the intersection of the cellular and molecular circles, it is possible, if the identification with material goods or precious metals is dominant enough, to descend to the hellish mineral realm. Instead of experiencing a lifetime of about 80 years until the next opportunity for liberation, the wait is 1000 times longer. Every body is composed of mineral elements and has access to their equivalent time perspective. The importance of precious metals like gold and silver, or gems like diamonds and rubies, stems from the sense of immense time which they encapsulate. If descent into the mineral realm is hell, Collin postulates that ascent into the higher electronic realm is heaven. The heavenly realm is always available, and may be compared with transpersonal or transcendent energies ready to merge with the self. The sphere in which all four circles of existence spin around their axes is a fifth dimension of eternal recurrence, or the revolution of things in their own place. A sixth dimension where all four circles spin around their meeting point is the world in which everything is everywhere and "all possibilities are realized".[193] Beings who live in a higher state than the four sensible worlds have gone beyond the sphere of

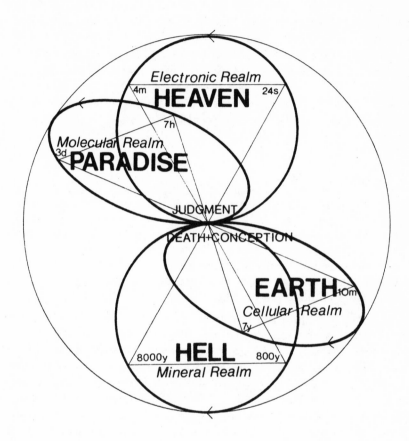

Fig. 47: Four Worlds
The four circles at right angles to each other signify the relationship between four dimensions of human existence. The horizontal circles represent, on the right the Cellular World of visible existence and on the left the Molecular World of invisible existence. They intersect at the moment of conception and death. The lower circle is the Hellish Mineral Realm of great density, and the upper circle is the Heavenly Electronic Realm of pure spirit. The four worlds of matter is a 'philosophical machine' to Collin. *(Collin, The Theory of Eternal Life)*

earthly beings and are free of the sun, the galaxy and the universe. Physical existence requires obedience to the cyclic laws of the various circles of being. In the context of the Universal Time Scale we cannot escape, even though it seems that movement from one octave level to another, finer level, constitutes heaven. Whatever the octave, the same laws are in operation relative to that dimension. The only liberation is beyond the world of such laws, into the timelessness associated with God. Liberation is unity with God.

At the present time the world is in a state of chaos which is beyond comprehension. The world is in great peril through:

1. Population explosion
2. Food Crisis
3. Resource Scarcity,
4. Environmental degradation, ecological imbalance due to burning fossil fuels, deforestation due to acid rain or pollution
5. Nuclear Abuse by design or accident from weapons and power plants
6. Science and Technology Unleashed
6. Political anarchy on a worldwide scale
7. Freak climatic catastrophes

The world population is in danger of self-destruction. Everyone alive now is reponsible for the state of affairs, and for any potential change of that state. Whatever the means by which a world age ends, it brings with it an inevitable necessity for deep revaluation. Whether the end of the World Age is a necessary step in the creation of an enlightened world, or an actual cataclysm, the reality of it must be faced. It is assumed that this is the first time such a crisis of preservation has occurred, yet persuasive evidence has been presented which proves that it is not the first time.

An age of darkness follows the end of a World Age, just as an age of darkness preceded the present cycle of civilizations. Whatever the cause of the End of the World, there are survivors. The enormity of the conflict which creates the End is too much to comprehend, and those who survive wander through the world reverting to primitive reality. Those prepared to understand and confront the End of the World are forced to develop rituals to carry on the meaning of The End from generation to generation. The purpose is multifold. On the mundane level it is to ensure survival on the principle that to know the problem is the first step to preventing its recurrence, but on a higher level it is to carry over into the next world knowledge of the sacred. The ritual of the end of a world is a unique heritage of all humans, and the death and burial ritual was often conceived as a reenactment of the ultimate event.

Can it be possible that the world as we know it may end? All it takes is a look at the daily news to see that the entire world is in violent chaos right now. People are killing each other in ever increasing numbers, as though the karmic rights of the underprivileged are being exonerated. The quantity of information available increases every day, and most individuals are being rapidly submerged in data. When large computers go down, planes crash and whole industries stop. People are unhappy amidst the greatest opulence ever imagined. We travel more each year on holiday than the greatest travellers the world knew five hundred years ago in a lifetime. Our annual income is more than a lifetime of wages fifty years ago. The world is already very different from the world we were prepared to grow up in as children. Many people wish it all to end.

There are many different theories to account for what is happening in our world today. Five of the more prominent theories follow. Much of the material they present is included within the wide-range of The Divine Plot.

Contemporary Theories of Universal History

The Divine Plot combines mechanisms from mythology, science, psychology, history, anthropology and many others, organized by the cosmic art and science astrology. Other ways of organizing the universal process are useful as comparison and show that the UTS integrates many of their ideas. These are *"The Reflexive Universe"* by Arthur M. Young, the inventor of the Bell helicopter; the Holographic Theory of Mind from *"The Invisible Landscape"* by Dennis and Terence McKenna, botanists, anthropologists and philosophers; *"Up From Eden"* by the transpersonal psychologist Ken Wilber; *"Earth Ascending"* by Jose Arguelles; and *"Exo-Psychology"* by Timothy Leary, the prophet of psychedelics. Although written from various viewpoints, the conclusions are very similar and consistent.

1. *The Reflexive Universe: Evolution of Consciousness*[193]
Arthur Young proposes a "theory of process" of seven stages in the sequence: Light, Particles, Atoms, Molecules, Plants, Animals, (Man), which has a distinctive pattern including a

"fall" or descent into matter. Although he starts with the mechanics of the torus form, the seven stages follow a V-shape with four Kingdoms of Freedom of action (Fig. 48), with molecules as the fulcrum at the depth of the descent with no freedom at all. Atoms and plants reflect each other with 1 degree of freedom, followed by particles and animals with 2 and light and man with 3. Young ingeniously correlates the model to quantum mechanics, the structure of the Periodic Table of the Elements, mechanisms in chemistry, physics, psychology and the natural world. Each Kingdom of organization is subdivided into seven Stages of potential, binding, identity, combination, growth, mobility and dominion. The grid theory is also compared with the mythologies which describe seven-fold processes of creation, including Iranian, Greek, Mayan and Egyptian myths and Genesis. He presents a Teleology of seven stages of human evolution of consciousness from Spirit-1 down to Soul-1 down to Mind-1 down to Body, and then as ascent from Mind-2 to Soul-2 to Spirit-2. His ultimate conclusion is that the photon of light falls into matter, there to undergo its transformations until in the process of the creation of the light recognizes itself.

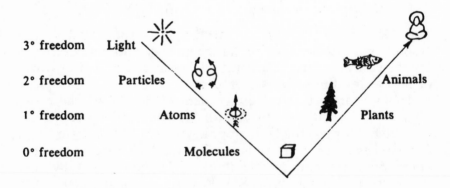

Fig. 48: Kingdoms of Freedom
The relative kingdoms of the natural world represented as a symmetrical fall from the uncertainty of photons to the total bond of molecules followed by an ascent from animals to humanity. *(Young, The Reflexive Universe)*

2. *"The Invisible Landscape: Mind, Hallucinogens and the I Ching"*[194]

The McKennas' theory is derived from shamanism via the effects of psychoactive drugs upon the psyche, and is a computer-generated time scale based on the Chinese I Ching. The universe is created by the interaction of two hyper-universes as a hologram is created by the interaction of two lasers, therefore every part contains the information of the whole – every atom is the brain of the whole universe.[198] Certain hallucinogens create transmitters which allow the mind to tap into the cyclic processes of DNA and RNA, possibly by activating melatonin and pineal serotonin. A cyclic recurrent universe on many different scales grows directly from the idea. Hallucinogens alter metabolism by affecting the electron spin resonance (ESR) of genetic molecules, and encourage the nervous system to resonate with the wave-form hologram of the universe. ESR molecules are superconductors of the holographic information storage system containing all genetic and experientially coded information within its wave pattern.

The mathematics is based on the hexagrams of the I Ching, creating 64 exponential time-scales which exist in the universe – all are collective and will all peak together in the year AD 2012. The concept is similar to The Divine Plot, particularly in the use of lunar months as the units for the time-scale. The following scales all peak together:

– a 4,300-year cycle from urbanization to modern science;
– a 384-year cycle in which science has dominated humanity;
– a 67-year cycle from the 1940's when DNA and nuclear energy were discovered, when there is more acceleration than from the Renaissance to the present;
– a 384-day cycle in 2011-2012 when there will be more transformations than in all previous cycles;
– a 6-day cycle at the end; leading to,

in the last 135 minutes, 18 barriers, comparable to the appearance of life, the invention of language or the achievement of immortality, will be crossed, 13 of them in the last 75×10^{-4} seconds.

Access to the quantum information system is movement into the Faustian universe, and psychedelics are one way to make the transition. The McKennas believe that humanity is in a unique position to accomplish a Resurrection into the Light of which the gnostics and alchemists dreamed.

3. *"Up From Eden: A Transpersonal View of Human Evolution"*[195]
Ken Wilber describes the path of transcendence according to
the perennial philosophy: the Great Chain of Being is a
universal sequence of hierarchic levels of increasing
consciousness from matter to body to mind to soul to spirit.
Transpersonal history is the unfolding of successively higher-
order structures. A circular map (Fig. 32) is divided into three
sections of Subconscious (pre-personal), Self-conscious
(personal) and Superconscious (trans-personal), a structure
identical to the individual astrological horoscope of Life★Time
Astrology and the Universal Time Scale. The sequence of stages
in the great chain parallels the twelve developmental stages of
The Divine Plot, but without dates, and uses inward and
outward arcs, as in the "descent into matter" of Young. The
message is the same: the universe is a whole and every
individual possesses the entire psychological evolutionary
reality of history.

4. *"Earth Ascending: An Illustrated Treatise on the Law Governing*
   Whole Systems"[196]
Jose Arguelles has created a series of holonomic maps presenting a theory of history and man based on a "psi bank", a
repository of all information parallel to the spiritual electron of
Charon, the ESR molecule of the McKennas and the torus of
Young. The maps combine principles from the binary DNA
triplets, Chinese geomancy, I Ching hexagrams, Benjamin
Franklin's magic square of 16, movements of tectonic plates and
the Mayan calendar with its pulse of 260 days, integrated with
the yearly cycle of nature. Many references are made to myth,
shamanism and the mantic arts in a spherical and rectilinear
model of a "planet art network" manifest through the global psi
bank.

5. *"Exo-Psychology"*[197]
Tim Leary's book is subtitled, "A Manual on the Use of the
Human Nervous System According to the Instructions of the
Manufacturers", and describes the purpose of life as
S.M.I.^{2}L.E., which is "Space Migration Intelligence Increase
Life Extension". Leary uses an eight-fold process and an
astrological model of two-times-twelve phases to describe from
a galactic perspective the biological development of the human
neurological system, its evolution on earth, and the direction of
its future in space. Leary also uses the quantum mechanical
model and the mechanism of genetic code, neurogenetics, to

explain how extra-ordinary mutations are being created. Leary recognizes that evolution is accelerating, but does not attempt to attribute dates to the process, although he insists that "the key to evolution beyond the larval forms is the understanding and control of time".

Leary believes in immanent space migration, the indefinite extension of life, and the necessity to reimprint the genetic template in order to make the next leap in understanding, which he calls "Neuro-Atomic Contelligence". The newly discovered freedom of quantum physics at the subatomic level is symbolic of a newly-acquired freedom of will, and implies, with Young and Charon, that "any system dominated by quantum mechanical fluctuations is conscious". The ultimate linkage is the black hole, the final vortex, "the linkage of the universe of everything with the void of everything".

The common goal of these five books is the discovery of a unified theory of the universe which includes humanity, presented from the viewpoints of the scientist, hallucenigenic anthropologist, transpersonal psychologist, artist and space-oriented philosopher. It is necessary to combine and synthesize many varied and even contradictory viewpoints in order to redeem the world.

Reincarnation is often used to rationalize difficulties in the world. It is easy to attribute the cause of disease to "karmic debts" inherited from previous lives. The lack of wholeness of life can be blamed on parents, social milieu, a time in history, government, religious education and many others, but the ultimate life lies within each of us as individuals. Each of us must take the entire history of the world on in our lives and redeem it, in order to liberate ourselves and the world. Freedom is in living in the present and incorporating all past and future in the moment.

UFO's and Space Fertilization

Whence this creation originated;
Whether He caused it to be or not,
He who in the highest empyrean surveys it,
He alone knows, or else, even He knows not.[199]

Since 1950, two related controversies have raged, both of which can be understood in the context of The Divine Plot.

The first was the barrage of reports of UFO's (Unidentified Flying Objects) seen by people all over the world. Sightings were usually of circular, disk or cigar-shaped objects moving through the sky at terrific speeds and performing impossible aerial antics. Many were seen by commercial or military pilots to move in ways which defied the laws of time and space. There have also been people who insisted they were taken into the saucers and examined by spacemen before being released. There have been so many cases of sightings that it is reasonable to consider the possibility, but there has been no proof of their existence.

The psychologist Carl Jung felt that flying saucers were collective projections onto the sky of feelings related to either the salvation or destruction of the planet, as well as being images of the totality of the self.[200] The circular mandala plays an experiential role in uniting apparently irreconcilable opposites and split-mindedness. Simultaneous sightings imply that different people are receiving similar ideas. Such images were also prevalent just before the year AD 1000, when there were many predictions of the end of the world. Jung states that when unconscious contents are resisted by consciousness, they can be projected onto objects which reflect that which had previously been hidden. The saucer symbolizes the circular nature of time itself as a totality.

Esoteric healer David Tansley presents a more intriguing explanation. Humans are manifestations in a multi-dimensional universe comprised of many levels of reality. Underlying physical reality are etheric forces, a scaffolding of energies upon which physical forms are built. Beyond the etheric lies the astral plane, and higher intuitive and spiritual levels of awareness. Theosophists posit two higher monadic planes, making a total of seven. Each plane is further sub-divided into seven parts, related to planetary spheres, yielding a total of forty-nine planes of manifestation, which recalls the numerological and mythological significance of the numbers forty-nine and fifty in the structure of The Divine Plot.

In esoteric teachings the symbols of the third and first etheric levels are half-moon and lenticular in shape, similar to that of the UFO sightings, and also a similar form to red blood corpuscles. The UFO sightings are in Tansley's conception a manifestation of forces which exist in the etheric level of reality attempting to communicate with or break through to our reality. Tansley even suggests that UFO's are a form of organic life.

If we recognise that the solar system we live in is the body of a vast entity, one in whom we live and move and have our being, it is ony a short step to consider the possibility that some of the UF0 forms we see, particularly those that are spheroidal lights, may be some form of cosmic corpuscles that flow into the body of the earth which is an organ of the solar man (system). . . if the consciousness of an atom in our body perceives a blood cell as a spheroidal travelling light winging its way across galaxies of cells, it is just possible to see in the UFO phenomena that occur around our planet, a similar pattern.[201]

UFO sightings are contact with finer and more subtle levels or reality which interpenetrate the gross physical plane, and in the framework of The Divine Plot, are access to other levels of the Universal Time Scale through the circular mandala shape characteristic of each level of manifestation. A popular explanation for mysterious origin is that of a visitation of earth by spacemen. Popularized by Erich van Daniken[202] and followed by hundreds of similar works, the theory attributes the origin of language, myths of sky battles and gods, and even consciousness itself to the influence of errant spacemen in prehistory. While most information advanced is allusive rather than concrete, many of the questions raised are relevant and perplexing. Megalithic monuments, earth marking and ley lines, primitive art of beings in what look like space helmets, indian legends of white gods descending from the sky, prophetic protestations from Ezekiel and the Book of Revelations and the unresolved enigma of the origin of life are all covered by Van Daniken in such a way that the entire issue is simultaneously absurd and profoundly stimulating. Until now there has been no answer to the questions he asks.

Rene Noorbergen finds traces of extra-terrestrial migration in Hindu accounts of the detonation of an atom bomb in 2400 BC, the use of x-rays in China in 206 BC, model aircraft found in pre-Incan sites, Egyptian drawings depicting a vacuum tube and a planetarium computer found in ancient Greece.[203]

The co-discoverer of the structure of the genetic code double helix, Nobel Laureate Francis Crick, hypothesized that life may have come to earth billions of years ago from an advanced civilization in another galactic system via an unmanned rocket, an interstellar Noah's Ark, carrying microbial spores. As a highly respected scientist, it was a shock to the establishment that Crick rejects the Oparin-Haldane mechanism that life arose by random accidents in the primeval boullion. The question of the origin of life is the greatest scientific mystery, and as Louis Pasteur proved, life does not originate from non-living matter.

Crick proposed that the doomed galactic civilization sent spaceships to many galaxies, knowing that the required chemical soup would exist on many planets in many solar systems. Bacteria can be frozen for the tens of thousands of years it takes for such an immense journey. Crick's theory is similar to that of the British astronomer Sir Fred Hoyle, who also believes that life has an extraterrestrial origin, and that bacteria may have come to earth through space itself. The still unanswered question is: if this is the case, how did life originate on the parent planet?

A fascinating idea is created by the integration of the hypotheses of UFO's and Space Fertilization. A model derived from electron microscope photographs of a virus looks strikingly like the NASA lunar landing module (LEM). (Fig. 49) The virus lands on a human cell and lowers its legs like the LEM lands on the surface of the moon. What if UFO's have already landed, but they are the product of a microscopic galaxy (an atom?), and are so small that they cannot be perceived by our eyes, but only by our perceptions tuned to the much faster and finer reality of such beings. The logarithmic relativity of such beings would mean that an entire world age for them would be the duration of a minor virus infection for us.

Just imagine it. The microscopic module has been sent from its galaxy from within the same human body and has landed upon the surface of a cell. The few bacteria (we are ourselves a very complex bacteria) land and colonize the cell system. Gradually they evolve, civilize the system, even populate neighboring cells, until they have an advanced civilization. In the final stages of the evolution of the civilization, they overpopulate, grow out of control like a cancer, discover atomic weapons, and finally overheat their environment, leading to a cataclysm, a trial by fire. The high temperature which accompanies brief illness would be the final conflagration of the bacterial society. They would send, just before their demise, scout rockets with colonists on long journeys to survive somewhere else in the universe. The situation is a familiar one. It is very possible that identical processes are happening in the microcosm, in the miniature world, as happen in the outer world.

There is no reason to assume that other galaxies and their inhabitants would be the same size as earthlings. On the contrary, it is possible that in other galaxies beings are so much larger than us that the solar system exists as an atom within their bodies, or that they are so much smaller that they would

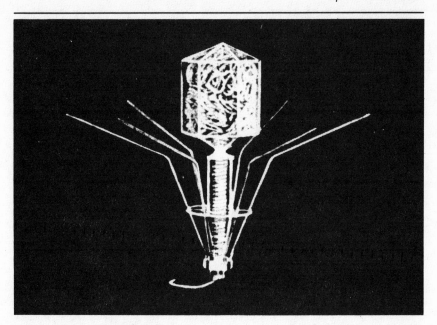

Fig. 49: The Viral LEM
The electron microscope reconstruction of a virus looks exactly like
the NASA lunar landing module.

exist within us. The relativity of dimensions of being is an
important concept in understanding our place within the
universe.

The powerful impact of UFO's and fertilizing spacemen must
be understood in the context of a recurrent universe. During the
last decades of the Twentieth Century television is so
widespread in the world that almost every individual alive has
either seen man landing on the moon, the most widely viewed
event in human history, or one of the many science fiction
movies along the lines of Star Wars. The capability of travelling
into outer space is proven, but the extent to which it can be
utilized constructively remains to be seen. Many people
fantasize the escape into deep space and other solar systems or
galaxies is the only solution to world problems. The fantasy has
become the primary myth of our age. The brilliant science
fiction work of Ray Bradbury, called *"The Martian Chronicles"*,
shows that humans from earth colonizing Mars and then
stranded there become the Martians that they are seeking. With
the concept of recurrent world ages it is entirely possible that
the collective myth of space fertilization is a matter of thinking
that we are fertilizing ourselves. It is still open whether there is
even one other solar system in the universe which has planets.

We may be alone.

Modern nations believe that they can dominate outer space, which gives the misleading notion that humanity can survive self-created ecological catastrophes simply by sending enough beings off of earth to inhabit other planets. While possible, it remains a rationalization. When each last world age terminates in a cataclysm, space fantasies are rife. The first conscious beings evolving thousands of years after the end of a world age would naturally utilize the powerful images of the spaceman-god with the universe at his command, yet having no even remote idea of the derivation of the image. We have literally fertilized ourselves in prehistory and attribute it to other beings. Early humanity after a cataclysm retains fragments of technological information, interbred domesticated animals and garbled languages – only these fragments of the previous world age. Humanity is a self-perpetuating myth.

The structure or programme which determines the form of not only galaxies and solar systems, but also life, is inherent in the mechanism of time. Life is not evolved, but is eternal – we have always been here in the same niche in the universal matrix. We can identify with higher or lower worlds, but all worlds are maya, illusions of reality.

Megaliths and Pyramids

The question of the origin of monuments such as Stonehenge, Macchu Picchu or the Great Pyramid are also clarified by The Divine Plot. Megalithic Stonehenge contains stones transported over hundreds of miles, across the Irish Sea. How can this be? Stonehenge is one of the few monuments which exists through multiple world ages. In every world age it is rediscovered, moved to a more propitious site, restored by adding extra rings of stones, and made a sacred remainder of the previous world age. Over many world ages it moves hundreds of miles and contains energies from many world ages, many purposes, and provides magical clues to The Divine Plot.

The same process operates for the Great Pyramid, rediscovered in ruins, refaced with new alabaster, revered, used as the basis for many other crude imitations, allowed to fall into ruin again, etc. The smoothness of the impermeable megalithic monuments is a testimony to multiple world ages. As in the idea of Schwaller de Lubicz that such monuments were continuously disassembled and rebuilt on new sites would support our contention. Such monuments are always mistakenly identified as tombs, but contain no proof of such an identity because they are the only transmitters capable of spanning the vast ages of multiple world ages. The Great Pyramid is astronomically sited, and the orientation of the ascending and descending passages imply that it was built when the pole star was Alpha Draconis, making its date about 2170 BC. But, since equinoctial cycles of about 25,000 years are repetitive, the date of its last rebuilding could equally be 29,000 years ago or 54,000 years ago. All such astronomically sited monuments are similarly confused by modern humanity.

A parallel type of evidence for repetitive history is the phenomenon of prophets. If an individual has the capacity to remember lives in earlier times or even during previous world ages through cycles of death and conception, a profound but challenging process confronts them. The prophet must learn prevailing languages and customs in which to express the ideas that time is circular. A prophet two thousand years ago trying to describe modern cities and transport would probably be considered totally mad. The dangers of civilization would be difficult if not impossible to express, except through the medium of parables or myths, which is why all prophets must couch their message in such forms. The ability to make predictions, or to present teachings which retain relevance through many generations is the primary quality which defines such beings. A similar profound memory of past lives and worlds is integral to prodigies, but the use of the information is not fully realized. Mozart would remember his compositions earlier and earlier each lifetime, until he was writing symphonies at five years old, before the age or reason. The understanding of the cyclic nature of time is the most profound mystery.

The End of Time

Strong is the system of the Pleroma; small is that which broke loose and became the world. But the All is what is encompassed. It has not come into being; it was existing.
Treatise on Resurrection, Nag Hammadi Gospels[204]

The paradox of The Divine Plot is that life cannot have originated without life. The universe cannot have been created without a universe. We cannot be here without having been here before. Creation, life and death are, as the Indians correctly surmised, illusions we invest with reality to make the world. We are composed of electrons which were present at the birth of the universe, and these pure energies will remain until the universe explodes in a Big Crunch and reforms into another universe. Once the divine nature of the plot of which we are the perpetuators, actors, set designers, producers, directors and audience becomes clear, the play may be experienced, loved and worshipped as it should be.

When we eat, the time in history of the origin of the substance is transmitted as a primary message. The closer to the origin, the purer and more spiritual the message. Water evokes the time when the planet was composed of vast seas; seaweed is a very primitive vegetable created in the earliest Virgo period in the Age of Creation; seafood evokes a later Scorpio period; while the meat of cattle is in the later Age of Mammals. Information from each period is communicated directly through the very substances we eat and breathe to sustain ourselves. We are what we eat. The entire past is omnipresent within, if only we can experience it directly. Humanity is divine, and divinity is inherent in our nature and in the mechanism of our world at every level.

In early history, humanity measured time by the sun or the moon. Some cultures developed lunar calendars, such as the builders of the megaliths in Europe, the Chinese, the Indians, the Jews, Islamic people or generally agricultural peoples. Others developed solar calendars, such as Egypt, Greece, Rome and western civilization. According to astrological symbolism, lunar cultures are primarily instinctive and unconscious while solar cultures place importance on rationality and consciousness. On the mathematical level, the two numbers are incommensurable, as the number of days in the lunar month (27.3) do not divide evenly into the number of days in the solar year (365.24). Life★Time Astrology is unique because it combines, for the first time, a temporal view of individual life and history which integrates the two required halves of the whole: solar and lunar, masculine and feminine, conscious and unconscious, left and right brain halves, and both rays of the holographic image. The mathematical constant of Life★Time Astrology is based on the fraction created when the moon is placed over the sun.

$$\text{Life} \star \text{Time Constant} = \frac{27.3 \quad \text{days in the lunar month}}{365.24 \quad \text{days in the solar year}}$$

Fig. 50: Coniunctio
The conjunction of the queen surmounting the king is a central image of alchemy. Beyond its symbolic meaning as the union of male and female, the Log Time Scale is based on its clear description of the mathematical formula of the number of days in the lunar month over the days in the solar year, making the ratio of .074744.

The most powerful and central alchemical image (Fig. 50) concerned the coniunctio of the King (Sol) and the Queen (Luna). While the psychological implications have been analyzed by Jung in particular[205], the symbolism is extremely rich and relevant. But the alchemists, in making gold, the spiritual body, transmitted not only a metaphor, but a mathematical equation which integrates masculine and feminine qualities. The basis of history, both individual and collective is the mystery of procreation.

The processes of history and the evolution of consciousness are both circular, spiralling and labyrinthine.

> Then it seemed like falling into a labyrinth; we thought we were at the finish, but our way bent a around and we found ourselves as it were back at the beginning, and just as far from that which we were seeking at first.[206]

The mysteries of time and being lead back to the sovereign Self, from where they started. After the descent from Unity into the eternal turmoil of multiplicity, the everpressing goal becomes the Return. The Return is the perpetually central theme of atoms, molecules, compounds, elementary life, complex life, humanity, moons, planets, solar systems and galaxies. In every pursuit of reality the motif of return is present, ever subtle and hidden, ever obvious, and always indescribable. It has given sanity and civilization to the world, but at the price of madness and chaos. It confuses and clarifies, expands and contracts, gives and takes, loves and hates. The path of being throughout time is variously Jacob's Ladder in the Kabbalah, the chain of causation Alaya, the movement of the planets through time and the double helix of genetic code. Every being, mundane or mythical, rich or poor, ecstatic or depressive, must confront the process of life and death. Whether it is seen, experienced, heard, felt, divined, ignored, worshipped or condemned, The Divine Plot involves us all.

"For time is just a delusion of
creatures who cannot cope
with eternity."
from The Supreme Law by
Maurice Maeterlinck

★*References*★

★*Chapter One – The Divine Plot*★

1. Oxford English Dictionary (unabridged)
2. Eliade, *Myths, Dreams and Mysteries* (London, 1968), p. 235.
3. Oswald Spengler, *The Decline of the West* (London, 1961), p. 425.
4. Mann, *The Round Art: The Astrology of Time and Space* (London, 1979) and *Life★Time Astrology* (London, 1984).

★*Chapter Two – Life History*★

5. Fraser, ed., *The Voices of Time*, (London, 1968), p. 91, quote by Sadogoshi.
6. Friedenthal, *Goethe: His Life and Times*, p. 418.
7. Eliade, *Myths, Dreams*, p. 54.
8. Marcus, *Freud and the Culture of Psychoanalysis* (London, 1983), p. 166.
9. Eliade, *Myths, Dreams*, p. 54.
10. Spengler, *Decline*, p. 3.
11. Mann, *Joseph and His Brothers* (London, 1950), p. 78.
12. Eliade, *Myth and Reality* (London, 1964), p. 85.
13. Ibid, p. 91.
14. Eliade, *Myths, Dreams*, p. 235.
15. Mann, *Joseph*, p. 6.
16. Collin, *The Theory of Eternal Life* (London, 1950).
17. Eliade, *The Myth of the Eternal Return* (New York, 1954), p. 144.
18. Blacker and Loewe, ed., *Ancient Cosmologies*, (London, 1975), p. 132.
19. Ibid, p. 123, from the *Mahabharata*.
20. Rig Veda, X, 29.
21. Blacker, *Cosmologies*, p. 128.
22. Thorndike, *The History of Magic and Experimental Science*, Vol. I (New York, 1941), p. 384.
23. According to the numerology of the Hebrew gematria, ShMITAH = 365 and ShMITA is 360, the number of days in the year and degrees in the circle, respectively.
24. Spengler, *Decline*.
25. Fraser, *Voices*, p. 111.
26. Thorndike, *History*, Vol. I, p. 384.
27. Malachi IV:1.
28. Jung, *Letters I 1906–1950* (London, 1973), p. 138.

29. Jung, *Aion*, CW 9, Part II (London, 1951), p. 81.
30. Blacker, *Cosmologies*, p. 162.
31. Corbin, '*Cyclical Time in Mazdaism and Ismailism*', *Man and Time*, Eranos Yearbook 3, edited by Joseph Campbell (New York, 1957, p. 157–60.
32. Wolben, *After Nostradamus* (London, 1973), p. 43.
33. Jung, *Symbols of Transformation*, CW 5 (London, 1952), p. 81.
34. Turville-Petre, *Myth and Religion of the North* (London, 1964), p. 276.
35. Donnelly, *Atlantis: The Antediluvian World* (London, 1950), p. 7.
36. Ibid, p. 7.
37. Robinson, *Is It True What They Say About Edgar Cayce?* (London, 1979), p. 119.
38. Donnelly, *Atlantis*, p. 316.
39. See Galanopoulos and Bacon, *Atlantis* (London, 1969).

★*Chapter Three — Eternal Recurrence*★

40. Porphyry, *Vita Pythagoras*, 19.
41. Russell, '*Time in Christian Thought*', Fraser, *Voices*, p. 68.
42. John 6:62, RSV.
43. John 14:3, RSV.
44. Pagels, *The Nag Hammadi Gospels* (London, 1979), p. 42.
45. Ibid, p. 46.
46. Nietzsche, Ms. 1066, March-June 1888.
47. Nietzsche, Ms. 1067, 1885.
48. Kollerstrom, *The Actual and the Real: A Way of Thinking About Eternity* (London, 1974), p. 149.
49. Nicoll, *Living Time* (London, 1952), p. 138.
50. Zukav, *The Dancing Wu Li Masters* (London, 1979), p. 318–19.
51. Plato, *The Republic*, 620.
52. Collin, *Celestial Influence*, p. 20.
53. Ibid, p. 21.
54. Ibid, p. 24.
55. *The Living Thoughts of Schopenhauer*, trans. by Haldane and Kemp, presented by Thomas Mann (London, 1939), p. 99.
56. Wendt, *Before the Deluge: The Story of Paleontology*, trans. Richard and Clara Winston (London, 1968), p. 119.
57. Ibid, p. 90–1.
58. Ibid, p. 105.
59. Knight, *Charles Fort, Prophet of the Unexplained*.
60. Alexander, International Herald Tribune, 18 November 1978.
61. Worshofsky, *Doomsday: The Science of Catastrophe* (London, 1979), p. 131.
62. Velikovsky, *Earth in Upheaval* (London, 1956), p. 128.
63. Jonas and Klein, *Manchild: A Study of the Infantilization of Man* (New York, 1970), p. 5.
64. Woodcock and Davis, *Catastrophe Theory* (London, 1980), p. 131.
65. Ibid, p. 15.
66. Ibid, p. 32.
67. Ibid, p. 81.
68. Ibid, p. 162.
69. Nicoll, Living, p. 149.
70. Esdras Gospel, *The Nag Hammadi Library* (Leiden, 1977).
71. Bohm, *Wholeness and the Implicate Order* (London, 1980), p. 9.
72. Ibid, p. 15.
73. Ibid, p. 25.

74. Dethlefsen, *The Challenge of Fate* (London, 1984), p. 75.
75. Spengler, *Decline*, p. 6.
76. Ibid, p. 7.
77. Sheldrake, *A New Science of Life* (London, 1981), p. 27.
78. Ibid, p. 95.
79. Ibid, p. 96.

★*Chapter Four – Life*★*Time Astrology*★

80. Jung, 'The Rediscovery of the Soul', *The Red Book* (unpublished).
81. Landscheit, *Cosmic Cybernetics* (Aalen, 1973), p. 56–7.
82. Du Nouy, *Biological Time* (London, 1936), p. 121; Collin, *Celestial*, p. 156; and Mann, *The Round Art*, p. 109.
83. Fischer, 'Biological Time', Fraser, *Voices*, p. 362.
84. John 3:4–5, RSV.
85. Jung, *Psychology and Alchemy*, CW 12 (London, 1966), p. 23.
86. Pagels, *Gospels*, p. 75.
87. Ferguson, *Brain/Mind Bulletin*, March, 1984.
88. Collin, *Eternal Life*, p. 66.
89. Fischer, 'Biological Time', Fraser, *Voices*, p. 325.
90. See Greene: *Saturn; Relating;* and *The Astrology of Fate*.
91. Imaginary quote by Goethe in Mann, *Lotte in Weimar* (London, 1965), p. 76.
92. Flanagan, *The First Nine Months of Life* (London, 1962), p. 22.
93. Needham, 'Time and Knowledge in China and the West', (Fraser, *Voices*, p. 112–3).
94. Piel, The Acceleration of History (New York, 1972), p. 21.
95. Ibid, p. 22.
96. Ibid, quote by H G Wells, p. 24–5.
97. Bennett, *The Dramatic Universe, Volume Four: History* (London, 1966), p. 166.
98. Ibid, p. 168.
99. Ibid, p. 169.
100. Huntley, *The Divine Proportion* (New York, 1970), p. 164–8.
101. Fischer, *Voices*, p. 372.
102. Ibid, Kalmus, 'Organic Evolution and Time', p. 338.
103. Calder, *Timescale* (London, 1984), p. 75.
104. Plato, *The Republic*, 144.
105. Von Franz, *Number and Time* (Wisconsin, 1974), p. 80–1.
106. Ibid, p. 82.
107. Schwaller de Lubicz, *Sacred Science* (New York, 1982), p. 207.
108. *Plotinus*, trans. MacKenna (London, 1962), p. 443.
109. Levi, *The Key to the Mysteries* (London, 1959).

★*Chapter Five – The World Age*★

110. Esdras Gospel.
111. Piel, *The Acceleration of History* (New York, 1972), p. 29; and Calder, *Timescale*, p. 157.
112. Leakey and Lewin, *Origins* (London, 1977), p. 254.
113. Toynbee, *A Study of History* (London, 1946), p. 48.
114. Piel, *Acceleration*, p. 29.
115. Laidler, The Observer, 19 April 1984.
116. *The Book of Revelations*, XX, 12–15, RSV.
117. Russell, *The Awakening Earth* (London, 1982).
118. Lenormant, *La Magie chez les Chaldeens*, trans. George Andrews.
119. Piel. *Acceleration*. p. 29–30.

120. West, *Serpent in the Sky* (New York, 1979), p. 105.
121. Ibid, p. 106.
122. Temple, *The Sirius Mystery* (London, 1976).
123. Ibid, p. 130.
124. Ibid, p. 85.
125. Ibid, p. 154.
126. Ibid, p. 155.
127. Ibid, p. 117.
128. Ibid, p. 113.
129. Ibid, p. 154.
130. Ibid, p. 89.
131. Graves, *The Greek Myths I* (London, 1955), p. 138.
132. Ibid, II, p. 85.
133. Ibid, p. 74.
134. Ibid, p. 156.
135. Leviticus, 25: 8–10, RSV.
136. Tansley, *Subtle Body* (London, p. 84–5).
137. Von Franz, *Jung: His Myth in Our Time* (London, 1975), p. 276.
138. Mann, *Joseph*, p. 124.
139. Landscheit, *Cosmic*, p. 26–7.
140. Auel, *The Clan of the Cave Bear* and *The River of Horses*.
141. Eliade, *The Forge and the Crucible* (London, 1978), p. 39.
142. Wilber, *Atman*, p. 7–8.
143. Jung, *Symbols of Transformation* (London, 1952), p. 151.
144. Wilber, *Atman*, p. 8–11.
145. Graves, *The White Goddess* (London, 1961), p. 128–30.
146. Wilber, *Atman*, p. 12–21.
147. Beard, *An Outline of Piaget's Developmental Psychology* (London, 1969), p. 17.
148. See Mann and others, *The Phenomenon Book of Calendars 1979–1980* (New York, 1979).
149. Wilber, *Atman*, p. 22–29 and Beard, *Piaget*, p. 17.
150. Calder, *Timescale* (London, 1984), p. 107.
151. Wilber, *Eye to Eye* (New York, 1983), p. 132 and Beard, *Piaget*, p. 57.
152. Plutarch, *Moralia*, p. 38.
153. See the works of Schwaller de Lubicz and West.
154. Davidson and Aldersmith, *The Great Pyramid* (London, 1925).
155. Wilber, *Atman*, p. 30–35 and Beard, *Piaget*, 45.
156. Ibid, p. 35–7 and Beard, *Piaget*, p. 98.
157. Ibid, p. 4–5.
158. Ibid, p. 45.
159. Cowen, *Rose Windows* (London, 1979).
160. Wilber, *Atman*, p. 56–7.
161. Ibid, p. 59–62.
162. Ibid, p. 66–7.
163. Eliade, *Eternal Return*, p. 148–56.
164. Wilber, *Atman*, p. 67–9.
165. Ibid, p. 71–3.
166. Matthew XIX, 28–30, RSV.
167. John I, 10, RSV.
168. Jung, 'Psychological Commentary', Evans-Wentz, *The Tibetan Book of the Dead* (London, 1960), p. xxxix.

★*Chapter Six – The Universal Time Scale*★

169. Sagan, *The Dragons of Eden* (New York, 1977), p. 16.
170. Jung, *The Structure and Dynamics of the Psyche*, CW 8 (London, 1960), p. 40.
171. International Herald Tribune, 27 December 1984 and Time Magazine, 6 May 1985.
172. Zúkav, *Dancing*, p. 94.
173. See Sheldrake, *New Science*.
174. Collin, *Celestial Influence*, p. 17.
175. Schopenhauer, op. cit., p. 30.
176. Young, *The Reflexive Universe* (San Fransisco, 1976). p. 262.
177. Zukav, *Dancing*, p. 94.
178. Charon, *The Unknown Spirit* (London, 1983), p. 50.
179. Ibid, p. 54.
180. Ibid, p. 64.
181. Scientific American, April 1980, p. 107.
182. Prigogine and Stengers, *Order Out of Chaos* (Boulder, 1984), p. 17.
183. Ferguson, *Brain/Mind Bulletin*, Vol. 8, No. 12/13, Jul/Aug 1983.

★*Chapter Seven – Reincarnation*★

184. Samannaphala Sutra, trans. T W Rhys-Davids.
185. Wilber, *Atman*, p. ix–x.
186. Ibid, p. 104.
187. Wachsmuth, *Reincarnation* (Dornach, 1937), p. 40.
188. Tansley, *Subtle Body*, p. 80.
189. Cheetham, *Prophecies of Nostradamus* (London, 1973), p. 38.
190. Ebertin, *Combination of Stellar Influences* (Aalen, 1940), p. 206.
191. Joshi, 'Avidya: A Psychological Interpretation', *Chakra*, Vol. 4, p. 170.

★*Chapter Eight – Up The Golden Path*★

192. Schopenhauer, op. cit.
193. Collin, *Eternal Life*, p. 121.
194. McKenna, *The Invisible Landscape* (New York, 1975).
195. Wilber, *Up From Eden* (London, 1981).
196. Arguelles, *Earth Ascending* (Boulder, 1984).
197. Leary, *Exo-Psychology* (Los Angeles, 1977).
198. Wilber, ed., *The Holograph Paradigm* (Boulder, 1983).
199. Feuerstein and Mitter, *Yoga and Beyond* (New York, 1972).
200. Jung, *Flying Saucers*.
201. Tansley, *Omens of Awareness* (London, 1977), p. 24.
202. van Daniken, *Chariots of the Gods* (London, 1968).
203. Noorbergen, *Secrets of the Lost Races* (London, 1978).
204. Crick, *Life Itself: Its Origin and Nature* (London, 1984).
205. Jung, *Mysterium Coniunctionis*.
206. *Nag Hammadi Texts*, p. 52.
207. Plato, *Euthydemus*.

★

★Bibliography★

Arquelles, Jose, *Earth Ascending: An Illustrated Treatise on the Law Governing Whole Systems* (Boulder, Shambhala, 1984)

Bateson, Gregory, *Mind and Nature* (London, Wildwood House, 1979)

Beard, Ruth M., *An Outline of Piaget's Developmental Psychology* (London, RKP, 1969)

Bellamy, H S, *The Atlantis Myth* (London, Faber and Faber, 1948)

Bennett, J G, *The Dramatic Universe, Volume Four: History* (London, Hodder and Stoughton, 1966)

Bergier, Jacques, *Mysteries of the Earth* (London, Sidgwick and Jackson, 1974)

Bergson, Henri, *Creative Evolution*, trans. Arthur Mitchell (London, Macmillan, 1913)

Berlitz, Charles, *Without a Trace: More Evidence from the Bermuda Triangle* (London, Souvenir, 1977)

Blacker, Carmen and Loewe, Michael, eds., *Ancient Cosmologies* (London, Allen & Unwin, 1975)

Blavatsky, Madame Helena, *The Secret Doctrine* (Los Angeles, Theosophical, 1947)

Bohm, David, *Wholeness and the Implicate Order* (London, RKP, 1980)

Brennan, J P, *An Occult History of the World* (London, Futura, 1976)

Calder, Nigel, *The Key to the Universe* (London, BBC, 1977)

------. *Timescale: An Atlas of the Fourth Dimension* (London, Chatto & Windus/The Hogarth Press, 1984)

Campbell, Joseph, ed., *Papers from the Eranos Yearbooks: Man and Time* (Princeton, Bollingen, 1957)

Charon, Jean, *The Unknown Spirit* (London, Coventure, 1984)

Cheetham, Erika, *The Prophecies of Nostradamus* (London, Spearman, 1973)

Cles-Reden, Sibylle von, *The Realm of the Great Goddess* (London, Thames & Hudson, 1961)

Collin, Rodney, *The Theory of Celestial Influence* (London, Robinson and Watkins, 1954)

------. *The Theory of Eternal Life* (London, Robinson and Watkins, 1950)

Cowen, Painton, *Rose Windows* (London, Thames and Hudson, 1979)

Darwin, Charles, *The Descent of Man* (London, John Murray, 1901)

------. *The Origin of Species* (London, John Murray, 1892)

Davidson and Aldersmith, *The Great Pyramid* (London, Williams and Norgate, 1925)

Dethlefson Thorwald, *The Challenge of Fate* (London, Coventure, 1984)

Divine, David, *The Opening of the World* (London, Collins, 1973)

Donnelly, Ignatius, *Atlantis: The Antediluvian World* (London, Sidgwick and Jackson, 1950)

------. *Ragnarok: The Age of Fire and Gravel* (New York, Steiner, 1971)

Dunne, J W, *An Experiment With Time* (London, A & C Black, 1927)

------. *The Serial Universe* (London, Faber and Faber, 1934)

Du Nouy, Pierre Lecomte, *Biological Time* (London, Methuen, 1936)

Eisler, Robert, *The Royal Art of Astrology* (London, Herbert Joseph, 1946)

Eliade, Mircea, *The Forge and the Crucible* (Chicago, U. of Chicago, 1978)

------. *Images and Symbols* (London, Harvill Press, 1961)

------. *Myth and Reality* (London, Allen & Unwin, 1964)

------. *Myths, Dreams and Reality* (London, Collins, 1968)

------. *The Myth of the Eternal Return* (Princeton, Bollingen, 1954)

------. *Shamanism: Archaic Techniques of Ecstacy* (Princeton, Bollingen, 1946)

Evans-Wentz, W Y, *The Tibetan Book of the Dead* (London, Oxford, 1960)

Fraser, J T, ed., *The Voices of Time* (London, Allen Lane/Penguin, 1968)

Frazer, Sir James, *The Golden Bough: A Study in Magic and Religion* (London, Macmillan, 1950)

Freud, Sigmund, *The Letters of Sigmund Freud 1873–1939*, ed. Ernest Freud, trans. Tania and James Stein (London, The Hogarth Press, 1961)

Galanopoulos, A G and Bacon, Edward, *Atlantis* (London, Nelson, 1969)

The Epic of Gilgamesh, trans. N K Saunders (London, Penguin, 1960)

Graves, Robert, *The Greek Myths*, Volumes I and II (London, Penguin, 1955)

------. *The White Goddess* (London, Faber and Faber, 1961)

Hall, Manley Palmer, *Secret Teachings of All Ages* (Los Angeles, Philosophical Research Society, 1968 (1928))

Hawkes, Jacquetta, *The Atlas of Early Man* (London, Macmillan, 1976)

Head, Joseph and Cranston, S L, *Reincarnation: An East-West Anthology* (New York, Julian Press, 1961)

------. *Reincarnation: The Phoenix Fire Mystery* (New York, Julian Press/Crown, 1977)

Hick, John, *Death and Eternal Life* (London, Collins, 1976)

Homer, *The Iliad*, trans. E V Rieu (London, Penguin, 1950)

------. *The Odyssey*, trans. E V Rieu (London, Penguin, 1946)

Huntley, H E, *The Divine Proportion* (New York, Dover, 1970)

Jacob, Francois, *The Logic of Living Systems*, trans. Betty Spillman (London, Allen Lane, 1974)

Jonas, David and Klein, Doris, *Man-child: A Study of the Infantilization of Man* (New York, McGraw-Hill, 1970)

Jung, Emma and von Franz, Marie Louise, *The Grail Legend*, trans. Andrea Dykes (New York, Jung Foundation, 1970)

Jung, Carl G, *Aion*, CW 9, (London, RKP, 1951) (Collected Works translated by R F C Hull)

------. *Alchemical Studies*, CW 13 (London, RKP, 1966)

------. *The Archetypes and the Collective Unconscious*, CW 9, Part I (London, RKP, 1959)

------. *C G Jung Letters, Volume One 1906–1950* (London, RKP, 1973)
------. *C G Jung Letters, Volume Two 1906–1961* (London, RKP, 1977)
------. *C G Jung: Psychological Reflections*, ed. Jolande Jacobi (London, RKP, 1953)
------. *Memories, Dreams and Reflections* (New York, Random House, 1961)
------. *Mysterium Coniunctionis*, CW 14 (London, RKP, 1963)
------. *Psychology and Alchemy*, CW 12 (London, RKP, 1966)
------. *Symbols of Transformation*, CW 5 (London, RKP, 1952)
------. and Pauli, Wolfgang, *The Interpretation of Nature and the Psyche* (London, RKP, 1955)
Kahn, Herman, Wiener, Anthony and The Hudson Institute, *The Year 2000* (London, Macmillan, 1967)
Kerenyi, Carl, *Dionysios: Archetypal Image of Indestructible Life*, trans. Ralph Manheim (London, RKP, 1976)
------. *The Gods of the Greeks*, trans. Ralph Manheim (London, Thames and Hudson, 1951)
------. *Prometheus: Archetypal Image of Human Existence*, trans. Ralph Manheim (London, Thames and Hudson, 1962)
------. *The Religion of the Greeks and Romans*, trans. Christopher Holme (London, Thames and Hudson, 1962)
Kollerstrom, Oscar, *The Actual and the Real: A Way of Thinking About Eternity* (London, Turnstone, 1974)
Landscheit, Dr Theodore, *Cosmic Cybernetics*, trans. Linda Kratsch (Aalen, Ebertin-Verlag, 1973)
Leakey, Richard and Lewin, Roger, *Origins* (London, Macdonald and Janes, 1977)
Leary, Timothy, *Exo-Psychology* (Los Angles, Starseed, 1977)
Levi, Eliphas, *The Key of the Mysteries* (London, Rider, 1959)
Lockyer, Sir Norman, *The Dawn of Astronomy* (Cambridge, MIT Press, 1964)
Luce, Gay Gaer, *Body Time* (London, Temple Smith, 1972)
Mann, A T, *Life★Time Astrology* (London, Allen & Unwin, 1984)
------. *The Round Art: The Astrology of Time and Space* (London, Dragon's World, 1979)
------, with Sesti, Giuseppe,Cowen, Painton and Flanagan, Mary, *The Phenomenon Book of Calendars 1979–1980* (New York, Simon & Schuster, 1979)
Mann, Thomas, *Joseph and His Brothers*, trans, H T Lowe-Porter (London, Secker & Warburg, 1950)
------. *Lotte in Weimar*, trans. H T Lowe-Porter (London, Secker & Warburg, 1964)
Marcus, Steven, *Freud and the Culture of Psychoanalysis* (London, Allen & Unwin, 1983)
Marwick, Arthur, *The Nature of History* (London, Macmillan, 1970)
McKenna, Dennis and Terence, *The Invisible Landscape: Mind, Hallucinogens and the I Ching* (New York, Seaburg Press, 1975)
McNeill, William, J, *Plagues and People* (Oxford, Basil Blackford, 1977)

Muck, Otto, *The Secret of Atlantis*, trans. Fred Bradley (London, Collins, 1978)

Neumann, Erich, *The Great Mother*, trans. R F C Hull, (London, RKP, 1955)

------. *The Origin and History of Consciousness*, trans. R F C Hull (Princeton, Bollingen, 1954)

Nicoll, Maurice, *Living Time* (London, Stuart and Watkins, 1952)

Noorbergen, Rene, *Secrets of the Lost Races* (London, New English Library, 1978)

O'Flahery, W O, *Hindu Myths* (London, Penguin, 1975)

Pagels, Elaine, *The Gnotic Gospels* (London, Penguin, 1979)

Pauwels, Louis and Bergier, Jacques, *The Dawn of Magic*, trans. Rollo Myers (London, Pantheon, 1964)

Pfeiffer, John E, *The Emergence of Man* (London, Nelson, 1970)

Piazzi-Smyth, C, *The Great Pyramid* (London, Isbister, 1880)

Piel, Gerard, *The Acceleration of History* (New York, Knopf, 1972)

Plato, *Timaeus and Critias*, trans. Desmond Lee (London, Penguin, 1965)

Plotinus, *The Enneads*, trans. Stephen MacKenna (London, Faber and Faber, 1962)

Prigogine, Ilya and Stengers, Isabelle, *Order Out of Chaos* (Boulder, Shambhala, 1984)

Ptolemy, *Tetrabiblos*, trans. and ed. by F E Robbins (Cambridge, Harvard University Press, 1971)

Renfrew, Colin, *Before Civilisation: The Radiocarbon Revolution and Prehistoric Europe* (London, Jonathan Cape, 1973)

Robinson, James M, ed., *The Nag Hammadi Library in English* (Leiden, Brill, 1977)

Robinson, Lytle, *Edgar Cayce's Story of the Origin and Destruction of Man* (London, Spearman, 1972)

------. *Is It True What They Say About Edgar Cayce?* (London, Spearman, 1979)

Russell, Bertrand, *History of Western Philosophy* (London, Allen & Unwin, 1946)

Sagan, Carl, *The Dragons of Eden* (New York, Random House, 1977)

Santillana, Giorgio de and Dechand, Herta von, *Hamlet's Mill: An Essay Investigating the Origins of Human Knowledge and its Transmission Through Myth* (Boston, Godine, 1969)

Schopenhauer, Arthur, *The Living Thoughts of Schopenhauer*, trans. R B Haldane and J Kemp, presented by Thomas Mann (London, Cassell, 1939)

Schwaller de Lubicz, R A, *Sacred Science*, trans. Andre and Goldian Vanden Broeck (New York, Inner Traditions, 1982)

------. *Symbol and Symbolic:* Egypt, Science and the Evolution of Consciousness, trans. Robert and Deborah Lawlor (Brookline, Autumn Press, 1978)

------. *The Temple in Man:* The Secrets of Ancient Egypt, trans. Robert and Deborah Lawlor (Brookline, Autumn Press, 1977)

Scott-Elliot, W, *The Story of Atlantis* (London, 1909)

Sheldrake, Rupert, *A New Science of Life* (London, Blond and Briggs, 1981)

Scholem, Gershom, *Major Trends in Jewish Mysticism* (London, Thames and Hudson, 1955)

Spence, Lewis, *Will Europe Follow Atlantis?* (London)

Spengler, Oswald, *The Decline of the West* (London, George Allen & Unwin, 1961)

Talbot, Michael, *Mysticism and the New Physics* (London, RKP, 1981)

Tansley, David, *Omens of Awareness* (London, Spearman, 1977)

------. *Subtle Body* (London, Spearman, 1977)

Tarling, D H and M P, *Continental Drift* (London, Bell and Sons, 1971)

Taylor, Gordon Rattray, *The Doomsday Book* (London, Thames and Hudson, 1970)

Temple, Robert K G, *The Sirius Mystery* (London, Sidgwick and Jackson, 1976)

Thorndike, Lynn, *The History of Magic and Experimental Science*, Nine Volumes (New York, Columbia University, 1941)

Toynbee, Arnold, *A Study of History*, abridged by D C Somervell (London, Oxford University, 1946)

------. *Change and Habit* (London, Oxford University, 1966)

------. *Mankind and Mother Earth* (London, Oxford University, 1976)

Trinkus, Erik and Howells, William, *The Neanderthals* (New York, Scientific American, December 1979)

Turville-Petre, E O G, *Myth and Religion of the North* (London, Weidenfeld and Nicholson, 1964)

van Daniken, Erik, *Chariots of the Gods* (London)

Velikovsky, Immanuel, *Earth in Upheaval* (London, Gollanz, 1956)

------. *Worlds in Collision* (London, Gollanz, 1950)

------ and the Editors of Pensee, *Velikovsky Reconsidered* (London, Sidgwick and Jackson, 1976)

★*Index*★

(The index is complete except for the proper names of individuals, gods and goddesses and historical events in the text and tables of Chapter Five.)